I0748780

ITALIAN SIGHTS

AND

PAPAL PRINCIPLES,

SEEN THROUGH

AMERICAN SPECTACLES.

BY

JAMES JACKSON JARVES,
AUTHOR OF "ART-HINTS," "PARISIAN SIGHTS," &c., &c.

NEW YORK
HARPER & BROTHERS, PUBLISHERS,
PEARL STREET, FRANKLIN SQUARE.
1856.

PREFACE.

"Simul et jucunda et idonea dicere vitæ."

Some of these "Sights" were penned several years back, while others are but of yesterday. I refer you, dear reader, for farther insight, to the chapters themselves. Hoping that, while you find amusement in the "Sights," you will not fail to "read, mark, learn, and inwardly digest" the Principles, I remain,

Your obliged servant

Ever at command.

The Author.

ITALIAN SIGHTS

AND

PAPAL PRINCIPLES.

CHAPTER I.

INTRODUCTION TO ITALY——GENOA——HOW MUCH TEMPER AND MONEY IT COST TO GET TO FLORENCE.

SUPERB Genoa, shall I ever forget thee? thyself but one of a series of beautiful entrances to a land favored of God and cursed of rulers! By thy gates I first entered Italy. What other country can boast such magnificent portals? Naples, Genoa, Venice, and the Alps, announce thy treasures on the very threshold of thy domains. By whichsoever side thou art approached, thou welcomest son and stranger to a plentiful feast provided by nature and spread by art.

Genoa the Superb! and superb she is; more beautiful even now, when her power has departed, than when to be a doge was to be more than king. The child of commerce has not been forsaken in old age, because she has not despised the hand that in her youth fashioned her to wealth and glory.

I like Genoa. I like it the more from its contrast with Marseilles. True, it has but few streets, but they are streets of palaces. Its other avenues are more like subterranean passages than streets, for the houses are so lofty that only a vertical sun can light their depths. Even this is in general shut out by projecting eaves that almost meet. Then they are so irregular as to defy all calculation on the part of a stranger who ventures to explore their intricacies. He doubles on his own track, and thinks himself going east, when his face is toward the setting sun. Then, too, he finds streets far above him; others below; some terminated abruptly by a rock; while many look as if they were about to leap into the sea. At one moment carriages are rolling along, a hundred feet over his head, on bridges which spring from one precipice to another. The next instant he stands at the base of a lofty palace, and yet finds himself looking into the chimneys of seven-story houses beneath. One edifice begins at an elevation where another terminates, and thus they rise, layer upon layer of buildings, far up the precipitous hills, down their sides, in their crevices, spanning their chasms, clinging to the rocks like shell-fish, or growing like moss wherever a foundation can be had. In many places the streets are walled in to prevent wayfarers from falling off. If you wish to arrive quickly at any spot, you must walk. Comparatively few streets are accessible to carriages, which makes Genoa the paradise of pedestrians. At one angle opens a most charming sea-view — the surf foams at your feet — if perfectly clear, the mountains of Corsica can be seen. At another are disclosed the forests of masts in the harbor, with a fleet of white sails studding the horizon, and an occasional steamer's pipe leaving behind it a comet-like tail of black smoke. Turn, and you see terraced gardens, fountains, statuary, bright flowers, and perhaps smiling faces from latticed windows looking down upon you. Farther back rise villas and vineyards upon the sunny hill-sides. Their summits are crested with a dark array of forts and bristling ramparts, standing out in strong relief against the clear sky. Genoa is a perpetual ascent or descent, but each pace brings with it something worth seeing.

I breakfasted at a café, amid an orange grove, loaded at the same time with the ripe fruit, bud, and blossom. At home it had already snowed in a latitude to the south of this.

Passing through the Strada Balbi, absorbed in admiration of the exterior of the noble palaces built by merchant princes, and recognizing in them not only a taste, but a humanity vastly superior to the castles of feudalism which had so recently attracted my attention on the Rhone, I was accosted by a rusty-looking individual, who, for the small consideration of three francs, proposed to introduce me into their interiors, and pilot me to all other lions of Genoa. He looked, withal, as honest as he was poor, so I told him to be on hand at an early hour the next morning. In the mean while, as there was some daylight left, he might commence operations with the most distinguished of the ecclesiastical museums, by the taste of man, rather than by the will of God, called churches.

On entering the Holy Annunciation, second in size only to the Cathedral, my eyes were fairly dazzled with the blaze of gold from the ceilings, and the rich colorings of the frescoes. This is, indeed, a magnificent temple, and as completely outshines the Madeleine at Paris in richness of ornament as it excels it in correct taste. The sumptuary laws of republican Genoa forbade its trading Crœsuses to expend their wealth in personal prodigalities. Being thus deprived of the more vulgar mode of display, they competed with each other in the erection of churches, each distinguished family building for itself a temple of its own. Thus the "Annunziata" is the monument of the wealth, and, if you will, the piety of the Lomellini family. It was built two centuries since, and gives one a strong idea of the comfortable position of a family which could afford, after having reared a sumptuous palace to itself, to invest its superfluous millions in a house of God, and keep up a befitting state for both.

The Carignan bridge, one of those that cross streets and not a river, uniting two mountains and passing over very lofty houses, was the work of the family Sauli, and leads directly to the church of Sainte Marie de Carignan, built also by them. Its origin was in this wise. The Marquis Sauli was the owner of several palaces, one of which occupied the site of the present church; but as he possessed no chapel of his own, he often went to mass in a church that belonged to his neighbor Fiesque. One day, finding himself too late, he laughingly complained to his noble friend of his disappointment.

"My dear Marquis," replied Fiesque, who had designedly anticipated the hour of worship to give force to his hint, "when one goes to mass, he should have a chapel of his own."

Sauli took the hint in good part, demolished a palace, and built on its foundation a church which cost enough to have satisfied even Solomon.

St. Laurent, the cathedral, pleased me greatly. The Saracens evidently had had something to say in its construction, for the Moorish and Christian styles of architecture are singularly blended in its interior. Like all the others, it is a museum, and the visitor is irreverently conducted by its officials for a small fee through all its sacred precincts, and unceremoniously invited to examine any thing curious without scruple, whatever may be its claims to sanctity. This system of making a mercenary show of the gifts of the altar, which prevails in all Catholic countries, struck me as peculiarly destructive of the respect due the temples of the Most High. One insensibly forgets their holy purposes in admiration of the works of man, or in irreverent ridicule at the absurd claims of false relics. Frequently the extravagant execution of some saintly picture or work of art is such as only to excite laughter. I saw a Madonna—not, however, in this church—holding in her hands, as a mother holds a babe when it first begins to know the pleasure of exercising its limbs, a naked adult Christ, of the proportion to her of a small doll, with the shrunken muscles, bowed head, and rigid attitude given in the Descents from the Cross. The Virgin had the appearance of holding him up to take a dance on her knees. My clerical cicerone pointed me out a portrait of Mary, painted by St. Luke. The apostle appears to have worked diligently in this line, if we can believe the claims of all the churches that possess original paintings of the mother of Christ. "Do you really think St. Luke did this one?" I asked. He shrugged his shoulders, half smiled, and called my attention to something more modern.

The side chapel of St. John the Baptist possesses the mortal remains—so they say—of the victim of Herodias; but as I expected, before my travels in the region of relics were terminated, to meet with a duplicate set, I only left half of my faith at this shrine. This is very rich and beautiful. A service was being performed in it for the soul of a criminal to be executed on the morrow. On account of the agency of woman in the death of the prophet of the wilderness, her sex are allowed to enter this chapel but once a year—not much of an interdiction, as it is perfectly open to the eye. Besides, if woman wished, it was man that performed the crime.

St. Laurent contains also the famous emerald dish given by the Queen of Sheba to King Solomon, and afterward preserved in the Temple. How it escaped the prying eyes of the ransacking lieutenants of Nebuchadnezzar the monks do not explain, but assert that from it Christ ate the Last Supper. It was found among the spoils of Cæsarea, upon the capture of that town by the combined armies of Genoa and Pisa in 1101. At that date, the Genoese, possessing more faith than avarice, took the "Sacro Cattino" for their share of the booty, leaving to the Pisans in exchange the entire mass of filthy lucre. It was brought to Genoa, where it continued to be held in such veneration that twelve nobles were appointed to guard it, or, rather, the tabernacle which contained it, each a month in turn. It was exhibited but once a year to the adoration of the crowd. Then a priest held it aloft by a cord, while its twelve guardians formed a circle around. In 1476 a law was enacted condemning to death whoever touched the holy emerald with any substance whatever. Unless the booty at Cæsarea was very large, the Genoese did not make a bad investment in their emerald, for within fifty years the Jews lent them four millions of francs on its security. In 1809, among the other valuables borrowed of Italy by Napoleon, it traveled to Paris, where it remained until 1815, when it was restored without difficulty, broken, and ascertained to be glass—an ancient specimen, undoubtedly, but worth something under eight hundred thousand dollars. It is still preserved on account of its souvenirs, and as a curious glass dish; but Genoa has lost, in losing her belief in the relic, a capital of nearly a million of dollars.

Faith in Catholic relics is essentially the substance of things unseen, for, when seen, faith vanishes.

St. Laurent possesses a rare merit for an Italian church. It is finished, although not quite seven hundred years old.

Enough of churches. My old friend was prompt to his engagement for the next morning. We passed from one palace to another with all the freedom of ownership, by the aid of a trifling fee bestowed upon their guardians. The liberality of the Italians in throwing open their collections to the entire world is worthy of praise and imitation elsewhere. It is done so unostentatiously that one feels at home within their halls. Great as were the masters that I passed in review—Genoa is rich in paintings—I felt still more interest in the various princely residences commerce had bestowed upon her successful sons. Her prizes were few, but they were worth drawing. There was the old Ducal Palace—the least pleasing, but grandest of them all—coldly aristocratic, like the government it represented; then that of Andrew Doria, with its charming garden, offering to the port as fine a view as it gives from its own unrivaled marble terrace. It was upon this terrace that the old admiral gave his famous repasts to embassadors, served in silver vessels which were renewed three times. At every change of course, the vessels were thrown into the sea. Fine fishing in those days, but I suspect the humbugging host reserved that right to himself; for, notwithstanding his frequent banquets, no shoal of silver ever made its appearance under his windows. Strozzi, at Florence, for want of a more refined method of exhibiting his wealth, used to seat his guests upon bags of dollars. It is to be hoped that they were cushioned.

The Durazzo Palace, occupied by the king on his visits to Genoa, is a fine specimen of a comfortable regal residence, not so grand as to be cold, nor so homely as to be unroyal. To facilitate the passage of their majesties from one story to another—in other words, to save stair-work—a sort of dumb-waiter boudoir has been contrived, into which they have simply to place themselves to be landed at any elevation they desire in their mansion. It is lined with yellow satin, and looks very safe and comfortable.

The Brignole Palace contains a galaxy of distinguished names. Titian, Paul Veronese, Paris Bordone, Louis Caracchi, Carlo Dolci, Guercino, Guido, and particularly Vandyck, have contributed liberally to adorn its walls. But the palace that pleased me most—it contained the fewest pictures—was the Balbi. It is the home of the most beautiful woman of Genoa. The exquisite bust of the Countess, which the guardian asserted did not do her justice—she must be ravishingly beautiful!—was in the principal salon. It was more like one of Power's inimitable heads of Proserpine than the bust of a real mother. Her children, in stone, were no less beautiful, and, as report said the truth had not been exaggerated, it was a laudable vanity to perpetuate the memory of so rare an assemblage of loveliness. We were taken into the boudoir and bedrooms, both displaying the taste of a cultivated woman; elegance and comfort so combined as to extort at first glance, from every visitor, an exclamation of envious admiration. Surely it is no wrong to wish for such a home. There were indications, too, that the Countess made it also the house of prayer. With the crucifix at the head of her bed hung a touching memorial of a lost child—a double remembrance of her hopes in heaven.

I will not compel my readers to ascend and descend as many steps, and to explore as many streets as I did with my venerable guide, for fear that they might do what he would never have done—drop me—at least, without his pay. At last I sought the "Arsenal of the Holy Ghost"—forgive me the incongruity of the name, for it is none of my making—to seek the famous rostrum of an ancient vessel found long since in the port of Genoa. It was supposed to be the beak of one of the galleys of Magon, brother of Hannibal, and broken off in a naval combat in this harbor in the year 524 of Rome. No one was allowed to enter the Arsenal without a permit. The sentinel, in deference to my antiquarian zeal, and my assurance that I would overlook all modern engines of war, let me pass. An officer, however, soon informed me that the "rostrum" had traveled to Turin. It should have been set up as a monument to Jason on some conspicuous classical promontory.

I had pretty well done up Genoa—at all events, its crust.

My guide was done up too. He had asked but three francs—I gave him four. In return, he said he should pray for my illustrious self every day of his life. As he was a good man, I was not sorry to hear this, but as he turned to go, doubts arose in my mind as to whether I should long have the benefit of them.

Many hard sayings are current of Genoa. Louis XI. said of its citizens, "The Genoese have given themselves to me, and I give them to the devil." They might have retorted that it was unnecessary, as in doing the former they had accomplished the latter. As for myself, I found every thing good at Genoa; I was satisfied with my hotel, my guide, table prices, and visit altogether, even to their Bedouins of the water, the boatmen. And yet the proverb—it must have come from the Pisans—runs to this day, "Mare senza pesci, monti senza ligno, uomini senza fede, donna senza vergogna;" which signifies, "Sea without fish, mountains without wood, men without faith, women without shame." If other Italian cities possess cleaner skirts than Genoa, I am yet to learn it.

Reader mine, did you ever read the advertisement of a Mediterranean steam-boat? There are numerous lines diverging from Marseilles east, west, and south, along the neighboring coasts, sailing under the French, Sardinian, Spanish, or Neapolitan flags, but they all sing the same song—sumptuous accommodations, spacious family saloons, an epicurean table, prompt dispatch, and great speed. Such is the burden of their chant. One may fairly be pardoned for indulging in the presumption that they are about to go on board of a craft that could claim a place, at all events, in one of our coasting lines of sea-steamers. But it is all a crafty snare. Lest you, my reader, should be deluded by the many adjectives of a steamer placard while on your classical tour, I will give you a charitable forewarning of what you may expect.

You say, Why not go on board, and test for yourself the description? Exactly because you can not. If you are able to distinguish in the distance your own smoke-pipe from the grove of others, you are lucky. The nearest you can get to it is a sight of a lithographic sketch in the agent's office of the accommodations, made, of course, to correspond with the advertisement. Indeed, an American is so accustomed to believe that a steam-packet is a steam-packet, that it does not occur to him to verify the description with the reality. He selects his place, pays two dollars where he would pay one in the United States, and thinks the affair settled. Not so. There is another charge for putting you on board, and a heavy one too; another for a health certificate, ditto for police; then you are told that you must pay two dollars to the American consul, and a sliding scale of from fifty cents to a dollar each to each one of the consuls of the several countries the steamer touches at. If you wish to land, you are compelled to do this, for although they often remain from one to several days in a port, they furnish no food on board during that time, notwithstanding the original fare terminated with a round sum per day charged for meals. In leaving Marseilles, it cost me nearly eight dollars to get on board the steam-boat, one quarter of which the American consul, whom I never saw, pocketed. He levies this tax upon his countrymen by an understanding with the officials of other powers that they are not to visé passports that have not his signature.

See us, then, alongside of the steamer, punctual to the hour of departure. Our first surprise was at her dimensions, which would have entitled her to the place of a launch in comparison with an Atlantic boat. It was the Castore, of Genoa, one of the best of the Sardinian line, newly refitted and in fine order. For a gentleman's yacht her size would have been unexceptionable, although above the water-line she was too lightly built for the stormy Gulf of Lyons. The baggage was piled up on deck, and a tarpaulin lashed over it, but not so thoroughly but that some of the trunks were exposed to a heavy rain. The whole mass would have gone a voyaging on its own account had even a moderate-sized sea come on board. Some hours after the time appointed we steamed out of port, distressingly surcharged with passengers.

The spacious family saloons were the frailest and most diminutive of state-rooms, alongside of the paddle-boxes, in dangerous proximity to the sea. The boat was very low in the water, and fitted up with berths after the fashion of the old steerage arrangements of the California steamers; that is to say, eight persons to occupy the room of two, and to pay the passage of sixteen. Below, the economy of space was still greater. The division was the reverse of that of our packet schooners. Two state-rooms for ladies were forward, and the cabin for gentlemen aft. In the former were crowded ladies, nurses, and children, in one promiscuous pile, so thickly brought together that the atmospheric air had no room to enter, or entered only to leave in disgust. In the latter the pressure was equally great. The berths were merely open shelves, of not the width of the shoulders of an ordinary sized man, and with no support to prevent one from imitating the motion of the ship, and rolling upon a neighbor stretched at full length upon a cushioned bench beneath. Floor and table had also their living freight, but this was after what was dearly paid for as a dinner had been served. The passengers are required to pay a price for meals, whether they partake or not, which would entitle them in Paris to a seat at the table d'hôte at the Hotel des Princes. The hours for eating are ingeniously contrived to fall upon that period when there is most motion and no one can come to the table, or else the steward hurries off the few cold dishes on the plea that, as there is no rack, his crockery will be broken. I had come on board at the hour notified for sailing, too early to dine on shore, expecting to eat the meal, for which I had paid, on board. It was not served until after eight o'clock ; I had breakfasted at nine, and, being an old sailor, felt disposed to assert my masticatory rights. In this I was joined by a young English lady, to whose appetite the sea had no terrors. By this time the boat was polkaing her way through the waters right merrily. Equilibrium was at a discount, and appetites in general as if they had never been. To nineteen twentieths of the passengers food was about as welcome as water to a mad dog, although an hour previous they had been mutinous with hunger. But the steward-contractor knew his game, and could calculate to a minute where for one dinner eaten he could save twenty. The berths were full of groaning victims of Neptune. We must eat in their midst, or not eat at all. The lady and myself were determined neither to be sea-sick nor to lose our dinners. A few attempted to follow our example, but one by one they came and went like ghosts, until we were left alone. The steward grew wroth at our pertinacity. We ate slowly, calling for all we could get—small matter that—to enjoy his vexation, ever and anon hinting that it was a shabby meal for so extravagant a price, and of course that he must have some gustatory surprise in store for us. He was a stout, surly Italian, a devout disciple of Mammon, and he watched every mouthful of disappearing chicken with all the eagerness of a hungry cat, dancing about, in the mean while, like a jumping Jack, to catch the falling dishes. In his anxiety for his beloved crockery, he would not have left me even a plate, had I not decidedly insisted upon the article, and something on it. He even had the impudence to insinuate that I was eating enough for two. I retorted that that was not surprising, as I paid for four. My lady friend was as agreeable as she was sea-proof—a polyglot in the most charming of bindings; so we made merry in English, French, or Italian alternately, as we charitably concluded we could most aggravate our penurious old purveyor. But he soon had his revenge. Distant sea-sickness we were fortified against, but the commotion of stomachs grew nearer and louder. At last an old gentleman immediately opposite, to whom, I doubt not, the smell of our viands had been a most unsavory incense, turned suddenly over, drew from his berth a nameless vessel, placed it within a few feet of our faces, and with a rushing, roaring noise, avenged his wrongs and the dyspepsia of fifty dinners at once. My fair friend had detected the coming storm sooner than I, and, by the time the liquid apparition had fairly appeared, was on deck. I saw only the gleam of her skirt as she turned the hatchway. Grasping blindly at the nearest edible, I rushed in pursuit. The remainder of the evening we devoted to admiration of the sublimity of a classical storm at the base of the moonlit mountains of the Italian shore, venturing no allusion to our inglorious retreat.

The steward was now complete master of the field. Man, woman, and child were at his mercy, and neither he nor his myrmidons would stir to their assistance without a fee. I remonstrated with him, not on my own account, for his covetousness, after the high price paid. "That entitles you only to a *passage;* we are not obliged to give you even a glass of water," was the reply, worthy of a Midas. A nice speculation he made of the wants of the helpless sea-sick. Every morsel to eat, every lemon to wet the lips, each cup of tea or coffee, or drop of brandy and water, brought him a Californian profit. Dumas says, in this same passage of ten hours he swallowed twenty-eight francs' worth of tea. It would have cost Dr. Johnson a fortune. Dismal were the groans and cries from the ladies' cabin as the night bore on. The boat behaved very well after the fashion of a sea-dog, but very badly in the excited imaginations of the sea-sick. Rip—rip, thump—thump, would go a sea upon her side, canting her over until those on the floor fancied they were transported to the ceiling; the engines meanwhile straining and tugging to pull her along, now jumping, now plunging, the boat creaking in every joint of her frame, until she became one chaos of sounds and struggles, and the ladies frantic with fright. "Steward! oh, steward! the bowl, quick!" "Coming, marm—all in use—in a minute." "Tell me, is there danger?" "Not at all; we are getting on finely." Another roll and general capsize of persons and liquids, enlivened by the sound as if of timbers twisting off, or a rock of a ton weight had hit her side. "Mercy on us, we shall sink—I am sure the boat will break in pieces—what shall we do?" A dozen calls for the unfortunate steward at once, for vessels, tea, and consolation. In his distraction, he hands the wrong article to each. At this juncture a heavy fall, struggle, and naughty exclamation in the gentlemen's cabin. Some one has been pitched from an upper berth on to the table, and thence on to his lower neighbor's abdomen. No one pities sea-sick men; they are at once the most helpless and the most disgusting of objects; all poke fun at them: a faint laugh, fresh gurgle, and all have relapsed into their previous condition of unutterable misery, the most despairing wishing that some Samaritan might be found to throw them overboard. For a few minutes there is a lull inside and out, but the rain soon descends afresh, the wind howls still more frightfully, the boat squirms like an impaled centipede, and the ladies wax more desperate than ever. "Do you call this a steam-boat?" at last exclaims one imperfectly, furious in her terror and sickness; "we would not go down the harbor in it at home. I hope it will sink as soon as we are all out of it." The steward looked aghast. He worshiped the boat, for it was as good as a gold "placer" to him. He was, too, a bit superstitious, and this staggered him. "Oh, you do wrong to say so, madam; it is the best boat in the Mediterranean." And he launched off into an eloquent eulogium on her merits, to which the lady retorted with certain invidious comparisons with transatlantic boats, to him utterly unintelligible. The storm abated, tempers grew sweeter, the demand for tea increased, and the steward was appeased. It continued to rain, and ventilation was impossible. At last even the rain ceased, and those able to stand went on deck. There was a call for the wherewithal for the morning toilet. Two wash-bowls were placed on the dining-table, which had just ceased doing duty as a bedstead, and some fifty passengers had the privilege of alternating at them, or going ashore dirty. We had entered the port of Leghorn, and were detained some hours before receiving permission to go ashore. Then the captain detained us some time longer before he would order his crew to leave off coaling to find our baggage, which they had stowed away among the freight. Finally, we were ready to be off. The crew demanded something for delivering to us our baggage, and the steward, not content with his previous fleecings, which he solemnly swore all went to the owners, informed us that his fee was so much a head; I forget how much, but it was a bouncing sum. We were too glad to put our feet over the gangway not to say Amen to every imposition.

The old proverb, out of the frying-pan, &c., was never more practically realized. Leghorn boatmen are a cross between New York hackmen and South Sea savages—a compound of importunity, extortion, and indifference. We tumbled right into their hands, of course, as their boats were the only bridge to the shore. We paid toll accordingly. They delivered us at the custom-house, where we were ushered up a narrow stairway into a dirty office, and confronted individually with our passports. After the Grand Duke's servants were satisfied that the Mr. Jonathan, Mrs. Jonathan, Miss Jonathan, and baby Jonathan, were the veritable Jonathans, of the same height, color, age, form of nose, and signature, as certified to by the Secretary of State at Washington, then we were graciously informed we could go about our ways in Leghorn by taking our passports to another office, and paying the lawful fee therefor. At the foot of the stairs we were beset by an avalanche of runners of every description. One made a dive at my passport, and ran off with it, saying he would soon bring it back, all right—for a fee. The hospitality of the hotel agents was beyond all description. Olympus itself never possessed half the advantages of their respective houses. One caught me by the left arm, another by the dexter; one swore that the other was a liar and would take me in; the other responded by declaring his rival to be the greatest rogue in Leghorn, which was equivalent to the climax of rascality the world over. All offered to perform for me every possible service. Cards were thrust into my hands and into my pockets. I was in bodily danger of being carried off by force, had not the hackmen overheard me declare that I would not go to any hotel, but direct to the rail-road. This created a diversion, for they rushed forward *en masse*, vociferating in Italian, French, and English like so many madmen. To witness the excitement, one would suppose that but one traveler ever arrived at Leghorn, and that he was made of gold. I retreated into the police station, and came to a parley, selecting, no doubt, the greatest rogue among them on condition that he would see me safe from the others. As I was to pay him quadruple fare, he became a stalwart champion. My baggage was turned upon the quay, searched, and found according to tariff. Each article was seized, and borne off to the carriage by whomsoever of the crowd the spirit moved. It was useless to remonstrate.

Every member of the cortège was bound to touch my money this day. We were divided between two carriages, and attempted to drive off. My coachman urged on his horses, but it was of no use. There was still somebody's claims to settle —more *bucksheesh.* I had already paid enough to have carried me through some of our American states, and had got only a few rods from the quay. The coachman fought stoutly for me, the crowd and he disputing at the top of their voices, until the din and excitement became overpowering. The police looked on as indifferently as if every thing was going on as well as could be expected. Any thing was better than being the centre of such a circle. I took out my purse. The sight of it was like oil on water. "How much does the beggar want?" He named the sum—sufficient for him to have lived on for a week. I passed it to him, and ordered the driver to go on. He drove rapidly to escape a fresh assault, for he wanted me entirely to himself. He contrived, however, to be too late for the train, and then he had a proposition to make. He would take me to Pisa himself for a consideration, put me through all the sights, and see me safely in the afternoon train for Florence. I cut down his price one third, and told him yes. He moved about it with an alacrity that convinced me that he respected the depth of my purse, and therefore he Jewed me. I was more glad to get out of Leghorn than I had ever been to get out of the Castore, an amount of pleasure not often condensed into the experience of one morning. But my baggage had all to be reopened, searched, and sealed up to avoid examination at Pisa, and another at Florence. The charge for this was cheap in comparison with the trouble saved. I have been in many sea-ports in various parts of the world, and in them all combined I never met with so much annoyance and imposition as were condensed into two hours at Leghorn. Not so remarkable either, when we consider that at

Leghorn a galley-slave's suit, that has upon it the mark of a murder or assassination, commands a premium among the criminals who sweep the streets, because it attracts notice and alms, as the badge of a dashing fellow, while he who is only distinguished simply by the stamp of a thief is considered but a pitiful chap, and is but too glad to obtain the right to wear the suit of deeper hue.

Was I wrong to be grateful to my coachman for having at last got me fairly out of the gates of Leghorn? He was a jovial, communicative fellow, and I mounted the box to chat with him. There was nothing worth looking at on the road, not even the Arno, which, where we crossed it, I should have mistaken for a ditch of dirty water if the driver had not explained its consequence. He loved America, the driver—he was thinking of his prospective "pour boire" when he said it—and wished he could go there. He was a Republican himself. He had about as adequate an idea of the institutions of the United States as he had of Timbuctoo. The Austrians he hated; the Grand Duke was a fool; the stiletto was his idea of a ballot-box, and the good time was coming when republicanism would avenge its recent humiliations. There were many like him all over the country, but they could do nothing so long as Austrian bayonets were in sight. I asked him about the brigands on the roads. "They call them brigands," he replied, "but they are Republicans." I should not like to rely upon their spirit of "fraternité" to spare my purse.

We arrived at Pisa punctual to the coachman's promise, and he drove us to an inn of his own selection to dine. I had given myself unreservedly to him for the day for two reasons: first, to save temper and trouble, and, secondly, to let its experience be a test for future operations. The lesson would be worth its cost. One must pay an initiative fee on entrance into society any where, and my plan was to condense all possible varieties of Italian tricks upon travelers into this one day, that I might start upon the morrow with clean eyesight. For the dinner—a shabby affair—we paid just treble the ordinary price, but it was economical at that, as it taught me how to deal with tricky hosts.

Jehu procured us a fresh coach, and drove us to see the lions. I always had an inclination for the Leaning Tower, and now was gratified to see that it had an inclination toward me of thirteen feet from the perpendicular—so they say who have measured it. As it has preserved this leaning toward mankind with impartial precision for six centuries, it is to be presumed that no future generation will be favored with any closer intimacy. Its proportions are very beautiful, so light and elastic that if it should tumble over, I believe it would pick itself up as sound as ever. From the Tower we passed to the Duomo. Here descended upon us one of the plagues, not of Egypt, but of Italy, in the shape of a cicerone, a race who seem to think that a traveler without their presence is as miserable an object as Peter Schlemihl without his shadow. My Genoa guide was a jewel, for he spoke only when he was spoken to, answered questions briefly and sensibly, and told only what he knew; but the tribe that waylay travelers on the thresholds of monuments are in general as great nuisances as were the money-changers on the steps of the Temple. However, as I was bent on learning the tricks of the trade, I let him pass me along in his own way. We got through the ranks of the maimed, leprous, blind, and vermin-infested horde which, in Italy, cluster about the entrances of churches, nourished there, as toadstools grow in the same soil that gives life to the monarch oak, without much depletion of the purse. They were reserving their final onset for our departure. After entering the magnificent church, worthy itself of a voyage across the Atlantic to see, it was amusing to detect the brethren of our cicerone darting at the sight of our party from behind columns and altars toward us, like spiders from their holes on their prey, and slinking reluctantly back upon seeing that we were already bought and sold. I inwardly chuckled over each disappointment, and formed plans how for the future I would examine churches unmolested, calling for a guide only in the last extremity. There was here an ancient statue of Mars baptized into a Saint Ephèse, but my cicerone was too good a Catholic to call my attention to this transformation, though the church that can convert even the stones should be acknowledged to possess miraculous powers.

From the church we passed into the baptistery, where the guardian was by no means disposed to allow us to be monopolized by our lawful owner. I was obliged to pay him something to let us alone. There was nothing to be seen, because a scaffolding totally eclipsed the dome, the building being then in that interesting state called restoration.

Next in order was the Campo Santo, the most interesting of the four monuments that constitute an architectural group unique even in Italy in beauty of location, artistic wealth, and historical souvenirs. Other cities possess edifices of equal or greater pretensions than any one of these, but none can boast four such gems assembled in one inclosure. Formerly the dead were admitted into the Campo Santo by paying a fee, but of course they never left it; there was nothing more to be made out of them. Now the living enter gratis, but the custode's hand must be crossed with silver before they can leave its sepulchral walls.

This cemetery dates from 1218, but was not finished until 1283. It is a vast rectangle, surrounded by porticoes with sixty-two semi-Gothic arches. The interior walls are covered with frescoes by the old masters, taken from scriptural subjects. The guide pointed out, with particular zest, a fancied resemblance between the portrait of Napoleon and the head of one of the damned writhing in the flames of hell. If this were accidental it was singular, as the resemblance was striking; but if the work of some restoring artist, it displays at once his ingratitude and bigotry, as the preservation of this monument is due to Napoleon. The earth which forms the field that fills the hollow square inclosed by the porticoes was brought from the holy places at Jerusalem in fifty galleys of the Republic of Pisa in 1228. It is now covered by a rich crop of grass of uniform height, like a mantle of green velvet. It has been long disused as a burial-place; but when used, it is said to be so strongly impregnated with acids as to entirely decompose the fleshy portions of corpses within forty-eight hours after their burial. One of these frescoes illustrates this statement in a somewhat painfully grotesque style. The magistrates of Pisa are assembled to witness the disinterment of three bodies that have lain in the earth longer or shorter periods of that time. The coffins are placed side by side and uncovered. The first two display different stages of decomposition too repulsive to describe. In the third appeared only the skeleton, the earth having picked the bones clean.

The floor and sides of the arcades are crusted with tablets and monuments of deceased Pisans; the records of virtues and talents are as bountifully accorded the dead as they are scantily awarded to the living. Master chisels of all ages, from John of Pisa to Bartolini and Thorwaldsen, have helped to perpetuate the flattering tale of ancestral virtue and beauty. It is an interesting spot as a museum of epitaphs, and a chronological exhibition of painting and sculpture for six hundred years, but for a burial-place far less beautiful and appropriate than the rural cemeteries of our own land.

I had almost forgotten the little church of the Holy Mary of the Crown of Thorns, a fantastic piece of architecture, beautiful in its way, but so prolifically spired as to correspond very well with its name.

On leaving the Campo Santo, the beggars made a final and desperate charge upon us. Two women in the very last stage of filth and rags seized me by the elbows, and by the love of that Virgin, of the neglect of whose worship they bore in their arms living evidence, demanded charity. Aside from any motive of benevolence, a few coins were well applied in stopping their tongues and sending them in pursuit of fresh prey. The guide proved the greatest beggar of all. He had forced himself upon me in the outset, followed me about for an hour, sold me a number of engravings of the monuments from his portfolio at double the shop price, and now, when I handed him a sum that would have drawn out of any Parisian showman a profusion of "merci biens" and an avalanche of bows, he bluntly said that his services were not half paid. The beggars, thinking their right to a stranger as good as his, renewed their importunities. I jumped into the carriage, threw him another piece of silver to silence his tongue, and ordered Jehu to cut short all farther claims by driving to the railway station for Florence. As we passed the inn at which we had dined, the landlord rushed out to demand a new contribution in the shape of a bill for water furnished for washing hands. Our driver thought this a little too strong even for an Italian Boniface, and summarily told him to go about his business, and be content with his first exactions. He then completed his contract by delivering us safely and in season at the cars, and went back to Leghorn with a weightier pocket than he had had for many a day, but not without attempting to demonstrate to me that he had not individually made much out of the operation. But a laughing eye and profusion of thanks were better evidence than his tongue.

There are certain days in a traveler's calendar in which no

amount of previous experience will keep him on the right track. He is doomed to be humbugged and cheated from sunrise to sunset—to be annoyed and crossed in every thing he undertakes—to have the weather all wrong, and to be the special mark for every species of pickpockets. At Leghorn there is no escape on any day. The only way is to quickly abandon yourself to your fate. The fewer struggles, the fewer scratches. On the morrow one can laugh heartily over the storms of its predecessor. It is usually the case, when one most wishes to indulge in quiet and sentiment, that he finds most noise and distraction. It is not until one is at "home" in Italy that he can profitably pursue his various tastes, free from the interruptions of the gallinipping gentry that pursue strangers with such relentless fury. It was amusing, after arriving at a comfortable hotel at Florence, to sum up the day's experience. We had had to satisfy six stewards, two boatmen, two sailors, three coachmen, and as many "pour boires"—a sum which every traveler knows has no limit in a "whip's" imagination—two landlords, six fees for baggage and passports, to have six trunks opened and searched twice within an hour, four guides, and ten porters, rail-road charges and beggars not included; some thirty-odd disbursements on a distance which, in America, would have been traveled over in two hours and a half, at a very moderate proportion of the same expense. And this was not all. Our progress through Leghorn was one continual street-row. Insatiable porters demanding more, and quarreling among themselves—commissionaires yelling in our ears in different tongues the praises of their several hotels—beggars whining their wants—the coachmen disputing with every body, and in vain endeavoring to whip a way through the crowd. Our baggage did not belong to us—our passports were not our own—we did not even belong to ourselves; and it was not until we promised, on our return to Leghorn—which God forbid

—that we would put up at as many different hotels as there were runners in the crowd, that we could get clear of this gentry. Even then they returned to refresh our memories by thrusting fresh cards into our hands. To add to the comforts of the landing, one of the ladies of my party had, in the goodness of her heart, promised to see a venerable spinster, who knew not a word of any language but the English, and had come thus far on her way to find a brother at Lucca, safe as far as Pisa. The old maid—I say it in its most respectful sense, for she was the impersonification of amiability and softness—had never before been out of sight of her village steeple. She had started by herself from England on this journey. The consequence was, that her solitary, antique hair trunk and calico bundle went to London, while she found herself at Paris. It took a week, and not a little expense, to get them reunited. An English family protected her as far as Genoa, and then consigned her to me. It was a pleasure to help her, she was so grateful; but, before we left Leghorn, we had two street contests on her account; that is to say, the porters perceived her weakness, which was to pay her way out of every scrape with an open purse, and made scrapes for her accordingly. It was no use insisting that she was one of my party. They would not stand that gammon. She must pay separately for every thing. I fought stoutly for her for a while, but it was of no use. At the custom-house, the officers, attracted by the singularity of her costume, which, perhaps, savored of Republican simplicity in their eyes, insisted upon ransacking her trunk and bundle from one end to the other. Every thing was turned out—bags opened—bundles unrolled—boxes emptied; it was a curious collection. The poor woman stood by, weeping bitterly, wringing her hands, saying, "O dear, what shall I do?" and refusing to be comforted. This but rendered the officers more suspicious. They were looking, evidently, for dispatches from Mazzini, or perhaps they expected to find Kossuth himself coiled up in one of her rolls of odds and ends, the gatherings of a long life of neatness and saving. Alas for them, they found only a yard or so of cotton, some pet remnant, which they measured, and finding it an inch wider than Tuscan law allowed, charged accordingly, and told the luckless female to repack her trunk. She was too bewildered to do it herself, so we did it for her. She made eight more charges in addition to my previous list before we discharged her at Pisa, but I laughed heartily when I heard her explain, after all, how she had thrown dust in the eyes of the officers of the customs by bringing a new silk dress in the piece, cunningly folded up in the skirts of some antiquated garment. She was not so unfit to travel by herself, after all.

If any one thinks that I have done injustice to Leghorn, I refer them to Dumas. He says, "I have been to Leghorn three times; the last two I was forewarned—I took my precautions, I held myself upon my guard; each time I paid still more dear. I never knew such a cut-throat place as Leghorn. One may escape being robbed on the Pontine Marshes sometimes, but at Leghorn—never."

CHAPTER II.

FLORENCE—ITS APARTMENTS—PALACES—STREETS AND THEIR CUSTOMS—THE PERGOLA AND THE MISERICORDIA—BALLS, ETC.

THERE is something in the very name of Florence that suggests refinement and pleasurable emotions. It is a delicious sound in itself, and of all others the most appropriate to the floral city of Italy. It recalls, too, the peerless queen of ancient sculpture, the Medicean Venus, and the triumph of modern art in Raphael's Madonna della Seggiola. Great names belong to its history, and its sons have bequeathed immortal works to mankind. It was then with involuntary respect and admiration that I entered, for the first time, the city of Dante and Michael Angelo, and trod the streets that had echoed to the footsteps of Galileo and Lorenzo the Magnificent.

There is something, too, peculiarly fascinating in the associations connected with Florence. We cluster about its name, at least I did, palaces and villas in charming profusion, a laughing landscape, treasuries of art, and a hospitality which makes it a paradise for exiles in pursuit of artistic ease or literary quiet. To crown all these advantages, it has long enjoyed the reputation of being the cheapest place in Europe. I had not long been a resident before I discovered that Florence was like the Arno, extremely variable in its looks, and constantly rushing into extremes. The first aspect is its worst. It so improves upon acquaintance, that, like a delicious fragrance, it always leaves behind a pleasing reminiscence.

The Arno, which divides it, is a most capricious river. One

day it swells to a fierce torrent, filling the wide space between the quays to almost a level with their embankments, and rushes along with terrific force, threatening to sweep before it the massive stone bridges which dispute its passage. On the next it shrinks to a most consumptive-looking stream, barely able to find its way over its own sands, and which a thirsty Arab might almost exhaust at one draught. During the ardent heats of summer it is lost amid clouds of dust. Then Florence empties itself into the country, for even the barber has his villa, and apartments, like tombs, gape for occupants.

My first object was to secure an apartment. It was the season when all the world returns to the city, and its inhabitants expect in four months to make enough out of the fleeting crowd of Americans, English, French, and Russians to live on during the entire twelve.

There was something seductive to even a republican imagination coupled with the idea of living in a palace, and possessing a garden ornamented with fountains and statues. Accordingly, I commenced my search with them. There was no lack; but their exteriors, with the exception of a certain graceful solidity, bore more resemblance to our ideas of prisons than luxurious mansions. I fancied them rather to be cut out of the solid rock than built up stone by stone. Such were the rival palaces of the Strozzi, Riccardi, Pitti, and the old republican stronghold, the Palazzo Vecchio. These were the types of all of the olden time, when every house was a citadel, and each family an independent power, struggling for life and fortune with its neighbor. Their proportions are fine, and their general appearance very imposing, but they are far from answering to our modern ideas of a palatial residence, especially if we have derived our taste from the beautiful structures of Paris. Their interiors are arranged on the same Titanic scale. Apartments so lofty that the eye fairly aches in the endeavor to trace out the ornaments of the ceiling, while the feet perish with cold on damp mosaic floors. The windows require a series of steps to reach their sills, and the doors and chimneys evolve a series of petrifying draughts that few modern constitutions are proof against. In general, the palaces are built on narrow, dark streets, guiltless of side-walks, and are impartially scattered all over the city, amidst characteristic styles of architecture of lesser pretensions. These have now degenerated into the abodes of poverty, so that, with the exception of a few modern innovations, no portion of the city can claim an aristocratic preference over another.

STROZZI PALACE.

The Strozzi Palace is the finest specimen of this type of mansions, from which cold magnificence and architectural effect banished comfort and sociability. It still belongs to the family that erected it in 1489, and looks as if it might continue to stand until Time, in its march reversing those figures, shall tell its age by thousands instead of hundreds of years. There are but three stories, but each story attains itself the height of an American house. Its interior arrangements are on a scale of gloomy grandeur, so much beyond the wants of even a Florentine noble, with his numerous train of dependants, that not many years since, some of the children of the family, in playing, discovered a suite of twelve rooms entirely unknown to the proprietor. The door had been walled up for two hundred years, and no one in this vast edifice had missed the space thus mysteriously closed. There is no garden attached to this palace. The interior forms a hollow square, paved with flat stones, with nothing to relieve the dungeon-like aspect of the massive walls.

There are ancient palaces of this character, but on a lesser scale, scattered throughout the city, which offer furnished apartments to strangers at prices cheap enough for the space they proffer, but too dear for the amount of comfort they have in store. If it be winter, the gardens are a nuisance, because the frequent rains keep them so damp as to be prejudicial to health. Italians, profiting by the experience of centuries, do not plant their squares and open spaces, as we do, with grass and shrubbery, but scrupulously exclude all vegetation, believing it in cities to be unwholesome. Their squares are either paved or Macadamized. Thus all the anticipated pleasures of orange groves and smiling gardens dissolve in Florence, during winter, like "the baseless fabric of a dream" before the superior considerations of health. The chief object is to obtain a sunny aspect. There are comparatively few such, and they command higher prices in consequence. The truth is, that the boasted Italian climate is as treacherous as a coquette. You never know when you are on good terms with it. It weeps and smiles in the same instant. On the shady side of the street you are frozen, and on the sunny side roasted. The breeze, when most wooing, is most to be suspected. In short, you must keep constantly on the *qui vive* to stop the numerous colds, rheumatisms, fevers, and pleurisies that are floating about in the atmosphere, before they can obtain a lodgment in your body. I dislike a climate that keeps one in a constant fuss. There are some so hospitable that the stranger can abandon himself without reserve to their keeping, taking no thought for the coming shower, and welcoming without suspicion the grateful breeze, whether it be that of noonday or midnight. With them, a current of air is not loaded with ills to the human frame, nor does a meridian sun prove false to its smiling face. Such is the climate of the Hawaiian group, the paradise of invalids and amateurs of a pure atmosphere.

The furniture in general of the furnished apartments appears to have migrated hither from the "*maisons meublés*" of Paris and the lodging-houses of London, after having been turned out of their doors as unfit for farther service. The attempts at neatness and embellishment are mournfully ludicrous; but, as the standard of an American for home comforts must necessarily be considerably lowered before he reaches Italy, he views these things with a less fastidious eye, and charitably pities their owners for knowing no better. Habits and tastes partake of the fluctuating extremes of the climate. In the birth-place of the chef-d'œuvres of art, and models of refined and celestial beauty, we find customs more disgusting and tastes more barbarous than among even semi-savages. Sights are daily seen in the most public places which, in the United States, would send their authors to the Penitentiary for a violation of public decency, while many streets—even those pretending to rank among the best—are almost impassable on account of their filthy condition. This arises from the neglect of providing in their houses what in England and America are considered indispensable adjuncts of even the meanest of habitations. When changes have been made, it has been owing to the demands of travelers, and the absolute necessity, if Italy would not starve, of catering to their wants.

Carpets, too, and fire-places capable of supporting a fire, are modern innovations. Florentines manage to live without both, when strangers from northern climes would be chilled to the very marrow. A few coals in an earthen dish suffice to keep their blood in motion, and if their feet are cold, they thrust them into woolen muffs. These are homely things to mention in connection with the classical soil of Italy; but, as all the world either comes or wishes to come hither, I am sure they will pardon me for mentioning a few things not usually to be found in travels or guide-books.

The distribution of the houses and palaces is the same as at Paris, into stories for separate families, only they rarely have "*porte cochères*," and less seldom, porters. It is very difficult, therefore, to find a friend after finding his house. No one pretends to know the names of the streets, for each corner has a separate christening. The houses throughout the city are numbered from one up to ten thousand, as may be, and, as the series is not always a neighborly one, a stranger is often greatly puzzled where to begin his search. Supposing the house found, he has before him a narrow door, by the side of which he finds a perpendicular row of bells, one answering to each apartment, and numbered accordingly. These bells communicate with the different stories, and from them descend stout wires to the door-latch, passing sometimes outside of the house, and sometimes in, so that every house has the appearance of being a telegraph office. You ring by chance one of these bells—one of the wires is set in motion, the door thrown open, and you find yourself in an unlighted entry, looking more like the entrance to some subterranean vault than to a gentleman's house. A voice from an immeasurable distance above calls out, "Who's there?" You respond, "A friend," or "A robber," if you wish to be waggish. If it be night, and you have forgotten to bring your pocket-taper, you must grope your way up an intricate and narrow staircase as you best may, or do as I have often done, beat a retreat in utter despair, for you can not see an inch beyond your nose. The custom is not to light the staircases—the exceptions are only the grand mansions. You have counted a hundred steps, omitting some in the agony of a battered shin, and at last find yourself at about what you consider the elevation which your friend, who is an amateur of sunlight, has selected for a lodging. Groping about for a bell, if you succeed in that search, a voice within, in a shrill key, demands again, "Who's there?" If satisfied that yours has an innocent ring, the door is opened, and you discover that your friend lives on the opposite side of the street, just one story higher. You prefer to meet him at Doney's, or at the Cascine, to undertaking again to find him in his lair. Indeed, the difficulties attending a domestic exploration are so well understood, that calls are considered as honored when returned at the Casino or any of the public rendezvous. An Italian talks very little about his home.

There are some neat and well-furnished apartments at Florence, but to be found, they must be diligently sought. The average of such as strangers occupy are as I have described, with two prices, according to the season, summer paying but half the rate of winter. An apartment in a palace of from twelve to twenty or more rooms, furnished, including silver and linen, with a kitchen ample enough for a regiment, and the privilege of a garden, costs fifty dollars a month. A Tuscan dollar is equal to eleven dimes United States currency. Apartments of more moderate pretensions, smaller rooms, and, therefore, more easily warmed, but large enough for a family, abound at from twenty to forty dollars per month for the winter. A bachelor can find passable accommodation as low as five dollars, and obtain by the year a fine suite of rooms, unfurnished, for fifty dollars. The best situations in new houses, including modern improvements, bath-rooms, &c., can be had for about thrice that sum. But there is a Florentine maxim which strangers would do well to keep in mind: "Let your house the first year to your enemy, the second to your acquaintance, and the third to your friend"—a new house, from the mode of construction, being considered unwholesome, as it takes a long time to dry. Villas go a begging. In the summer they are comfortable, but in winter damp and chilly. Where houses are built almost exclusively of stone and mortar, with a copious provision of currents of air, this must be expected.

The market is well supplied, at low prices. At the cafés and restaurants, a breakfast costs eleven cents, and a good enough dinner thirty-three. At the table d'hôte of hotels, fifty-five, and an excellent meal at that. But, for those who wish to avoid the annoyances of providing for the table, the "trattori," or public cooks, supply meals of every quality and cost, served up at any hour in any part of the city. For one dollar and a quarter per day, a friend of mine was well served for five persons with a dinner consisting of soup, three courses of meat, several of vegetables, wine, and a dessert of pastry and fruit. Clothing and most other articles are cheaper than in the United States, and the services of the best professors in music, languages, and education generally, can be had for about one half the price. In short, if one can reconcile himself to Florentine habits, sharp wine, water so hard that it makes you fear that you will eventually become a stalactite, the loss of politics and newspapers, and odors that are the more aggravating from being unnecessary, Florence is the city for the money.

This is not all. There is another annoyance, which, as it is the exclusive property of pretty women, I mention, that they may go forewarned. It is as bad in many other European cities, but there is in it something more ludicrous at Florence than elsewhere.

Fashion tells the ladies, with reason, that they must not walk. The streets generally are in too uninviting a condition for such an operation, where skirts are to be employed, and Bloomerism has not yet made its advent here. Besides, it is apparent that they were intended only for carriages and beggars. There are a few places where they might walk, were it not for the abominable habits of the male population. Foreign ladies frequently attempt it, and it is forgiven in them by the Florentines on the score of their being strangers and knowing no better. Old and ugly women can do it with impunity any where, at any time. But let a lady of even ordinary attractions attempt it by herself, or in company with others of her sex, and if she be not vexed, astonished, mortified, and amused before she regains her own roof, it will be because she proves an exception to an otherwise general rule. When she least expects it, some impudent clown or peasant suddenly pokes his ugly, dirty face right under her bonnet, makes a mock kiss, cries "boo," or some such intelligible sound, or compliments her with a "cara" or some equally loving epithet, and walks innocently off, with his hands in his pockets, before her astonishment has had time to jump into indignation. If she escape these low vagabonds, she is sure to attract the race of gentlemen, who, having nothing else to do, amuse themselves by following ladies. The less impudent dog them at a distance, but near enough to let them know that every motion is watched and commented upon. The bolder pass and repass, to take a good stare; walk ahead, that they may return and meet them, saying flattering things in an under tone, with the intention of being overheard. The boldest come alongside, and let fly a complimentary volley, without any compunctions, much amused if an inexperienced damsel involuntarily jumps aside at such an unlooked-for tribute to her attractions. There was one young Florentine who made himself quite conspicuous at this sort of pastime. He could speak a few words of English, and had a mania for running after foreign ladies, and launching upon their astonished ears the extent of his philological acquirements. His vocabulary was confined to a few flattering ejaculations. One day he overtook an English lady and her daughters. He was but a pint measure of a man, but he boldly gave chase, and, coming up, called out, "Very good," "very much pretty," "I like," "you handsome," rattling on as fast as his tongue would permit. First he would be on one side, then on another, now heading them, now sailing round, and cutting such absurd capers that the ladies could not refrain from smiling. This he took for encouragement, and plied his battery of admiration more vigorously than ever. The lady, at last arriving at her own door, suddenly entered, while he, more intent upon her than his own ways, pitched over a donkey, that laid him sprawling in the street. This, with a hint that a little birch would be applied to his skin the next time he ventured upon a similar experiment, cured him for a while; but the last I heard of him he was on the watch to waylay some American ladies as they descended from their carriages, popping up suddenly under their noses like a phantom, with his everlasting "very much pleased," and "charming ladies," from which amusement nothing short of a thorough drubbing is likely to cure him. The plain truth is, that a pretty lady, though safe from violence, is not safe from impertinence at any time of the day in Florence. Consequently, she must keep a carriage if she would go out, so that whatever economy there may be in Florence, in other respects, over other capitals, it is, in the main, lost in the extra expense of horseflesh. Or, in other words, the difference of prices between Paris and Florence in the essentials of housekeeping enables one to keep a carriage in the capital of Tuscany.

There is still another indispensable expense, if a family desire to enter within the charmed circle of "society," and this is a box at the Pergola, in one of the three tiers classified as noble. Although it costs a stranger a third more than a Florentine—this same ratio obtains in every thing else—it is not a costly affair. One hundred and twenty-five to one hundred and fifty dollars will pay the cost of a season of several months, and this expense may be reduced by imitating the example of the Florentines, and letting the box on nights when not wanted. You may dispense with receptions "*chez-vous*," but it is an unpardonable sin in the world of fashion not to be at home at the Opera. The world goes to the Opera as to a *réunion.* There they pay their visits, chat, laugh, partake of refreshments, turn their backs upon the stage—in short, almost drown by their conversation the music. The Opera is nothing; the assemblage of fashion every thing. A box, then, at the Pergola is really an economical affair, as it saves the expense of society under one's roof; it is a most amusing one, from the variety of ranks, nations, and toilets there represented. The English astonish there, as every where, with their brilliant colors, forests of plumes, and bizarre costumes; the Russians with their mines of precious stones; the Germans with their fair hair and brilliant complexions; the Florentines by their princely jewels, laces, and velvets, drawn from their imperishable hereditary stores; the French eclipse all by their matchless elegance, seemingly so simple and unstudied; while the Americans please all from their rarity and general good taste.

The theatre is so constructed that while one half of the audience of the boxes can, if they choose, look toward the stage, the other half are necessarily turned toward the imperial box, which is quite a hall of itself. Of course, the architect never contemplated in his design the spectacle as the main object of the edifice. It is merely an auxiliary. If an opera, it attracts attention only from novelty or the harmony of particular strains. But the ballet, which is introduced between the acts of the Opera, rivets the attention of all. It is strange, but true, that a Florentine audience prefers poor dancing to good music. While the American, Miss Maywood, was with them, they had a legitimate excuse for their passion, for a more elastic, untiring, and, the Italians say, graceful danseuse never appeared on any boards. They exalt her above Cerito, Ellsler, and even Taglioni. But what carried them away nightly into a tempest of applause was the perfection of her time. The music and her limbs moved in such entire accord as to seem but one impulse. "Bravas and encores" thundered over the house. Hands, feet, and lips were all in violent commotion in all quarters. No eloquence could have excited the susceptible Florentines to half such a pitch of "furore" as her legs. Bouquets as large as wine-barrels were precipitated upon the stage, their numerous ribbons fluttering gayly in the air as they fell, like the pennants from a masthead. She fairly staggered under their weight. On one occasion, the prima donna, having vainly essayed to carry off a monster bouquet, gracefully drew it behind the scenes by its ribbons, courtesying as she backed across the stage, amid the cheers of the spectators. At Maywood's benefit it took three carriages to carry away the floral avalanche tumbled at her feet.

There are nine theatres and Operas in the little city of Florence, but, with the exception of the Pergola, of no pretensions to fashion or elegance. The Cocomero is a very humble and unsuccessful imitator of the Théâtre Française at Paris. At all there is a price of entry, in addition to which another sum is demanded for seats not in the parterre. There are two Operas where the Tuscans can listen to the music of Mozart, Rossini, or Donizetti for five cents, and the cheapest of the theatres did provide a night's entertainment for a trifle less than three cents, commencing at eight and terminating past midnight.

It is at the Opera, perhaps, that the attention is first drawn toward a society which ranks in the annals of Roman Catholic benevolence second only in good works to that of the Sisters of Charity. Not unfrequently, in the midst of one of Maywood's marvelous pirouettes, the sharp tone of a bell strikes upon the ear. All listen. If it sounds but once, it is the signal of an ordinary accident; if twice, a grave casualty; if three times, a death. It is the bell of the Misericordia. From all parts of the house, spectators rise one by one, and abruptly leave. Probably the gentleman with whom you are conversing, if an Italian, excuses himself, takes his hat, and departs. The audience turn toward the stage, and in a minute the interruption is forgotten.

The Society of Misericordia is one of the purest and noblest charities with which the Christian religion has blessed the world. It took its rise in 1244, when the plague ravaged Europe. For six centuries it has maintained its existence, true to the holy principles of its original foundation, a fact, perhaps, without a parallel in the history of humanity. It represents, in different proportions, the aristocracy, the liberal arts, and the people. The artisans of Florence, moved by the contagions that desolated their city, leaving multitudes of sick without

THE BROTHERS OF PITY.

succor, and of dead without burial, were the first to conceive the sublime idea of its institution. The wealthy added their donations, and the society soon took rank among the most important institutions of charity.

The Brethren of Pity, or the Misericordia, are under the direction of seventy-two members, called "Capi di Gardia" (chiefs of watch). These regulate the works of charity, the administration of its revenues, which are considerable, and the distribution of alms. They are composed of ten prelates, fourteen nobles, twenty priests, and twenty-eight artisans. Under their immediate orders are two hundred and eighty "giornanti," or journeymen, secular and ecclesiastical. Forty of these are always on service. There are, besides, inscribed on their lists, voluntarily, the names of more than twelve hundred other brethren, called "buonevoglie," whom they can call upon at any moment to assist in their charitable labors.

The office of the Misericordia is in the Piazza del Duomo. Each brother on duty keeps there, marked with his name, a box containing his black robe, which covers him from head to foot. They are such as penitents formerly wore, with openings only for the mouth and eyes, in order that the incognito of charity, recommended by Christ, shall be strictly preserved. As soon as the signal is heard that their services are required, the members on duty assemble at their office, assume their mournful habit—which no one can see for the first time without being strangely affected—receive their orders, and proceed to the scene of their duties. Some are required to carry the diseased or wounded to the hospitals, or other places, as need may be. Others devote themselves to nursing in the homes of the ill and infirm poor. They often pass days and nights at their bedsides, bestowing upon them those attentions which try even the constancy of friendship and the affinities of blood. In every place, at any hour, wherever an accident calls, a groan is heard, or there are misery and suffering to be relieved, the Brothers of Pity are required, by their voluntary bond of good deeds, to bestow their alms and their offices. It matters not what may be the origin of the poor victim, or whether he confesses Christ, Moses, or Mohammed. Their charity blesses alike all men, without distinction of race or religion. They bury the unknown dead, carrying themselves the corpse to the sepulchre. The scaffold even does not repel them from fulfilling, in its broadest extent, the spirit of their vows. They are to be found at the latest moment beside the criminal, consoling and preparing him for his doom; and, after his head has fallen under the axe of the guillotine, gathering up his mangled remains, to bestow upon them a Christian burial. Priest and layman, noble and mechanic, unknown perhaps to each other, and unrecognizable by their nearest relatives, bear upon their shoulders the same litter, containing, it may be, a poor cripple, abandoned by all the world beside. Knowing his benefactors only by the uniform which proclaims them to be ministering angels to suffering mankind, he prays to their common Father alike for all. The spectator of the mournful cortège, be he prince or beggar, respectfully uncovers his head as it silently passes along the street. Often, when unknown hands have borne away the head of a family to the succors poverty too often denies to her children under their own roofs, or perhaps to his burial, the afflicted mother finds that the same hands have left behind them alms that will nourish her through her first sorrows, and linger forever in her grateful memory.

The Grand Duke is a member of the society, more in name than in action, though he is said occasionally to assume the habit and visit the bedside of the dying, leaving behind him a clew to his rank by the extent of his bounty.

But, as with every other creature of man, useful as it undoubtedly is, and meriting the warmest eulogiums, yet it is not without its evils. It was established during a period of great public calamity, when human nature shrank affrighted from the duties it was called upon to perform. The ties of blood had lost their power, wealth had grown alike feeble, while misery, disease, and despair rioted in their career of selfishness, profligacy, and death. Then religion intervened, and, with her parable of the Samaritan, rekindled in the heart of humanity that ardent love of the common neighbor which led to the holiest rivalry in charity, and most touching self-abnegation the world had as yet witnessed on so comprehensive a scale. Its benefits during pestilence are incalculable, because it is during seasons when ordinary benevolence fails that its sublime energies take their loftiest flight. They lead the forlorn hope of humanity, and cheerfully mount the breach to contest with death, in its most appalling forms, their right to save its victims. But when the world treads its usual course, the ordinary sentiments of human brotherhood had better be left to their natural action. Corporations in benevolence, as in commerce, tend to weaken individual responsibility or enterprise. If an accident occurs, is is rare indeed that the sufferer does not find a Samaritan among the sympathizing crowd, prompt to bind up his wounds. But, should a brother of the Misericordia be at hand, he anoints the victim with oil from his crucifix, and thus seals him as his own. The neighbors, disburdened of the compassionate calls of their own consciences, cease to interfere, for he is no longer a waif upon the shores of humanity, but a wreck in charge of his spiritual and medicinal underwriters. The brother hastens to give the alarm to his assistants, but it sometimes happens that, before they have time to don their habits and arrive at the side of the sufferer, he has passed beyond the reach of their help. However, these casualties are of rare occurrence, and it is doubtful if any other system of benevolence would be found better adapted to the wants of Tuscany—habituated as it is to the guidance of a hierarchy that forbids individual action and responsibility in all matters of civil and religious policy—than that practiced by this organized militia of charity.

The Pergola retains its motley and brilliant world until near midnight, when it scatters itself among the various soirées, receptions, and balls which Florence proffers with so much hospitality. A singular feature of Florentine society is its cosmopolitan character. Elsewhere, the native element predominates; but here it is but one star in the firmament of fashion, often eclipsed by the superior magnitude of those that have wandered hither from foreign spheres. Representatives of all the nations of Europe here meet in social rivalry, each striving to outshine the other, while adding to the pleasure of the whole. Consequently, society furnishes a variety, brilliancy, and piquancy not readily to be found in other cities.

The nobles have established a sort of club, called the Casino, which possesses a fine suite of rooms in the Piazza Santa Trinita. Any stranger properly recommended can become a member, by the payment of a trifling fee for the benefit of the servants. There is no restaurant or reading-room, but it affords an agreeable social rendezvous, with facilities for cards and billiards. It is under the patronage of the Grand Duke; and, during the winter, balls are given. The court generally attend, and the etiquette is of that easy good-breeding that makes every one feel at home. They form a very agreeable addition to the hospitalities of Florence.

The chief attractions, however, are the court balls at the Pitti. The Grand Duke, with politic liberality, throws open his vast and beautiful *salons* frequently, during the fashionable season, to the society of Florence. No billets of invitation are issued, but notice is sent to each foreign minister when the balls are to occur, and he notifies those of his countrymen whom he judges suitable to be presented. Their names are sent in to the Grand Chamberlain. The Americans, having no representative, are obliged to apply to him personally. The Chevalier Ginori is always prompt to perform for those of respectability the service which properly belongs only to a representative of their country. Those who have ever been presented go freely to all the fêtes without farther ceremony. The foreigners or Florentines, not yet presented, assemble at nine o'clock in one of the halls, where they await, with their minister, the entrance of the Grand Duke. Each nation has a place apart. The Grand Duke, reversing the usual awkward courtly etiquette, which requires the inexperienced stranger to be presented to the sovereign, and *back* out from his presence, walks round the circle, hearing the name of each person, and occasionally stopping to make some observation. The whole affair is very quickly dispatched, and the parties hurry off to the dance, which is kept up with great animation until about two o'clock.

No city in Europe surpasses Florence in the magnificence of its toilets (at least, so it is said); not so much in the dress as in the displays of ancient lace and jewels. In viewing the *élite* of Florentine aristocracy on a gala night, one would suppose that each alone possessed the key of Aladdin's cave. The balls of the English and French courts may be more brilliant in their *tout ensemble*, but, for sociability and good taste, those of the Grand Duke stand foremost. The charm of Italian society is that it immediately melts all reserve, while it retains a tone of chivalrous courtesy. You are unbent, in spite of yourself, when once the presentation is passed. It is really delightful to see the easy familiarity of the best-bred Italians among themselves. It is not elaborate, like that of Frenchmen, taking its cue from the head, but is a genuine inspiration of the heart. Personal freedoms are not bestowed, as among the Anglo-Saxon race, with an emphasis that all but upsets the recipient, and makes him as fearful of meeting a "good fellow" as he would a mad dog, but are given with all the delicacy and grace of young girls Our ways, to be sure, are not like their ways, and we rather shrink from a whiskered and mustached exquisite, who, after knowing us one day, calls us by our Christian name, on the second " my dear," and, upon meeting after a brief separation, rushes into our arms, landing an affectionate kiss plump on our lips, hugging us in the mean while with all the ardor of a just accepted lover. Despite this risk, however, there is about them an undefinable courtesy, which, without meaning or costing much, or savoring even of English " home" hospitality, fills up the chinks of social intercourse admirably, and makes a smooth surface often out of very unpromising materials. Possessing lively imaginations, quick perceptions, and great elasticity of spirit, with a natural taste for the beautiful in whatever they study, they give an Epicurean relish to society more delicately flavored than the sparkling tone of France, so like its own Champagne. They are proud, sensitive, and trifling; but, in their anger, courteous, and if they waste time, it is gracefully done. The more I see of Italian character, the higher the estimate I put upon its moral and intellectual capacities. If it does not correspond to our standard, charity requires us to ask why. When we have penetrated the spell that makes it what it is, we prize our own institutions the more, and pray for the time when Italy shall throw off her bonds, and contest on equal terms with the free nations of earth for that moral supremacy which alone constitutes true greatness.

CHAPTER III.

FLORENCE ARCHITECTURALLY AND HISTORICALLY, WITH GLIMPSES AT ITS DEAD LIONS.

FLORENCE possesses enough beautiful architecture to make the reputation of a dozen American towns. This is to be expected of a city where Giotto, Arnolfo, Brunellesco, Michael Angelo, and Raphael were the architects, and labored on both public and private edifices. But, for all this, Florence, viewed internally, has, for a European capital, a somewhat mean aspect. It is too condensed. With few exceptions, its numerous palaces and churches are hidden in obscure streets, with seeming indifference to external effect, notwithstanding their architectural merit and delicate ornature. It is difficult for the eye to measure their beautiful proportions or to appreciate their labored elegance, because it has not space in which to grasp their harmonious unity.

The taste for narrow, dark streets, with eaves so projecting as greatly to interefere with the free passage of light, has not even yet been wholly superseded by the modern love for more wholesome and cheerful neighborhoods. The old lords were satisfied to find a foundation sufficiently firm and ample for their massive habitations. The present nobles live where their fathers did, or, if they build, are much inclined to imitate them. Thus the villas Poniatowski and Borghese, both modern, occupy situations which no one of America's "upper ten thousand" could stomach for a day. Then, too, a goodly portion of the palaces in general is devoted to the baser uses of trade. Even the oldest names do not hesitate to retail wine from their cellars through a little iron trap-door to any one who knocks thereon. This is, however, a time-honored patrician practice, and sanctioned by classical usage, for the old Roman lords did the same.

The general dispersion of the mansions of the nobility throughout the town is not without beneficial results. It prevents the isolation of the rich and poor into distinct quarters, and makes them better acquainted. If the grand effect of palaces is somewhat diminished by indiscriminate herding with meaner edifices, the general appearance of the place is improved. Hence, although we may find many incongruous spectacles in the neighborhood, and sometimes about even aristocratic mansions, such as stables and mechanics' shops beneath, vegetable and meat stalls against their walls, and more filthy sights and smells at their base, or awkward festoons of family linen suspended from the chamber windows to dry, yet there is a very welcome absence of those squalid abodes of filth and poverty which distinguish certain quarters of more democratic cities.

The most characteristic specimen of that species of architecture which gives to Florence so anomalous an aspect is the Pitti Palace. The front is usually regarded as the back, and, at first glance, from the immense size of the rough-hewn stones, its apparent simplicity, and vast extent, it upsets all one's previous conceptions of a regal residence. But farther and closer inspection convinces one of its architectural superiority over most of the lighter and more fanciful palaces we find elsewhere. It has about it the imposing aspect and strength of an aristocratic residence, yet it would equally befit the governmental wants of a republic. Solid and graceful, in its harmonious combination of strength and beauty, it is not excelled, in these respects, by any other royal residence in

Europe. It was commenced in 1440, by Brunellesco, for Luca Pitti, an enemy of the Medici, desirous of eclipsing their wealth and power by giving an imposing token of his own. He

PITTI PALACE—FRONT VIEW.

wished also to build a palace on so capacious a scale that the court-yard alone should be able to contain the entire palace of his rival Strozzi. He finished by ruining himself, and his palace passed into the possession of his enemies. By them it was completed as we find it, though the family were nearly

PITTI PALACE—REAR VIEW.

two centuries about the work. The side toward the garden is a very striking contrast to the other, possessing the same elements of solidity, but so arranged as to be in unison with the smiling vista of flowers, groves, and statues beyond. A stranger, seeing one side only of this building, would go away with as obstinate and false an idea of its *tout ensemble* as did the knights of the ancient legend who looked only on the silver or gold surface of the shield toward them, and be as fully inclined to battle to the death for his but half-formed opinion.

The peculiar situation of Florence, in the hollow of many hills, with its bisecting river running seaward through a rich plain, hemmed in by picturesque ranges of the Apennines, and studded as thickly with white villas as are the heavens of a clear night with stars, makes its first view, from whichsoever side it is approached, novel and charming. Come upon it how and where we may, whether from the distant mountain, the overhanging hill, or the verdant plain, the impression of its beauty is equally vivid. It has as many aspects as a kaleidoscope, and it would be a nice point to settle upon the best. If there be any fault to be found with the general landscape about Florence, it would be that it is overcharged with art. Nature appears only under cultivation. The geology of the soil is seen chiefly in the structures that man has reared. The very surface-rock is exhausted or covered with vineyards, while the agriculturist's hand leaves no spot of ground untouched. The forest trees have a garden-look. The roads are narrow, tortuous, and confined by high stone walls. Industry stops only before the sterile or precipitous mountain summits which make either horizon of the valley. In short, the suburbs are like the expanded blossom, while the city resembles the shrunken seed-pod.

It is no easy matter for Florence to stretch herself out to modern notions of comfort. Her efforts at widening her streets remind one of the yawns of a dozing giant. Houses which are as solid as the quarry itself are not to be trimmed or moved off like the frail structures of America. They were built to last, not years, but centuries, and they are fully determined on completing their destiny. Still something has been done, and modern Florentines begin to have a faint idea that there exists sunlight somewhere in the region above them. Within a few years, the principal business street of the city, leading from the Cathedral Square to the Place of the Grand Duke, has been remodeled into a fine wide avenue, which would do credit to Paris. Formerly it was so narrow that carriages could not pass each other. Yet a modern English author laments the change, while so many churches remain unfinished, as if the completion of a façade was to human beings a consideration of more importance than a supply of the pure air of heaven. Of late, we have had an abundant crop of those amateurs of good old times, who would fain persuade the people that when they herded like swine, fought their lord's quarrels, and begged at convent gates, they were better off than with the comforts of the nineteenth century about them. They may be willing to replace the cottage by the hovel, the model lodging-house by the damp and unwholesome habitations of the Middle Ages, that the cathedral and palace may be built to gratify their architectural taste ; but we doubt if one of them would consent to reduce his own household standard to the level of the Elizabethan age, exchanging his Champagne for coarse beer, and his Brussels carpets for dirty rushes, however much he may prate about the petrifying influence of modern sensuality, as shown in the luxury of boudoirs and pride of reception-rooms.

The oldest monument of Florence is the Baptistery of St. John, the primitive church of the city, dating its consecration to Christ from the sixth century, but having, at least in part, a prior origin as a heathen temple. This we should consider a very respectable antiquity were Rome not so near. Ancient art and architects worked slowly, so it was not until six centuries later that it was completed as we now find it. The Greek artists of the ninth century, dispersed from Constantinople, left traces of their tastes for mosaics every where. It is to them that the Baptistery is indebted for its long and meagre figures of Christ, the Virgin, and the Saints in a sea of gold. But to me its most interesting feature is that it perpetuates the memory of a generosity worthy of a Christian monument like this. While it exists it will rebuke the spirit of unworthy jealousy among artists, and long after its destruction the memory of the disinterestedness it consecrated will, it is to be hoped, continue to find an abiding place in the hearts of men.

In 1330, Andrew of Pisa was charged with the execution of the southern gate of bronze. He completed his labor in 1339. It produced so great a sensation from its beauty, that the government of Florence, with the foreign embassadors, went in solemn state to visit it, at the same time conferring upon Andrew the honors of citizenship.

There were two more gates required to complete the edifice. It was resolved to offer them to the competition of artists of all nations, in the hope that something might be realized which should correspond with the beauty of the work of the first. Each artist who received the commission was to receive also from the republic a sum sufficient for his subsistence for a year, at the expiration of which time he was to present his design Among the artists that offered themselves were Donatello, Lorenzo de Bartoluccio, Simon de Bolle, Brunellesco, and other celebrated names of that era. These were all admitted to the contest without objection. There came also a young man named Lorenzo Ghiberti, an itinerant goldsmith and carver, who had been encouraged to present himself by the Lord of Rimini. The judges asked him what he had done. This was a difficult question for him to answer, for as yet he had modeled only pretty playthings in wax and clay for the children of his patron. Ghiberti, discouraged by the severity of the judges, was upon the point of abandoning his project and returning to Rimini, to work upon the frescoes ordered of him by Malatesta, its tyrant, as it was the fashion then to call the petty lords, when one of his competitors, interested by his youth and energy, interceded for him. He was received, more to encourage his ambition than in the belief of his becoming a rival. This was, however, all he desired. The money was handed him for his year's expenses, and he devoted himself to the task.

At the expiration of the year, the thirty-four judges, all first rate artists, assembled to decide upon the designs of the claimants.

Donatello, Lorenzo de Bartoluccio, and Brunellesco equally divided their suffrages. On which of the three the work should have been bestowed, would perhaps have proved to the judges as difficult of solution as to unravel the Gordian knot, and perhaps they would have been obliged to decide the question on the same principle of division, had not these three artists solved the problem for them. The sketch of Ghiberti lay there beside their own. It had been pronounced very beautiful, but not worthy of competition with theirs. Retiring into a corner, the three conversed earnestly together for a few minutes. Their course was soon taken. Coming forward, they respectfully represented to the judges that, in justice to art, they could not receive the prize while a design like that of Ghiberti's was before them. Upon their honor and conscience, his was the superior, and to him rightly belonged the award. The judges, already favorably impressed, were readily persuaded by such disinterested testimony, and to Lorenzo Ghiberti, owing to the unparalleled generosity of his rivals, was decreed the execution of the gates. Art could not fail to prosper when genius was guided solely by justice.

Ghiberti worked forty years on his task, commencing it in his youth, and finishing it when he was old and bent. His own portrait, as he completed his work, was incorporated by him in an ornament in the middle. It cost him a lifetime, but it rewarded him with a fame more durable even than his own doors of bronze, which Michael Angelo pronounced worthy to be the gates of Paradise.

Opposite these gates we find a monument of a grace so remarkable that even in Florence its comeliness has passed into a proverb. "Beautiful as the Campanile" is the term employed when all other comparisons of splendor fail to a Florentine. It unites all the delicacy of finish of the richest lacework with the solidity of stone. Time has mellowed the original brightness of its varied marbles into a pale gold tint, leaving, however, perfectly distinguishable its checkered mosaics, which rival in delicacy the finest work of Hindostan. The Emperor Charles V. best described its marvelous beauty when he declared that it should be put under glass, and shown only on holidays. It is seemingly too fair and delicate to withstand any climate, however delicious, yet centuries, as they roll by, thus far have served but to deepen its beauties, without detracting from its perfect lightness and freshness of design.

The Campanile is the bell-tower of the Duomo, which it adjoins. The same style of decoration has been employed in the exterior of this immense building, which, like a lion couchant, lies spread out on the Piazza to which it gives a name. The dome—finished by Brunellesco in 1436—is the largest in the world. It served as the model for that of St. Peter's to Michael Angelo, who, despairing of excelling, hoped only to rival it, and desired that his tomb should be so placed that he might continue to gaze upon it even in death. "Farewell," he exclaimed, when called to Rome by Julius II., to complete

THE CAMPANILE.

St. Peter's; "I go to try to make thy sister, but I can not hope to make thy equal."

When the Florentine Republic, in 1298, designed the execution of this magnificent work, they decreed as follows: "Whereas, the chief aim of a people of great origin being to act in a way that, from its outward works, every one should recognize both its wise and magnanimous manner of proceeding, we order Arnolfo, chief architect of our city, to make a model or design for the complete rebuilding of St. Reparata, with the greatest possible magnificence that the human mind is capable of conceiving, since it has been decreed in council, both public and private, by the most able men of this city, that nothing should be undertaken for the community which did not correspond entirely to the ideas of its most enlightened citizens, united together to decide on such subjects, and moved by one and the same mind, the grandeur and glory of the country." This formula is worthy of being transplanted to transatlantic shores as a legacy to the sovereign people of the New World, from the shades of the departed republicans of the old.

The Duomo, or Cathedral, also called "Holy Mary of the Flowers," fully corresponds to the spirit of the document, with the exception that six centuries have not sufficed to furnish it with a façade, or complete some of the minor portions of the dome and the exterior gallery. It is, however, a truly magnificent monument of the taste and piety of the citizens of the old republic, whether we take in at one glance its colossal dimensions, doubled in size under the magic effect of moonlight, with its vast dome rising between us and the heavens, like a newly-created satellite for the earth, or, by the strong light of day, bewilder the eye in the vain effort to comprise into one look its interminable and delicate tracery. The exterior is as highly finished as the Campanile, and quite as worthy of a glass case. The interior is an anomaly among Roman Catholic churches of Italy for its severe and grand simplicity. It pleases me the more that I find it a church, and not a museum. It is the noblest specimen extant of the Tuscan Gothic; perhaps a little too cold, but great and consistent throughout in its proportions and decorations.

Singularly enough, the Duomo contains the monument of a

THE DUOMO.

notorious heretic and mercenary soldier, who owed his employment and honors from the Florentine Republic to his success in fighting against it. This was John Hawkwood, an Englishman, the general of the celebrated Black Bands that, in the fourteenth century, sold their swords to the highest bidders. John Hawkwood passed from the service of the Holy Father at Rome, the vicegerent of the Prince of Peace, into that of the Florentines, whom he served for twenty years. So stoutly did he battle for them, that the Church admitted him to honors next to saintship; but not for his piety, for he was a sad reprobate and brutal soldier, with but a faint respect for the ministers of religion.

At the sack of Faenza, which he abandoned to his troops, he found two of his bravest officers fighting for the possession of a poor nun, clinging, in her terror, to the crucifix of the high altar of the convent. Hawkwood promptly restored discipline by stabbing to the heart the guiltless cause of the affray.

One day two monks paid him a visit at his chateau of Montecchio. "The peace of God rest upon you," said one of them to him. "The devil take you, with your gift," bluntly replied Hawkwood. "Why do you give us so rude a reception?" meekly asked the poor brother. "Eh!" he rejoined, with the usual profane exclamation of the English race, "do you not know that I live by war, and that the peace that you wish me would make me starve?" It is easy to conceive that it must have been by other acts than these that he won the favor of the Church.

At the rear of the high altar we find the last work on which Michael Angelo labored. It represents Joseph of Arimathea taking the body of Christ from the cross, and was destined by the sculptor for his own tomb. Death did not give him time to finish it, and the unscrupulous chanonines of the Cathedral, in their pious zeal for the adornment of their church, so it is said, seized the unfinished block of marble for their high altar; and thus robbed the great artist of what would have been his most appropriate monument.

The power of genius to make every thing it touches its own

was never more fully exemplified than by the effect of Michael Angelo's name upon this city. Florence seems to belong to him, and not he to Florence. There is a touching familiarity, too, in the associations that speak of the heart, as if Florence loved as well as honored its great master. And yet there was in him more of the prophet Moses than the apostle John.

CHURCH OF SANTA MARIA NOVELLA

Buildings which in themselves have a just claim to fame, are wider known from his opinions than from their own merits; and travelers visit their shrines, not to criticise them, but to admire what Michael Angelo praised. He was wont to call the stately church of Santa Maria Novella—beautiful without, and full of good things within—his wife; and that of San

CHURCH OF SAN MINIATO UPON THE HILL.

Miniato upon the Hill, as charming and picturesque a little chapel, both in situation and decoration, as can be found any where, his rustic sweetheart. The first—like a good, honest mother of a family—still retains those qualities that made her dear to his soul; while the rural San Miniato, lovely as ever in its position, has faded like a superannuated belle, and is now visited only from the reputation of those charms that once won the love of the stern and captious architect. It is deserted even by the clergy. A peasant woman retains the key of the inclosure, and the stone mistress of Michael Angelo is now exhibited by an old crone, but too content to receive the smallest gratuity.

The imagination has almost as much to do with the reputation of Michael Angelo as with his works, in giving both that character of sublimity and grandiose effect which was evidently his aim, and for which he frequently sacrificed the nicer details of truth. In statuary, he seems to me to strive after some unattainable end, as if his conceptions overpowered his means of execution. We detect at once the force and depth of his imagination. The spiritual truths he would convey start out from the very stone, with all the energy of form and character with which they sprang into life from his teeming brain. This is particularly true of his unfinished works, which furnish the hint, and leave to the beholder's mind to complete the idea, with a perfection of moral and artistic attributes that the chisel would vainly strive to express. It is thus that Michael Angelo, by creating the motive, incites to thought. By his wonderful grasp of genius, coupled with an intensity of imagination seldom equaled, creating, as it were at will, ideas too vast and comprehensive to find a birth-place in any minds whose fires were not lighted direct from heaven, but which, when flung, as it were, into existence by the hot haste of an energy too impatient to polish them into the perfection of material shape and beauty, startle and amaze by their deep truth, he triumphs over the ordinary understandings of men. But when he condescends to work at details, we find he approaches the more common standard of art. The best Grecian sculptors excelled him in anatomical truth. He is inferior even to the Apollo and Venus, which with connoisseurs rank as antiques of the second class. The perfect symmetry and delicate finish of our own Powers are equally remote from his chisel. He exaggerated the merely physical, until, as in his Moses, it reached the unnatural, and even impossible. The Prophet of the Jews, in his hands, it is true, attained a terrific grandeur; but in divesting him of the natural features of man, he did not exalt him to a god. It is the head of a ferocious satyr, horns and all, and not that of an inspired legislator. No such countenance as his could have looked upon the Almighty and lived. The sculptors of antiquity never conceived a type of evil more repulsive. An image of brutal appetites, furious passions, and colossal dimensions, with the vulgar expression of majesty that springs from the merely physically great and pre-eminently bad, he has indeed created; but the lawgiver of the chosen tribes—he who conversed face to face with God as with a friend, until his features shone with the glory of heaven—no Christian mind can recognize in the Moses of Michael Angelo.

In the muscular developments of his women he partakes of the coarse taste of Rubens, as may be seen in his bronzes in the Louvre and statues in the Chapel of the Medici. We look in vain for the softness and harmony of outline most attractive in the daughters of Eve. His women are fit only to mate with Titans. The anatomy of his men is equally overdone; but the marble, nevertheless, is so inspired with the lofty conceptions of its sculptor, that the first sensation of physical coarseness is quickly forgotten in admiration of the power of his creative mind. In no example of chiseling sentiment from stone has he been more successful than in his Bacchus, in the Uffizii. He has labored painfully, but successfully, in polishing his marble to the smoothness of the natural skin, overcoming, as if by a strong effort, his predilection for the colossal to produce to the world a statue whose lightness of limbs, and life-like size and attitude, shall remain through all time a convincing proof of his ability to cope, in their own range of art, with the master sculptors of Greece. But the wondrous skill of this statue lies not so much in the drunken lassitude of its limbs, swelled with the inebriating juice just drained from the bowl, as in the perfect expression of joyous intoxication which gleams upon features verging toward sottish drunkenness. Intellectual beauty and physical grace have not wholly departed. Enough remains to show the perfection of the sober man, while the senses, just sinking in the cup, are struggling in their last gasp, but so faintly that they make no noise, for they feel themselves to be hopelessly gone. Rare statue, this—a Father Mathew in marble! for I know not any living apostle of temperance who discourses more eloquently, or argues more logically, than this silent stone. Every spectator must feel that drunkenness is disgusting and brutal even in its most poetical aspect.

The admirers of Michael Angelo, in their enthusiasm for his genius, have long claimed for him the habit of working straightforward from the block—smiting the stone, as it were, into shape, under the impulse of the idea graven on his mind. In some instances he may have attempted this, which would account for so many crude works from his chisel. Lately, however, accident has brought to light many curious studies of statues and models in wax which belonged to Michael Angelo, and prove that even his genius was subjected to the universal law of laborious detail, where the end sought was perfection.

His last will was characteristic of the man—a model of brevity, but a bone of contention among his heirs, if they were at all inclined to be avaricious. "*Lascio l'anima a Dio, e la mia roba ai più prossimi parenti.*" "I leave my soul to God, and my property to my nearest relations." His descendants —one of whom is a painter, and professor in the Florentine Academy—still occupy the Buonarotti mansion, where they preserve, with religious veneration, many relics of their distinguished ancestor.

There is a monument in Florence—a simple slab of marble, reposing under the shadow of its magnificent Cathedral—which interests me far more than its mighty dome or other *chefs-d'œuvre* of its material art. It recalls something more than the memory of those that will to themselves glory by earthly fanes, limiting their grasp to this sphere, which, if it be the foundation, is equally the grave of their triumphs; for it links itself with the mind of him who, though born of earth, measured heaven and hell in his philosophic glance; the poet, patriot, and theologian, whose genius has spread itself wherever human language is heard, and there is soul to feel or thought to comprehend; building himself a memorial in the grand temple of universal humanity, which will claim him for its apostle and prophet through all ages. This monument, so simple in itself, so grand in its associations, is the stone on which Dante was accustomed to sit, during warm summer evenings, to catch the cooling breeze.

The historical souvenirs of Florence cluster thickest about the Piazza del Gran Duca. From whichsoever point the city is viewed at a distance, there are two objects, rising far above all others, that form its most characteristic and conspicuous landmarks. These are the dome of the Cathedral, profoundly grand, like the faith that gave it existence, and the stern, lofty tower of the Palazzo Vecchio, lifted toward the skies like the defying arm of a giant. To view the last in its most commanding aspect, we should enter the square by the street leading to the Post-office, and directly fronting the old palace.

FLORENCE, FROM SAN MINIATO.

Then this huge but harmonious mass of stonework, so firmly rooted to the soil, and mounting so high toward heaven, with its emblazoned arms of the deceased republic, and its giant statues, fit guardians of its gloomy portal, calls up vividly from out the past the turbulent, but great and free, associations of democratic Florence; its endless animosities of Guelph and Ghibelline; its haughty aristocracy, and fierce population; the incorporated crafts and mercenary soldiery; its spasmodic changes from the rule of the people to the tyranny of princes, until the old square is alive again with the clang of mailed men, the rivalries of artists, intrigues of politicians, and the shouts of its mercurial population.

In 1298, scarcely sixteen years after the Florentines had won for themselves a Constitution, they decided to build a City Hall to accommodate their magistrates, and also to support a belfry which should be conspicuous throughout the surrounding country, and give the signal for the rallying of its democracy. Arnolfo di Sapo was ordered to build the palace, but forbidden to place a single stone of its foundation upon the earth that had sustained any portion of the house of Farinata di Uberti, which the people, in their hatred of all that bore the name of Ghibelline, had razed to the very dust. The architect, in consequence, was compelled to crowd this palace of the people into an irregular, though vast pile, leaving the place accursed by them to be forever trodden under their feet, in token of their vengeance.

During the republic, this palace lodged the chief magistrate, or Gonfalonier, with his eight priors, or assistants, two of whom had charge of each of the four quarters of the town. Their duties lasted two months, during which time they were compelled to devote themselves wholly to the service of the republic, not being allowed to leave the palace, and receiving the moderate salary of less than one dollar and a half per day. Although at the head of the republic, they were its prisoners, or at best but apprenticed servants, and not allowed any portion of the liberty of which they were the chosen guardians until their terms of office had expired. They ate in common, each being provided with two domestics, and having at their orders a secretary, likewise confined, to record their deliberations. If some such rule were adopted at Washington, we should have less "Buncombe," and more business, among our legislators. Notwithstanding the parsimony of the Florentine commonwealth toward its officers, it won for itself the surname of the Magnificent, from its great deeds in art and war.

The principal hall of the palace was made to accommodate at their ease, when they met to discuss national affairs, not less than one thousand citizens. It was constructed with such rapidity that Savonarola was accustomed to say that angels worked as masons. The republic enjoyed its stronghold but for a brief period, for thirty years later it became the residence of its tyrants.

The name of Savonarola recalls one of the strangest and most tragic events history has preserved. Savonarola was born in 1452. From infancy he manifested an austere disposition, with an ardent desire to connect himself with the Church. A vision, as later with Loyola, decided his career. He was then twenty-two years of age, and one night, having dreamed that a shower of ice had fallen upon his naked body, he suddenly awoke, and resolved to dedicate himself to the service of God, who had in this manner signified the extinction in his heart of the warm passions of youth. The next morning, without informing his friends or even his parents, he fled from his native place to Bologna, where he took the white habit of St. Dominic. He remained here for some time, but his talents and devotion made so slight an impression upon the monks, that, when the war broke out between Venice and Ferrara, they drove him, with a number of others, from the convent, as being so many useless mouths.

Savonarola came to Florence, where he found an opportunity to preach during Lent at the church of San Lorenzo. His eloquence, if he then possessed any, made so little impression that he began himself to doubt of the legitimacy of his call for a divine mission. He then retired into a convent in Lombardy, where he applied himself to the interpretation of the Holy Scriptures until he was recalled to Florence by Lorenzo de Medicis.

The time which he had passed in retirement had been so well spent in study that the true depth and power of his genius speedily began to manifest themselves. His dryness of manner and rigidity of gesture had disappeared. The first essays of his eloquence were so enthusiastically received, that the belief that he was chosen of God as his mouthpiece to his people again moved within him. The times were ripe for a prophet. At the head of the Church was a pope, the parent of so many children that he was nicknamed the father of his people. Religion had become a cloak for all manner of debauchery, while Italy was rent in pieces by the violence of its factions. Then Savonarola, as if foreseeing the reformer of Germany who was soon to arise, boldly asserted that the Holy Catholic Church was about to be cleansed from its pollutions; that Italy would be beaten with rods, and that these events would be accomplished previous to his death, which would take place before the termination of the century. It was then 1490. The boldness of these predictions, the apparent proximity of their fulfillment, joined to the imposing oratory of the preacher, struck awe into the hearts of his audience. Luther fulfilled his first prophecy; the Medici and Borgias the second; as for the third, we shall see in what manner it was accomplished.

Savonarola continued to preach and prophesy with such effect that no church in Florence, not even the Duomo, which of itself could contain the population of a city, was sufficiently capacious to hold his audience He was compelled to divide them, as has done an equally eloquent clergyman of Rome of our day, the Father Ventura, into classes, according to their sex or age, devoting separate days to men and to women, and even to children. So rapidly did his reputation for sanctity augment, that he could not pass to and from his convent to the church without a guard to clear a passage through the dense masses of people that struggled to kiss his robe and receive his blessing.

This devotion dispelled any doubts which might have still haunted him of his being the chosen oracle of the Almighty. Henceforth all timidity and hesitation were banished, and he assumed the inflexible tone of severity and denunciation which, in being consistent with his supposed mission, was also most natural to his character. No rank intimidated or ecclesiastical authority awed him. He was the direct messenger from God, and therefore bound to speak the words of sober truth with equal freedom to man, prince, or pope. Had his mind been tempered with the sound reason that guided the German reformers, the energy and courage that was common to both would have made of him a Calvin for Italy. But his ardent temperament, characteristic of his race, and the mainspring of his influence over a nation more prone to feel than to reason, urged him on from one step to another, until, in his enthusiasm, he believed himself superior to the laws of nature, and accountable only to Him whose agent he assumed to be. His pride, however, was based upon the unyielding strength of moral right, and his energies directed solely toward the reformation and freedom of his countrymen.

In 1490 he was nominated Prior of the Convent of Saint Mark. It had been the custom with his predecessors, on the occasion of their elevation to this dignity, to present their homage to Lorenzo de Medicis as the supreme chief of the commonwealth, and to beseech him to grant to their order his powerful protection. Savonarola was too zealous a republican to recognize an authority which he considered as usurped, because not founded upon the suffrages of the people. He refused to go. His friends, with politic zeal, sought to persuade him. Even the haughty Medician prince employed artifice and courtesy to induce him to take a step which, if omitted, he felt would wound both his pride and popularity. Savonarola gave one answer to all: "He was Prior of God and not of Lorenzo. He had therefore nothing more to expect from him than had the meanest citizen."

Until this opposition, Lorenzo had ruled supreme in Florence since the conspiracy of the Pazzi. He could neither overcome nor forgive the obstinacy of Savonarola. The poor monk had become as powerful as the sovereign prince. He sought to interrupt his sermons by a threat conveyed through five of the principal citizens. The rejoinder was a discourse more violent than any of its predecessors, at the conclusion of which he announced to the people the death of Lorenzo as nigh at hand.

The austerity of Savonarola was not confined to his political and religious principles. Equally republican in his manners, he applied the stirring notes of his eloquence and the force of his example to awaken the people from the excessive luxury and sensual pleasures into which the licentiousness and extravagance of the Medici had plunged them. Florence had become another Capua. Its new princes, in establishing their power, had corrupted its citizens. Gold and amusements had been lavished upon them until the Spartan spirit had been extinguished, and the erotic morals and depraved taste of degenerate Athens awakened instead. Savonarola laid the axe with bold strokes to the evil tree of knowledge. Its root was to be drawn out into full daylight and consumed in the flames. He chose the season of Lent to commence his crusade against the debasing superfluities of social life. Never was his eloquence more effective. Florence brought out its stores of licentious literature, its obscene paintings and disgraceful statues, its laces, jewels, velvets and golden habits, the treasures of its pride and sensuality, and heaped them together in the public squares. Even Fra Bartolomeo contributed the instruments of his art, which until then he had employed in pandering to the vicious caprices of his countrymen, threw them upon the pile, and vowed before God henceforth to apply his genius solely to his service. How faithfully he kept his oath, the chaste and spiritual productions of his pencil, now alone to be seen in the galleries and churches of Florence, sufficiently attest. His fame and his works were alike purified by fire. Savonarola, followed by a crowd of women and children chanting the praises of Almighty God, left the Duomo, and marched in triumph from pile to pile, applying the torch to each, until nothing was left of the wealth and art there garnered for destruction but ashes, which the winds soon scattered to the four quarters of heaven. Daily these sacrifices of vanity and lust were renewed, until luxury trembled for her existence; but, like all unnatural and violent excitements, the enthusiasm soon passed away without other permanent impression than as a memorial of the extraordinary ability of the monk in causing the public mind to vibrate for a while in unison with his own.

Eighteen months after the prediction of Savonarola, Lorenzo the Magnificent found himself on his death-bed. This was the 9th of April, 1492. Then the prince recalled to mind the Prior of Saint Mark, who had so boldly defied his power and so truly foretold his end. From him only would he receive absolution. The monk this time obeyed his summons, but not more promptly than he would have hastened to the bedside of the humblest sinner of Florence that solicited extreme unction from his hands. The dying Lorenzo disburdened his conscience by a long catalogue of deeds, known and unknown, for which he would have in vain sought for a warrant in the word of God. Savonarola promised him absolution upon three conditions. "Name them," demanded the prince, grasping eagerly at stipulations apparently so much lighter than he had reason to expect.

"The first," said his confessor, "is that you acknowledge a full and firm faith in your Creator."

"I do," quickly answered Lorenzo.

"The second is, that you restore, as far as possible, the property that you have wrongfully acquired."

After a momentary hesitation, Lorenzo replied, "This is right; I will do it."

"The third is, that you render back to Florence her liberty."

"As to that, never," said the dying man; "I would sooner be d—d." Lorenzo turned his back toward the monk without uttering another word, and died a few hours after.

This event augmented, if possible, the prophetic reputation of Savonarola. Other causes contributed also to increase his influence. The evils which he had prophesied were in store for Italy, began now to assume so lowering an aspect as to dispel the doubts of the most incredulous. Roderick Borgia was made pope. Charles VIII., marching to the conquest of the kingdom of Naples, regarded Florence with no friendly eye. Savonarola was deputed to meet him. He approached the unscrupulous King of France less as an embassador than as a prophet, predicting to him victory if he restored the ancient liberties of Florence, defeat and disgrace should he confirm its yoke. The descendant of Saint Louis paid slight regard to one he regarded as a fanatic intermeddling with matters of public policy. Florence was betrayed into his hands, and he did not leave it until the decree which sequestered the property of the Medici and placed their heads at a price was annulled. The monk was again right. In less than a year, Charles VIII., with sword in hand, was forced to open for himself a bloody and disgraceful road back to his own kingdom.

The fall of Peter de Medicis placed, as it were, the civil power wholly into the hands of Savonarola. He received the commission to prepare a constitution. Then it was that his democratic ideas became fully apparent. He established his new system of government upon the most liberal and popular basis that had as yet been presented to the citizens. The grand principle was that of choice by the entire people for all offices of trust or honor. The citizens elected delegates who represented their views in the general assembly, for the accommodation of which Savonarola caused to be built the famous hall in the Palazzo Vecchio, which, as we have seen, could accommodate a thousand representatives.

Successful at home in all his measures, triumphing over the court of France, and showing himself no mean antagonist of even distant England, the fearless monk prepared to enter the lists against that colossus of evil, Alexander VI., who then disgraced the papal throne by an example of crime and debauchery which revived the recollections of the most scandalous eras of heathen Rome. The resistless tones of his eloquence reached the Vatican. The Pope, unable to gainsay the charges of his accuser, thought to silence him by the usual weapons of papacy. He fulminated a bull, in which he retorted upon Savonarola the charge of heresy, and forbade him to preach. Savonarola eluded the injunction by bringing forward Dominic Benvicini, a disciple, who had sufficient ability and courage to fill his pulpit and use his weapons. But the master was not of a temper to remain long silent. His reason and his cause soon divorced him from the mystic influence the Church of Rome holds over all her followers, or, more justly speaking, he found a refuge amid her subtle doctrines for his ecclesiastical rebellion. Upon the authority of the Pope Pelagius, that an unjust excommunication was without efficacy, he declared that he had no need of absolution from the interdiction of Alexander VI. Accordingly, on Christmas, 1497, he reascended the pulpit, and asserted that Christ had inspired him to refuse obedience to the mandate of the Pope, on account of the criminality of its author. Thenceforward he continued to preach against the successor of St. Peter with increasing energy and license. He had now attained the height of his influence. The people no longer regarded him simply with the veneration due a prophet, but exalted him to the rank of a new Messiah, and knelt in awe as often as he passed through their midst. His mien, however, became sad and humble like that of the Man of Sorrows. Perhaps, while a consciousness of his approaching fate stirred within him, he mourned more for his country than for himself.

A second and more formidable brief was forwarded from Rome. Alexander VI. threatened to confiscate the property of all Florentines within the pontifical territory, and to put the republic under interdict, and to declare her the spiritual and temporal enemy of the Holy Catholic Church, if the magistrates did not silence the contumacious monk. This threat was the more emphatic, as Cæsar Borgia was in their neighborhood with a powerful military force. Accordingly, they bowed before the coming storm, and passed the order for Savonarola to suspend his sermons. He obeyed without demur, because resistance would have been to infringe the laws which he had himself prepared for the republic. In his valedictory discourse he took a feeling farewell of his beloved auditory. But Alexander VI., not content with his silence, sought to root out his influence and principles by sending to fill his pulpit a preacher from Rome, of great reputation and devoted to his interests. It was in vain, however, that he attempted to be heard. The moderation of Savonarola was not imitated by his followers. From zeal they soon passed into folly. Florence became one field of fanatical excitement. To his other high claims upon the love and devotion of the people, Savonarola now added that of a martyr for truth. Reason lost all weight in the spiritual conflict, and the supernatural began to mingle in the strife. There were tales of visions; rumors of miracles and prophecies that were fast being realized. The zeal of the votaries of Savonarola, which he was unable either to check or guide, drew him into a vortex of absurdity, which the sincerity of all parties alone saved from becoming blasphemy. They went so far as to claim for Savonarola the power to raise the dead, and offered to put him to the test on a corpse in the vaults of the Cathedral.

This was not long on its way to the ears of Francis de Pouille, his reverend opponent from Rome, a man of equal determination and greater fanaticism. More than this, he was ready to die for his cause, provided that his death could insure its triumph. He answered the vague rumors of the supernatural powers of Savonarola by a formal challenge to enter jointly with him into a fiery furnace, in the face of all the people, and leave to God the recognition of his elected servant by preserving him unharmed amid the flames. The Brother Francis was not deluded by an exaggerated religious faith, for he made this proposition simply to tempt Savonarola to a proof of mutual inspiration, which he well knew must end in the destruction of both. His object was to destroy an uncompromising enemy of the Church even at the cost of his own life, and thus save a multitude of souls from being led further astray on the road to eternal perdition.

Savonarola was not, however, to be duped either by his own claims to inspiration, or the artifice of his rival in so strange a proposition. He had proposed no trial himself. There was no sufficient reason why he should accept one. But when the tide of religious phrensy begins to rise, no mortal can assign its limits. What the master declined to accept, the disciple eagerly rushed to seize. His old substitute in the pulpit, Brother Dominic Benvicini, confident in the direct intervention of the Almighty, on his own responsibility announced his readiness to accept the trial of fire. This devotion was not at all welcome to the Brother Francis. It was the principal whose life he balanced with his own, and not that of a second, with whom to have died would have cost him the coveted triumph of his sacrifice.

The feverish agitation of the public mind kept pace with these events. Florence literally went mad. The magistrates, who would willingly have stopped the increasing folly, discovered that their sole resource was to guide, for it was too late to arrest the scandals. As soon as it was known that the Brother Francis refused to immolate himself with other than Savonarola, two Franciscans, Nicolas de Pilly and Andrew de Rondinelli, volunteered to take his place. The parts in this anomalous duel were now filled, and the people waited for the termination of this unholy contest in a state of excitement that would brook no disappointment. To have removed the principals from the city would have exposed it to a fearful tumult. The anxiety of the populace to behold so extraordinary and terrible a spectacle was not alone that vulgar curiosity which finds its daintiest nutriment in sights of mortal agony, but it was allied to the mysterious and supernatural; for though there were doubtless many scoffers, there were fewer hearts that did not beat tremulously with vague hope or expectation of an exhibition of divine intervention, unknown in the history of man since the days of the prophet Daniel. The most incredulous minds could not have been indifferent to a sight which was shortly to test the exact meaning to be attached to the parable of the mustard seed. Even in our own age, we have seen those who believed in the literal power of removing mountains by faith alone. If the mountains did not cast themselves into the sea at their bidding, it was owing solely to the deadness of their faith. Here was to be an exhibition of rival faith, sincere on both sides, which was to do more than cast mountains into the sea. It was to triumph over the most destructive element known to man, and convert the flames of a furnace into garments of celestial glory.

The authorities of Florence, by undertaking to control this strange business, lent to it, though unwillingly, the august sanction of their official position. It was now under the direction of the state. Dominic Benvicini, on the part of Savonarola, and Andrew Rondinelli, who, to obtain the preference over his brother monk, Nicolas de Pilly, proved that he had anticipated him in his offer to represent Francis de Pouille, were the chosen champions. A committee of the citizens were elected to decide upon the day and place, and make the necessary arrangements. They fixed upon the 7th of April, 1498, on a spot contiguous to the Palace of the People, in what is now the square of the Grand Duke.

Although several days were yet to elapse previous to the trial, the people crowded the square in such masses that it was impossible to erect the furnace, until, by the aid of numerous troops, a sufficient space was kept clear for the work to proceed.

The portico of the Lanzi, on the right of the Palazzo Vecchio, so famed for its graceful proportions and the ancient and modern statuary it shelters, comprising the Judith of Donatello, the Perseus of Benvenuto, and the Rape of the Sabines by

John of Bologne, all worthy of their position close by the David of Michael Angelo, was divided into two compartments for the rival clergymen and their respective partisans; for friends they could not be called who would stimulate them to such an act. In front, at the distance of a few rods, a wooden scaffold was erected of twenty-four feet in length, ten in width, and five in height. Upon this scaffold was piled dry fagots, pine knots, and other combustible materials, so arranged as to leave two separate passages or corridors the entire length of the platform. Through these, encircled by the flames, in plain daylight, so that the spectators could see them enter at one end and walk out unscathed by the fire at the other, provided their faith made them as incombustible as asbestos, the two reverend fanatics were to pass. The preparations were all in earnest; the fires were to be as fierce as the most inflammable substances could make them; there was no opportunity to arrange a false miracle, or to spare either candidate from an equal test of the fiery ordeal.

On the day appointed, Savonarola called upon all his proselytes to assist at a solemn mass. The Franciscans, on the contrary, quietly took their places in the stall provided for them without any public ceremony, as coolly and unconcernedly as if assembling for any of the ordinary offices of their religion. The mass ended, Savonarola, instead of replacing the host in its tabernacle, kept it in his hand, and, leaving the church, advanced toward the place of trial. He was followed by all the monks of his convent, chanting hymns, and a vast crowd of citizens who favored his cause; the most ardent of whom, so confident were they of a miracle in favor of their champion, carried themselves the torches with which to fire the pile. Dominic walked with them, the most confident of all, smiling and often kissing the feet of a crucifix which he held in his hands.

There was not an eye in Florence on that day that did not seek to rest on the scaffold. Not only the square and streets were crowded to repletion, but the balconies and roofs of houses, and even the distant platform of the Campanile, the towers of the Bargello, and the roof of the Duomo, were encumbered with spectators. Well they might be, for it was a sight not likely to be seen twice on earth.

Dominic Benvicini stepped forward and announced that he was ready to enter the furnace. There was a hesitation on the part of the Franciscans. It is possible that they were appalled by the steadfast assurance of Dominic, and sought for some subterfuge to escape from the consequences of their own defiance. They charged their opponents with sorcery, and protecting themselves by charms and talismans. To disprove these accusations, Dominic allowed himself to be examined by physicians, threw off his clothes, reclad himself with those furnished by the judges, and again asked Andrew Rondinelli if he were ready. Obliged now to leave his stall, he came forward as if prepared to make the trial, when, glancing at his adversary, he stopped abruptly and refused to go farther. At that moment Savonarola had placed in the hands of Dominic the host. Rondinelli exclaimed that it would be a sacrilege to expose the body and blood of the Savior to be burned. Besides, if Dominic should escape, the miracle would not be conclusive, since it was not the rebel monk, but the well-beloved Son of God that was spared by the flames. He declared, in consequence, that, unless the Dominican renounced this supernatural aid, he would renounce the proof.

Savonarola insisted upon the presence of the host. Rondinelli refused to yield his position. Both parties engaged in a warm and fruitless argument, which lasted four hours. In the mean while the spectators, who were exposed to a burning sun, grew impatient, and loudly manifested their displeasure at the delay. They had come to see others burned, and not to be burned themselves. To put an end to the tumult and strife, Dominic Benvicini said that he would give up the host, and make the trial with a simple crucifix. No objections could be alleged to this, as the crucifix was only the image and not the real presence of the Savior. Once again it was announced that the trial was about to commence. The people forgot their fatigue, and as loudly applauded the infatuated monks as if they had been awaiting the entrance on a stage of some favorite actors.

Every avenue of escape from the fiery proof seemed now closed to both parties. They started together, but at the same instant, as if Heaven had forborne to the latest moment to see to what extent the folly of men would go, a violent storm, which had been gathering unseen, burst over the city and deluged it with rain. The fire was instantly extinguished. In vain they applied fresh torches, and brought fire and inflammable substances from the neighboring houses. Torrents of water continued to fall and put out the flames. There was more to fear from a deluge than a conflagration.

The spectators, who had been wrought up to the highest pitch of excitement, now vented their rage at their disappointment upon the parties, accusing them both of having conjured up the storm. They, in their turn, retorted upon each other the same accusation. The multitude began to look upon them as charlatans who had played them a dirty trick. Notwithstanding the rain which continued to fall, no one would obey the order of the magistrates to retrie to their homes. They continued their menacing outcries, and threatened a serious disturbance. A guard was given to the two adversaries to insure their safety to their respective convents. Savonarola escaped violence by holding aloft the holy sacrament, but Rondinelli was saluted with a shower of stones, and cries of rage and contempt. He finally reached his sanctuary half murdered, and with his clothes torn into shreds.

The people that had so lately exalted Savonarola to a level with Divinity, in their desire to expiate their own weakness, now turned upon him with the usual unreasonableness of those who have more to forgive in themselves than in others. That rain-storm, in preserving the spectators from being accomplices in a blasphemous trial of the natural laws of Providence, had at the same time washed away every vestige of his former sacred prestige. With a fickleness and ingratitude that does human nature signal dishonor, they forgot his eminent services and great virtues. They forgot, too, that the defiance came not from him. They saw not in the extinguishment of the fire the disapprobation of Heaven, but the magic art of a false prophet. From walking with angels, they fell at once to sport with demons.

Francis de Pouille, the adroit agent of Alexander VI., profited by the reaction to arouse against Savonarola every enemy that interest or bigotry could create. The partisans of the exiled Medici hated him, because his democratic institutions prevented their return to power. Many of the clergy believed him accursed of God so long as he remained under the anathema of a pope. With them, the authority of the Head of the Church was independent of all personal considerations. The Franciscans saved their own credit in the proportion that they took an active part against him. They cried "Stop thief!" lest they should themselves be considered as robbers. If he had any friends left besides the brethren of his convent, they were to be found only among the few in Florence whose reason was neither to be duped by fanaticism nor disgraced by passion. These few were unable to protect him.

Savonarola lost no time, however, in seeking to regain his position. On the very next day he ascended the pulpit to explain his conduct, and do away the evil impression created on the preceding by an intervention of nature as unexpected by him as by the people. But they drowned his voice in ferocious shouts. On every side was heard, "Down with the excommunicated! down with the heretic! death to the false prophet!" from those who, less than twenty-four hours before, had knelt before him, too happy if they could but touch the hem of his garment. He sought refuge in his convent. The crowd followed him there, swelled at each step by new enemies. They burst open the gates, demanding their victim. He opened his cell and stood before them. For an instant they wavered, for they had long been accustomed to tremble before him. A friendly voice, prompt at touching the right chord in the aroused public mind, might have saved him. But none was raised. The zealots of the Medici faction threw themselves upon him, shouting, "To the stake with the heretic! Let us gibbet the false prophet!" These ominous notes were repeated by a thousand voices as they dragged their former idol to a shameful death. But his end was not yet to be. The magistracy, informed of the tumult, had assembled in haste some troops. They rescued him in part by force, but more by the assurance that justice should promptly take its course.

The fickle multitude had not long to wait their prey. In forty-two days only after the failure which had so enraged them, on the twenty-third of May, they again assembled in the same place to witness a spectacle still more terrible, for its memory would forever remind heaven and earth of their cruelty and injustice. Another scaffold had been erected. Upon it, bound to a post, were the three victims whose dying agonies were to replace the previous loss. These three were Jerome Savonarola, Silvester Maruffi, and Dominic Benvicini, the disciple, faithful in death, as he had been through life, to his master.

This time there was no disappointment. The fire burned fiercely, and human nerves crackled and snapped in the flames. But the spirit triumphed over the flesh. Hymns of praise arose amid the smoke, and bore toward heaven the evidence of a faith which took no heed of bodily anguish in the superior consciousness of approaching celestial joys. Savonarola, with his eyes turned toward heaven, expired without a groan.

He was no sooner dead than the populace repented them of their sacrifice. His enemies continued to blacken his fame, as they had calumniated his life. But the people missed their benefactor and counselor. They could not recall their victim, but they could honor his memory. Each year, on the anniversary of his death, the place of his scaffold was found strewn with flowers by invisible hands. It was said that angels thus celebrated the fête of the martyr. This tribute continued to augment yearly, reviving the memory of the liberal principles and austere morality of Savonarola, until it led to renewed religious commotions. The supreme power had returned to the Medici. Cosmo I. was resolved to put an end to this pretext for popular demonstrations, but he dared not encounter openly the public sympathies. He employed art. Ammanato was ordered to erect a fountain on the site. It is to him that we owe the colossal statue in marble of Neptune with his pigmy steeds, which has, through the succeeding centuries, continued to pour its limpid stream upon the spot so indelibly stained by fire.

A strange event happened some fifteen years ago to one of the bronze figures of the size of life which adorn the edge of the basin. For two months it was missed, and not the slightest clew could be obtained to the cause of its disappearance. At last it was discovered that it had been stolen during the night by an English amateur, but the means which enabled

FOUNTAIN OF NEPTUNE, PALAZZO VECCH'

him so adroitly to carry off without detection from a public square a statue weighing one ton, remained as great an enigma as ever.

Opposite the fountain is the Post-office, and over the windows of delivery is an antique projecting roof or porch of wood, unsupported by columns, and which looks momentarily as if about to tumble upon the heads of the letter-seekers beneath. It would not be strange if it did, for it dates back nearly five hundred years, and was made by the compulsory labor of the enemies of Florence, whose spirits doubtless, even at this interval, would be rejoiced to grind the descendants of their conquerors into dust, in revenge for the brutality to which they were subjected. They were Pisans, to the number of two thousand, that had been taken prisoners at Gallotto, where one thousand of their fellow-citizens were left dead on the field. The two thousand prisoners were conducted to Florence in forty-two carts. At the gates they were ignominiously taxed a shilling a head, the duty levied on cattle. Afterward they were drawn in triumph, with trumpets sounding, through the city, and forced to descend in the square of the public palace and kiss the statue of Marsocco, the lion emblem of the city, as they defiled in its rear. Two of the prisoners, unable to endure the humiliation, strangled themselves with their chains. The others were required to build the shelter mentioned above, which has ever since been called the Roof of the Pisans.

CHAPTER IV.

THE ARTS AND ARTISTS AT FLORENCE.

Perhaps there is no trade that has more tricks than that of the picture-dealer. It is worth while coming to Florence, if one have a taste for the fine arts, to learn something in this line by way of caution, particularly at a time when gullibility commands so high a premium in all that relates to the relics of antiquity and the works of the "great masters." The amount of trash annually palmed off on the discerning critics of Russia, England, and America, on the authority of great names, is truly astonishing, and, too, for sums of money that would create an El Dorado for modern artists. Whatever is either rare or beautiful is sure to beget a corresponding passion, for the gratification of which it becomes necessary to fabricate counterfeits. Thus Italy, which has given birth to the finest works of art, has also produced the most ingenious race of imitators. Gems, precious stones, vases, coins, statuettes, bas-reliefs, bronzes, and paintings, all genuine, antique, or original, are multiplied with such an extraordinary facility that it really seems as if they were rather the perennial crop of nature than the labor and study of man. The manner of the reproduction of paintings is more wonderful than that of the phœnix, for the new do not await even the ashes of the old. Nor may any one pride himself upon being an infallible judge of an original, when he remembers that Guido had among his pupils so successful an imitator that the scholar was enabled to substitute for the incomplete original his unfinished copy, which Guido continued to labor upon as his own. Neither does it follow that an original painting by a great master is necessarily a good one. If each had great merits, they had also characteristic faults. Guido often commenced and finished several paintings on the same day, to provide means to indulge his passion for gaming. Others painted as rapidly by candle-light. So that it does not follow that because an artist immortalized himself by certain productions which in his peculiar style have never been excelled, every touch of his pencil is equally worthy of his genius. Many "gems," whose originality can be well established, and which have cost their purchasers their weight in gold, would, if their genealogy had been lost, have been deposited among the unsightly lumber of the garret, while others of really tenfold more merit hang unnoticed on walls simply for want of the name of a "great master." The temptation, therefore, to picture-dealers to indulge in this sort of baptism is irresistible. If the painting be too fresh, a worm-eaten frame, a skillful smoking, an ingenious story as to its discovery in some old convent, or purchase from some dilapidated family, for whose gallery Titian, Paris Birdone, the Caracchi, Salvator Rosa, or Domenichino painted, make it a great deal more original than the original itself. If any lingering doubts should exist in the mind of the amateur, who, while examining a bad copy or the work of a feeble imitator, has his mind more occupied with the impression that the *chef-d'œuvres* have produced upon him than the subject before his eyes, which he envelops with the halo of their great names, it is speedily dispelled by the certificates of high tribunals and professional judges, who, for a consideration, are but too ready to attest its legitimacy. In this manner, many a picture, that cost the purchaser but a few dollars, has been triumphantly borne off, at as many thousands, by gentlemen of taste and fortune, to greet the admiring eyes of the learned amateurs of the old masters in Europe or the United States, or, what is quite as likely, to extort a smile of derision at that taste which could find merit in such dilapidated and obscure daubs. In this way a great wrong is often done to great reputations, for they are made responsible for the sins of their counterfeiters. The best specimens of the earliest masters are more valuable as records of the progress of art than for examples of its perfection. Thus Cimabue and Giotto shine chiefly by contrast with their predecessors. But the angelic beauty of the faces of Beatico Angelico is proverbial, and so with Perugino, Da Vinci, Andrea del Sarto, and Raphael, there are individual peculiarities of style so exquisitely perfected that they must forever remain "masters" in those arts.

The progress of painting has been gradual, each great artist and celebrated school adding something toward its various degrees of perfection. No one is equally good in all, or always equal to himself A correct knowledge of anatomy and perspective was attained by slow degrees, while coloring varies with the taste or feeling of each master. Those world-renowned pictures of Titian and his school, that so dazzle by their beauteous and harmonizing tints, are not remarkable for their close resemblance to common nature. They form, as it were, a nature of themselves, or create one to us by selecting those aspects which we most rarely see. I doubt if any man would wish the complexion of his wife to be of the same tint as Titian's Flora, and the idea of her resembling one of Vasari's Madonnas, or Michael Angelo's Titanic women, would strike him with horror; but worse than all would be his fate were one of Rubens's Flemish nudities, with her adipose proportions, crooked legs, and bruised flesh coloring, to step from her canvas and claim him for her liege lord. Neither would he like any more to acknowledge that Bacchanal-looking infant, called the Holy Child, which we see in the Pitti, by the same pencil, for his own, for fear that his friends would suspect him of having substituted the bottle for the nipple in the rearing of his offspring. Raphael's and Perugino's trees are as flat as petrifactions. Bronzino's flesh might often be mistaken for putty. Fra Bartolomme's figures, at least some of them, astonish more than they please by their colossal dimensions. We all wish that Guido had found smaller hands and less expansive throats for his models—that Carlo Dolci had put less jewelry and finish upon his holy women—that Paul Veronese, in his Marriage of Cana, had not placed men on roofs so steep that you are nervous from fear that they will slip off; and, lastly, let me say it with reverence both for the subject and its otherwise faultless treatment, that Raphael had given to his Madonna della Seggiola that inimitable *divine* expression which he has bestowed upon others of his Madonnas, and which, in general, characterizes his earlier holy faces, and makes him peerless in this, the highest aim of art. The Seggiola Madonna is a beautiful woman, surpassingly beautiful, but conscious of the fact, and with the faintest twinkle of coquetry in her eyes, averted from her child to demand the admiration of the spectator. But this very expression, beyond the copyist's art or the skill of the engraver, proclaims the marvelous genius of the artist. He has given the world, in this painting, the highest type of the natural mother. If, in doing this, he has robbed her of her celestial glory, he has but made her the more lovely inhabitant of earth. She is not the virgin mother of God, but the loving wife of man.

Thus, if we were to indulge in captious criticism, we should lose one half the pleasure artistic genius holds in store. Its true test is its power over us as a whole. That must be good which for ages has continued to hold the world spell-bound by feeling, and which to criticise in mechanical detail requires close study, developing, as it were, a qualm of conscience in the necessity of sinking the noble art to reach the lower.

Florence, more than any other city, may be said to live on its pictures. True, architecture, statuary, and mosaics each contribute toward her support, but the chiefest resource is painting. Her own citizens probably know less of the galleries, as freely open to all the world as if they were the common property of mankind, than my own countrymen. What private collection rivals the Pitti? Arranged in chambers that are truly marvelous in themselves for the delicacy and magnificence of their ornaments, we find those superb originals which have been made, by copies and engravings, so familiar to the world. There are about four hundred pictures, but among them more chef-d'œuvres of the Italian school than any other collection in Europe, with the exception of the Louvre and the Escurial. My own experience on first beholding other celebrated galleries has been that of disappointment, because my imagination over-painted the reality, and it has only been, as it were, by degrees that I have been led to estimate their treasures at their true standard. The number, too, of worthless or uninteresting pictures which swell their catalogues strengthens this effect. But at the Pitti it is quite different. On entering the hall of Lorenzo *il magnifico*, I felt myself, as it were, in the presence of the Genius of Painting herself. It was like coming suddenly upon a landscape so beautiful that the tongue becomes dumb from inability to express the fullness of the sensations of the soul. Each painting invited attention, and each was a rival to its neighbor. No one thinks of talking aloud in those halls. They are subdued into silence by the solemnity of art. The souls of those masters who gave such life and power to canvas seem still to linger about their favorite works, enjoying the silent homage of generation after generation of their fellow-men, as they come up from distant lands to learn from them new conceptions of truth and beauty. There, too, we see those superb portraits, each a passport to immortality to painter and sitter: Raphael's Leo the Tenth and Julius the Second; Titian's Cardinal Ippolito dei Medici; his mistress, more beautiful even than his Urbino Venus; the portrait of Cornaro, the advocate and example of longevity; the Venetian gentleman in black; Lotto's Three Ages of Man; Subterman's magic touches, and Rubens's famous group, all as if ready to step out from their frames, and play their parts over again in the rôle of life.

To do justice to this gallery would be to write the history of art in its greatest excellence. The Uffizii collection embraces a wider range of objects. It is a museum, and incloses within its halls an epitome of the history of the world for the last three thousand years. There Niobe, in her imperishable grief, with her dying children struck by Apollo's darts; the Queen of Loveliness, faultless, if she had been left, like her sister of Milo, as antiquity bequeathed her to modern eyes; her companion in beauty, the Apollino, the Faun, the Wrestlers, and the Mysterious Slave, have all found an asylum. The classical ages were prolific in statues. It strikes one oddly that the moderns should house with such sacred care every relic of the ancient chisel, whatever may be its merits, while they turn their own productions so unceremoniously out of doors. Two thousand years hence, they too will probably be taken under shelter as too venerable to bear farther exposure to the ravages of the climate, while skillful hands will be employed to restore them to their original symmetry.

The busts of the Roman Emperors are exceedingly interesting, commencing with Pompey, who, by the way, never wore the imperial robe, and terminating with Constantine the Great. Julius Cæsar's head struck me as of the Henry Clay order. There are two of his busts, and both show, by the manner of dressing the hair, his anxiety to conceal his baldness, which made him more covetous of the honor of receiving from the Senate the right of always wearing the laurel crown on this account than for conquering the world. Vespasian looks like a hale old gentleman, "all of the olden time." He has a firm, fatherly sort of countenance. Titus was decidedly the handsomest gentleman of them all—an imperial Bayard—and well bears out his reputation of being "the delight of the world." There is a Nero of about six years of age, a chubby, innocent face, very unlike his matured physiognomy after having murdered his mother, friends, and most of his relatives. Hair-dressing must have been well understood at ancient Rome, for among the busts of the empresses and their daughters there are fashions to be seen which are really worthy of revival by modern beauties.

The Hall of the Bronzes contains a veritable mystery, found at Arezzo in 1559. Books have been written upon it, but its elucidation is as remote as ever. It is an Etruscan bronze of the size of a St. Gothard dog, with three heads: the first is called that of a lion, but is more of the dragon order, and is, at all events, a nondescript; the second grows from his back, and is that of a goat; the third is that of a serpent, which forms the tail, and, turning over the back, bites one of the horns of the goat-shaped head. Its attitude is fierce and threatening, half crouching, as for a spring. Modern writers have christened it the Chimera, and no doubt it is quite as comely an animal as that we often bag after a chase of a lifetime.

To my mind, Michael Angelo appears to better advantage in his unfinished than his finished statuary. He appears to have so thought himself, if a judgment may be formed from the number he left in the former condition. There is about them the stamp of a powerful genius, of conceptions too grand for mortal execution. The hand that struck out those rough sketches could have fashioned the solid stone at will; so conceive our imaginations, as they complete the works that he began. But when he finishes, he exaggerates; he delights in huge muscular developments, and strains after anatomical effect. His men and women are Brobdignags, with voluminous folds of flesh, into which a Lilliputian could creep and hide. His eye measured every thing on a Titanic scale, as if his aim was rather to astonish than to please. The easel-paintings that claim to be his show the same bent of genius. He despised this branch of art as frivolous, and fit only for women or children. The Tribune contains his famous tondo of a Holy Family, painted for the Doni. It bears more the character of the chisel than the brush—hard, bold, strained in attitude, and of a color positively disagreeable. He was right when he estimated himself as too great for the details of oil painting. But, perhaps, the true secret of this opinion was his unwillingness to pursue a branch in which his rival Raphael excelled him so greatly.

The Tribune is to the Uffizii what the Holy of Holies was to the Temple of Jerusalem. In this sanctuary are assembled the gems of art. Perhaps no other room of its size in the world contains such a collection of masterpieces of painting and sculpture. But these are subjects to which description is inadequate to do justice. To be appreciated, they must be seen and felt by appreciating power. Each spectator may experience different sensations, as tastes differ, but all will confess to the opening to them of a new world of beauty.

The study of painting is much like that of human nature. The character of the artist can be read in the treatment of his subjects. They give the reflection of the inner soul. His passions, prejudices, and weaknesses, as well as his great and good points, appear on the canvas. A painter, like a tragedian, must feel what he would express, if he would paint truth. Any thing short of this becomes cold and mannered. In seeing but one picture, we see the incomplete man or artist. Who, in gazing upon the "Esperanza" of Guido, would recall the fierce painter that, in composing his "Crucifixion," eager to catch and transfer to his canvas the expression of dying agony, in his delirium of art snatched a knife and stabbed in the side his helpless model, bound to a cross to represent the dying Savior? The poor wretch was murdered, but Guido caught the parting breath, completed his picture that night, and fled. He was missed, and three days after his studio was forced open in the search for him. There were found the painting, now at Bologna, and the corpse, still lashed to the cross, in a state of decomposition. Years of exile sufficed to expiate his crime. He was suffered to return to Rome and resume his art, for the popes could better spare a hecatomb of models than one such artist, of whose death Canova said that Heaven gained at the expense of earth. Guido was a sad profligate. Genius is a light lent by Heaven to illumine the earth. He who returns it not to its shrine as pure and bright as when received, may hope from its mercy, but must tremble before its justice.

In the Tuscan school there is a painting by Lucio Massari, who flourished between 1569 and 1633, that pleased me greatly—perhaps I should say amused—from the manner of treatment of a subject which has exhausted the invention and genius of artists, from St. Luke to our day. It was a Holy Family, and their employment was decidedly original, so far as the imaginations of painters have run; though, when we consider their poverty, and that both Joseph and his son worked at a mechanical trade, nothing more likely than this was likely to occur in their household duties. Still, the ideas connected with the Holy Family, daguerreotyped as they are in our minds by the devotional masterpieces of Raphael and the teachings of our catechisms, are so foreign to Massari's very natural treatment of the subject, that it seems not only irreverent, but ludicrous. The scene is a brook in the neighborhood of Nazareth, overshadowed by trees. The Virgin is scrubbing the family linen on stones, after the usual fashion in these countries, and laying it aside in a tub. The infant Jesus is picking out the articles one by one, and handing them to St. Joseph, who is hanging them up to dry. The attitudes of the three are very natural, and suggestive of a rural washing-Monday.

The Dutch school, which is so minutely true to nature in all its homely aspects, furnishes some most extraordinary examples of the grotesque when it aspires to sacred subjects. In an adjoining hall we find the raising of Lazarus, by Nicholas Frumenti, in 1461—a painting in the form of a tabernacle. The costumes of the fifteenth century are sent back to do duty in the first. A monk, with a book in one hand, is helping Lazarus to rise. He has just opened his eyes in his coffin, and is represented as precisely in that ghastly condition when he may be supposed to fully justify the scriptural relation in regard to his physical condition. Mary, overcome by the odor, has covered her mouth with her robe ; a soldier looks on with an expression which literally seems to turn his nose upside down ; while the spectators generally are much more disgusted with the smell than astonished by the miracle.

In the hall of Baroccio there are four of the richest tables, in fine stones and gems of the manufactory of Florence, in existence. The one in the centre of the hall is the richest in the world. It was commenced in 1613, and employed twenty-two workmen incessantly for twenty-five years, costing upward of one hundred thousand dollars, and using up a mine of topazes, onyxes, agates, lapis-lazuli, pearls, and other valuable gems.

Nothing more magnificent can be conceived; but I was much more interested in the eagle of the twenty-fourth Roman legion, in the collection of bronzes, and the kitchen utensils and silver vessels of the Consul Flavius Artaburius, marked with his name, and dating back some twenty-two hundred years. I could not help thinking what a nice point it would be for the lawyers to decide, were any descendant of the family to claim his ancestral plate of the Grand Duke.

Besides the Pitti and Uffizii galleries, there are others, belonging to noblemen, always open to the public, such as the Corsini, Strozzi, Ferroni, and Torrigiani, each possessing some celebrated paintings. The private galleries have, however, greatly diminished before the seductions of British and Russian gold. The renowned Rinuccini gallery was lately sold at auction, and attracted purchasers from all parts of Europe. Never was a name turned to better account. With many amateurs, a bad picture, with a great name, is a greater prize at a thousand pounds sterling, than a good picture, equally original, but lacking the weighty testimony of celebrated authorship, at a hundred dollars. There were fine pictures in the Rinuccini gallery, and their merit shed a golden halo upon all their companions. It was considered an infallible test of merit for a picture that it had hung in the Rinuccini gallery; consequently, paintings not worth ten dollars sold for hundreds. The bait took so well that the gallery appeared inexhaustible, like the stock of a deceased epicurean's wines. Even now, the custode will tell you, in showing you the remaining paintings, that the best are still unsold, offering a Raphael for fifteen thousand, and a Michael Angelo for ten thousand dollars. There are left, however, two undoubted Salvator Rosa's, well worthy the attention of the lovers of his style, which may be had at not a very extravagant price.

Florence lives upon strangers, and paintings are the great

attraction that draws them hither. Without its galleries half its population would starve. They are to it an inexhaustible placer, so long as the rage for copies exist. The public taste centres on a comparatively few subjects. Sassoferato's blue-mantle Madonna, Carlo Dolci's poetry and devotion, the Madonna della Seggiola, Titian's Flora, and a few others, are multiplied without end. Nearly one quarter of the year is lost to copyists at Florence on account of the numerous fête-days, when the galleries are closed. Of the best pictures, it requires from one to two months to take faithful copies; consequently, there can be made of each but a few annually from the original itself. Such, too, is the number of applications for permission to copy, that artists, who follow in turn, are often obliged to wait several years for an opportunity. The Madonna della Seggiola is engaged from ten to fifteen years in advance—a compliment which, on a much briefer scale, would quite turn the head of any dancing damsel at a ball. From this it will readily be inferred that good copies must be comparatively rare, and yet, within this century, there have been enough made in Italy of celebrated pictures, one would suppose, to reach from New York to New Orleans.

I do not know the number of artists and students in Florence, but they are a legion. Nowhere have they better facilities for pursuing their studies. If there be any drawback, compared with other schools, it is the scarcity of good living models. The liberality of the government provides an Academy of Design, and the use of the galleries, easels, &c., gratis. Private owners are no less generous. And, for a student or poor artist, Florence is the most economical of cities. It is really surprising upon how little they can exist in comparative comfort. I use the word *comfort* in the *artistic* standard, which would not suit every body. Less than fifty cents a day will suffice, divided as follows: for a chamber, scantily furnished, he pays five cents a day; six cents for his breakfast, and sixteen for dinner, leaving quite a balance for other necessaries. Mr. Powers pays two hundred and twenty dollars annual rent for an establishment which in New York he could not hire for less than several thousand dollars.

Good artists residing in Florence have another advantage in possessing the market, as it were, of the world. Hundreds here purchase works of art from the fact that their attention is here first awakened to its value as a source of pure gratification. Besides, example is contagious. I have known a friend, who proposed, on his arrival, to limit himself to a few cheap copies, carry away nearly one hundred original paintings.

But modern artists of merit have much to contend against. The cheapness at which copies are furnished drives them from the field of originality to labor in that of mere imitation, because there are now but comparatively few purchasers of original pictures at prices which really recompense an artist. Good copies, too, sometimes command a price much beyond what the artist could expect from an original composition; as, for instance, one thousand dollars is occasionally paid by a discriminating patron for the same subject of which he could get a copy, which would pass equally well with the public, for fifty dollars. Very tolerable copies of the favorite paintings are manufactured for from ten to sixty dollars each. The secret is this. The artists are Florentines, having homes, and perhaps food, furnished them by their families. It costs them the merest pittance for a support, and if they gain a few pauls, say fifty cents per day, they are satisfied. It is pitiable to see art so reduced, while their labors are of doubtful benefit to the world in general, except so far as they may foster a taste which will ultimately demand for its gratification something higher than a feeble imitation of the standard of past centuries.

In Italy, however, this competition for daily bread, instead of excellence, produces disastrous effects. With few exceptions, the original native artists produce nothing worthy even of being classed above the standard of mediocrity. They labor, however, under the great disadvantage, in point of comparison, of being in company, as it were, with the acknowledged masters of the world. The gulf between them has become lamentably wide.

If modern copies and paintings in Florence can be counted by myriads, there seems to be equally a mine of old copies and originals as inexhaustible as the coal-pits of England. For centuries Italy has been furnishing the rest of Europe with pictures, yet the supply still remains as plentiful as its beggars. Lumber-rooms are stored with them; streets are lined with them; every tailor has his gallery; each Italian gentleman his heir-looms; in short, Florence is a vast picture-shop. One would imagine that every man, woman, and child, for the last century, had been born with pencil in hand. There is no possibility of diminishing them. Hercules could clean the Augean stables, but it would be a greater exploit to empty Florence of its pictures. I know one dealer who has sold *twelve thousand* in England alone—at least he says so—and yet his rooms are full to repletion, though he is diminishing his stock to give up business. Cargoes go annually to the United States. We are treated to the arts much after this fashion. I am relating a true story. A speculator arrives, and gives out that he is a purchaser of pictures by the wholesale. A flock of crows can not light sooner upon an open corn-bag than do the sellers upon him. He is not after good pictures, but the trash that can be bought for the value of the wood in their frames. They are brought to him by wagon-loads. He looks at the pile, and makes an offer according to its size. In this way he buys several thousand daubs at an average of a few dimes each, spends as much more in varnish, regilding, and a little retouching, sends them to America, where they are duly offered for sale as so many Titians, Vandycks, Murillos, or other lights of the European schools. One lucky sale pays for the entire lot.

No other art affords a wider scope for fraud. This arises from the conventional values placed upon different styles. One amateur seeks age, and gloats over worm-eaten frames and dilapidated canvas; another detects beauty amid what to others appear but hopeless masses of dirt and varnish; others buy by proxy, and pin their taste to another's interest or vanity; comparatively few buy with discrimination, consequently the cheat and counterfeiter have a wide field. Besides, as the values of all such objects must be graduated by an arbitrary scale, or are the result of a caprice, they feel no compunctions at levying the greatest possible amount of tribute the purchaser's purse or gullibility will stand. There are fair dealers, but Italian reputation in general, in this respect, is of a slippery character. After all, it does not seem to be a heinous sin, if faith is created in the coveted genuineness of any article, when it quadruples the pleasure of the buyer and fills the purse of the seller in the same ratio. Without it there would have been no profit to the one or joy to the other. The merits of the picture would have remained unknown, and two good bargains lost. Still, I have known a dealer to carry his trickery beyond the reach of any charitable extenuation; as, for instance, to have a fine copy, in a frame, exposed as a sample, for which a buyer was found, at what appeared a reasonable price, the bargain concluded, and the purchaser's name marked by himself on the back of the picture. Upon receiving it at home, however, he could not believe his own senses, so inferior did it appear to the one he selected; but on the back there was the evidence of his own handwriting. Upon investigation, however, it was proved that the seller had two pictures in the same frame, the outer one being good and the inner bad, and that he had withdrawn the former and sent the latter.

With all its drawbacks in the shape of trash and trickery, Italy still offers to the amateur of good pictures his best field. This is not surprising when we consider that, for four centuries, it has abounded in artists of real merit. The disciples of the great masters multiplied their works and diffused their genius broadcast over the land. Many of them lived and painted to a great age. Titian employed his brush until his death, which only occurred when within a year of completing a century; Michael Angelo died at eighty-nine years of age; Guido at sixty-seven; the prolific Carlo Dolci at seventy-two; and Guercino at seventy-six. Raphael lived to be but thirty-seven, but, whenever he appeared at the papal court, he was followed by a train of fifty of the first artists, his scholars, many of whom acquired great distinction. Lanzi, in the last century, finds some three thousand Italian artists worthy to be mentioned in his History of Painting. It will readily be believed, therefore, that Italy still contains an ample supply of good paintings. These are only to be found by bestowing time and patience to the search. It is of no use to be turned aside by the bait of a great name, for, if authentic and worthy of its origin, the picture is sure to be prized at many thousands of dollars, and to find competitors for its purchase from all parts of Europe. Such pictures have their history and genealogy as carefully recorded as that of the noblest of families, and to change owners becomes an event in the history of art; and ten to one, supposing yourself tempted into such a purchase, you would find that a substitute has been palmed upon you, while the original is slumbering peacefully in some gallery of Russia or convent in Spain. There are, however, good paintings still to be had, originals, which might change places to advantage with many that are stamped as celebrated in the public galleries, and at prices much under the rates that modern artists would demand for similar excellence. They have the advantage, also, of having stood the test of time in their coloring. When such are discovered, the shortest way of treating for them is to politely smile at the owner's tale of their origin as an agreeable fiction; to impress upon him that you buy pictures, not names, and are guided merely by your fancy in your choice. When he discovers that your taste is purely individual, and that the genealogy of the brush makes no impression upon either your purse or imagination, he becomes reasonable, and acknowledges he knows no more about the paintings than that he purchased them at such a time and at such a place, and believes them to be of such a school; he is quite sure to conclude by accepting one quarter of what he first asked. Indeed, I have known a dealer fall from one hundred and sixty dollars to *four*, rather than miss the sale. He probably bought it for as many francs. Those who deal most with the English pretend to fixed prices, but they actually rise and fall like a Nova Scotia tide. The only rule is to fix upon the price you are willing to pay for the gratification of your whim or taste, and abide by it. The probability is that even then the dealer will be delighted with your custom; but you will do better yet, if you can afford it, to leave discretionary orders at remunerating prices with your countrymen artists for original productions. This will stimulate them to rival or surpass the excellence of the ancient art you so much admire, and be a patriotic contribution toward American fame. Americans have already taken the lead in bust sculpture. They often receive a thousand dollars for a bust, while the best Italian artists are content with a third of that sum. It is gratifying to perceive that the same comparative difference of prices obtains between the original productions and copies of American and Italian painters. While we have such artists in Italy as Page, Tilten, White, and others that might be named, we need not despair of an American school which shall, in time, win a respectable rank in comparison even with the past.

It may be doubted whether painting will ever again be cultivated in any country with so much enthusiasm as it was at Florence at that period when science, genius, and wealth combined to give it its greatest excellence. The Medician sovereigns impoverished their country, but they made it the home of the arts, which, however, they degraded to mean ends. Painting became a passion. It was employed for every purpose. Bread itself was not more common. Not only the interiors of houses were decorated throughout, so that not a vestibule or passage-way was left unpainted, but even the exteriors, from the eaves to the foundation, were so beautifully frescoed, that their designs and colors, even now, after the lapse of centuries, excite our admiration by their beauty and freshness. In his chamber or in the street, at church or in his shop, above him, around him, on his garden walls, whichever way a Florentine turned his eyes, he beheld the marvelous results of the art which lent to stone and mortar all the attractions of the natural landscape, and the artistic creations of the most numerous and varied assemblage of talents the world had then beheld, within the walls of one small city; but he was not content with even this deluge of the art. The most common domestic utensils were submitted to its adorning hands. He painted his furniture, the trunks and boxes which contained his clothes and family stores. The bucklers of their warriors, the shields for the tournament, and the trappings of the horses, were decorated by the hands of the best artists. Painting was to his refined imagination what gold was to the barbarous Mexican. It was displayed every where. In Rome and throughout Tuscany, no girl married who did not bestow with her dowry, by contract, and classed among the family jewels, some celebrated painting, usually a Madonna. If the real flesh and blood proved uncongenial, the husband had always the resource of falling back for consolation upon the virtues of the ideal woman, which, unlike the living, improved with age, and were at any moment transmutable into gold.

So conscious are the Tuscan and Roman governments of the importance of conserving within their territories the best productions of their celebrated masters, as an attraction for foreign travel, that they allow no paintings whatever to be exported without an examination by a professional tribunal. There is no difficulty in obtaining their authorization for paintings in general; but to procure permission to take away an undoubted original of the first water would be as difficult as to obtain an invitation to visit the Emperor of Japan. These will not leave Italy again until some future Napoleon makes them the forfeit of broken treaties or the ransom of kingdoms. They are best where they are, and, like the ruins of classical Italy, should remain forever on their natal soil, to attest her former greatness, and stimulate her sons to revive her ancient renown.

Perhaps in the entire range of criticism there is nothing more ludicrously uncertain than the decisions of would-be authorities in painting. This arises partly from the fact that it is as easy to find a good artist as a true connoisseur, and partly from the empirical or interested judgments of amateurs. Centuries of acquiescence in the claims of some celebrated original of a famous collection are no defense against its authenticity being stolen from it, or at least disputed at the eleventh hour. The public galleries are filled with contested pictures, and few of the private are allowed to possess a gem uncontradicted by some rival amateur, more jealous to establish a name than to possess true merit. These controversies enlist not only authors, but nations, in their respective causes. In a number of instances, the proofs and merits are so equally balanced, that it would be doubtful if the artist himself could, should he return to earth, unhesitatingly point out his own offspring. Andrea del Sarto copied Raphael's Leo the Tenth so truthfully that it was marked in order to distinguish it from the original. Those, therefore, whose artistic triumph depends not so much upon the excellence of their painting as upon the great parentage they claim for it, must live in constant fear and trembling, lest their laurels be rudely snatched away when they least expect it. At all events, the clouds of doubt are constantly arising in the public mind to darken their pictorial horizon. They may esteem themselves fortunate if criticism, which by some inexplicable modern process invariably becomes more luminous as it recedes from the era of its subject, leaves them a few pencil-marks or dashes of the brush of their adored master. Generally, the admiration of ages is criticised away, until nothing is admitted but tolerable imitation or an impaired style. Ask two doctors the nature of a disease, and the probabilities are far more that they will agree in opinion than that two professional picture-dealers will coincide as to even the school of a good painting. I have amused myself more than once in testing this by asking their opinions on an acknowledged painting. The first would decide it to be decidedly of the Bolognese school, for technical reasons that appeared incontestable; the next comer would be as sincere in favor of some other school, with an equally good argument; and so the changes would be rung through every variety of generic art, leaving the anxious novice in most ungratifying uncertainty, until he has acquired sufficient mental independence to be satisfied with what is good for its own sake, without puzzling his brains over dubious genealogies and the endless intricacies of an art which, in its meanest sense, is nothing but deception.

Rome, Florence, and Naples have long waged a mutual warfare in regard to the originality of certain pictures. London glories in costly originals of the Continental schools in her National Gallery, over which John Bull periodically goes into ecstasies, while her best critics pronounce them to be wretched forgeries, underrating the real merits and exaggerating the faults of their supposed authors. The Corsini Gallery at Florence has long boasted the Wheel of Fortune of Michael Angelo, though the most astute critics insist that the Tribune alone has the sole specimen of his easel-painting in existence. Be this as it may, there are others sufficiently like their father to claim to be his children. Recently a dealer has bought at an old-clothes fair, for seven pauls (seventy-seven cents), a twin picture, which, being cleaned, he now brings forward to dispute the palm of originality with that of the Corsini, which he pronounces to be a copy. Michael Angelo could touch nothing without stamping it, in a greater or less degree, with the power of his genius. In the oil paintings that claim to be his, his contempt or indifference to this branch of art are equally shown; for there is not one of them which, if called by another name, would afford pleasure from those sources that appeal most forcibly to the public mind in painting.

CHAPTER V.

CARRIAGES AND THE CASCINE AT FLORENCE, WITH A SLIGHT DISSECTION OF SOCIETY.

At Florence, Fashion is an easy dame. She does not demand much, but when she speaks she must be obeyed. She lets you alone while under a roof, and has no preferences in the way of a habitation. You may eat maccaroni three times a day, and she does not take it to heart. If you lodge close to the eaves, and are obliged to make your nocturnal ascents up a narrow stone staircase by the light of a pocket taper, she whispers it not in Gath, nor talks of it at Askelon. She respects economy within doors, even to the extent of pitching comfort out of the windows. Should you shiver the winter through over a few half-dead coals in an earthen pot, her eyes see it not; nor would she take note of your dress, were it gayer than Jacob's garment, or fouler than the beggar's rags, so that it be worn within the charmed hour when you are considered, by a fiction of etiquette, invisible. This laxity has, however, its limit. If you do not wish to be considered upon a par in social importance with an Egyptian mummy, you must circulate with the world after the sun has warmed the eastern bank of the Arno. Fashion then summons her train; not on foot—for no one walks in Florence, except by way of parenthesis—but in carriages.

Two things, then, are essential to respectability; an equipage, and a box at the Pergola. So long as you do not possess one of these two, you are without the golden circle—a mere nobody—though Crœsus were your grandfather, and the blood of Augustus warmed your veins. Florence boasts, in consequence, the most numerous, stylish, and, at the same time, cheapest turn-outs of any capital. It is unnecessary to own a carriage, when fifty dollars per month provides not only one with a fine span of horses, but coachmen and footmen in a livery of your choice in addition. Even a whole stud of horses does not involve a ruinous expenditure.

Neither is a title of nobility an insurmountable affair. The pert little town of Fiesole, the germ of Florence, and old when even Rome was young, has established itself in the trade of manufacturing titles of nobility, to raise a fund for the repair of its roads. Four hundred dollars will buy the parchment, title, seal, coat of arms, with a genealogy thrown in when required, of a count, baron, or other patent of nobility not infringing upon the superior claims of the families of the Popes, which have made princes almost as common in Italy as generals in the United States. After all, the attraction is not so very great. One American, however, I am told, has made an investment in this fancy stock, and with John Bull it is not an unknown weakness.

An Italian cherishes the distinctions of rank to a degree that makes him a fit neighbor to the Orientals. His vocabulary of titles is most sonorous and imposing, but in his eagerness to pay court he is apt to overshoot the mark to a most ridiculous extent when in contact with the Jonathans of America. One soon becomes an "illustrious lord" in Italy, and the commonest apartment a palace, so dubbed by the tongues of the sycophantic throng, whose aim is to explore your purse. Fools and princes, so Kendall says, are the only individuals that ride in the first-class cars in Germany. As Americans of late have earned in Europe the reputation of spending money like both those classes, they must not be shocked if their ears are saluted with adjectives in general familiar only to the latter personages. There is, however, a special inconvenience attending them when at the head of a bill. They cost more than even Jenny Lind's notes.

Fashion in Florence, it is true, imperatively demands carriages. She likes to have them do her credit, but does not refuse a hack. The numbered Jehus know this, and as there are no side-walks, or, where there are any, they are so narrow as to throw one still farther toward the middle of the street, they drive rapidly among the pedestrian throngs, aiming, in particular, to frighten the ladies or soil their dresses, so that, in self-defense, they may be forced to ride. The hackmen are the sturdiest of all the beggars. There are no fixed fares; custom gives about thirty cents the hour for a fine open carriage, and if they can not get that, they are content to take less. It is amusing to watch with what perseverance they will walk their horses alongside a newly-arrived group of strangers, following up their quarry, as a pointer does his game, until they are fairly bagged. Ride you must; and, after all, it is almost as cheap as shoe-leather.

Fashion has done something more than demand carriages; she has provided the loveliest of all drives for them—a sort of rural exchange, where they all centre, from whatever quarter they may depart. Florence, compared with most capitals, is small—a mere tenth part of Paris; yet she contrives to assemble, on the right sort of a day, not less than several hundred carriages, of all kinds, at the Cascine. Some pretend to have counted fifteen hundred on one occasion, but I have never seen half that number. Most of these are no vulgar turnouts, but equipages of every style and fancy, expressly got up for competition in taste and display of thorough-bred horseflesh. It is a sight peculiar to Florence, and to strangers quite as attractive, while to citizens far more so, than all her galleries of antique art. In its own way it is a school of morals and manners. A friend of mine, thinking, upon his first arrival, to make a nice display of four-in-hand driving, went up to the Cascine with his bloods, but found himself but one of seven similar establishments. It was useless to think of astonishing, by any equestrian display or skill, the owners of forty fancy horses and upward, drawn from the best stocks of England, Germany, and Arabia, with equipages of every style of elegance, not excepting the unrivaled New York trotting-wagon, which all over Europe maintains its superiority as the best model for grace and speed. The Cascine boasts of several of these, all fine in their way, with horses to match. It owes their introduction to a transatlantic lion, now a fixture in Europe. To him it is indebted, also, for the most extraordinary vehicle—called a drag, I believe—ever contrived for pleasure. The body resembles a section of a stage-coach, got up in a coupé fashion, with blinds to the windows, and kept as closely shut as a Turkish harem. The interior of this singular contrivance is a perpetual mystery to all beholders, and must have been originally devised for the airings of the Man in the Iron Mask. The exterior, however, has no secrets. It is mounted upon a heavy set of wheels, clumsy we should say in the United States, and well calculated to stand the rigors of mountain roads. Back of the coupé portion is a high, strong seat, occupied by two servants in livery. On top, and chained to it, are four dogs ; in front, and higher still, much like the elevated seats of one of our leviathan sleighs or a circus-wagon, is another, occupied by the owner, who drives four beautiful and spirited black horses. There are numerous cupboards about and underneath for baggage, and, I presume, a kitchen battery, to be used in traveling, while the exterior generally is hung around with spare whipple-trees, and other duplicate portions of those parts of the vehicle which were liable to give way, for the readjustment of which a portable blacksmith's shop is provided, the whole giving the vehicle the appearance of being turned inside out. The entire carriage forms the most extraordinary combination of utility, oddity, and ornamental ugliness ever put on wheels.

But, before describing the lions of the Cascine, it is necessary to explain what it is. In literal English, the farm-houses or dairies of the Grand Duke, but, in reality, the most charming drive in Italy. They commence immediately outside of the walls, by the Leghorn Rail-road station, and extend along the Arno for two miles. The bank of the river is laid out as a beautiful walk, overshadowed by magnificent trees, among which is a superb species of pine, with a clean, noble trunk, and top that spreads out like an umbrella. The forest on this side is a narrow belt, but kept in fine order, and intersected by the most level and easy of roads, giving, for the space, a charming variety of drives. Farther to the right are the extensive lawns, trimmed in English style, and contrasting sweetly with the bordering groves. Among them are interspersed the dairies from which Florence derives its purest supplies of milk and butter. At intervals, little temple-shaped summer-houses bestow upon the landscape a classical look. The eastern horizon is bounded by the Apennine range of mountains, thickly dotted with villas and villages, brought by the clearness of the atmosphere to within an apparently very neighborly distance. The half-way point of the drive is laid out in a circle, the interior of which forms a fine promenade, and a station for the military bands which play on several afternoons of each week. Around this circle the carriages all gather. No orders are given. The coachmen know that to take a drive means to go to the Cascine, and to go to the Cascine is to perform the tour, and then join the grand group to listen to the music, chat, flirt, descend and walk along the river's bank, or to lade one's self with the most fragrant of bouquets, assiduously proffered by unsentimental-looking flower-girls at prices that seem almost of fabulous cheapness in contrast with floral sales elsewhere. But with the Florentines flowers would appear to be too vulgar an attraction, for few but strangers display taste in this respect. With them, however, it can not ever be said to be a matter of choice, for, like carriages, they must receive the offered bouquets in self-defense. By some incomprehensible singularity, the flower-girls are among the grossest and most ill-favored of the peasantry; or, if they are fair specimens of the peasantry, the rural Tuscans are remarkably deficient in good looks. Even when one has a pretty face, and turns it to profitable account, she runs the risk of having it peeled by the knife of some jealous rival. This actually took place a short time since, because it proved to its possessor worth, in the sale of flowers, something more than twice that of her enraged and homely competitor. What do you suppose was the sum total of the monthly gains that excited the one to a deed that sent her, or, rather, her agent—for she did it by proxy—to the penitentiary, and the other to the hospital? Eleven dollars!!!

But, as I was saying, the flower-girls are as pertinacious as hack-drivers or picture-dealers. They do not demand money, only you must accept their flowers; if you will not take them, they arrest you by the collar, and decorate your button-hole with a dainty bunch, and then slip modestly off, declining all recompense, knowing that bachelor-nature can never long hold its purse-strings closed against the language of flowers. This they repeat every morning. If you breakfast at Doney's, the Delmonico of Florence, a fresh bouquet is on your table as soon as you are seated. If you escape this, you are overtaken in the street, or at the Cascine, and decorated, despite all modest resistance, with the infallible sign of a newly-caught stranger. After all, it is a very pretty and innocent affair, barring the advertisement it holds out of a greenhorn to be plucked.

The Cascine is so arranged that carriages, horsemen, and pedestrians have each their distinct avenues. Seats are plentifully supplied, and also cosey, shady nooks, most agreeable to lovers or the recluse. Why is it that the sovereign people of America do not sufficiently regard their health and pleasure to create for themselves similar grounds? In the plenitude of our political wisdom, we pity the subjects of the sovereign princes of Europe, but we forget that those said despots throw open to the masses galleries, palaces, and particularly gardens, such as no private republican wealth can ever hope to rival. The poor of Europe are more liberally supplied in these respects than the rich of America. Are these advantages as nothing in the scale of individual happiness?

But to return to the Cascine, or, rather, to its fashionable throng. I had driven twice around its shady avenue, wishing the while that public taste in America was equal to the creation of similar results, and now found myself near the centre of the circle of carriages. The Austrian band was playing a polka, to the time of which little children were hopping merrily on the greensward. A bright sun—it was in December—warmed up the Arno and the hills. Although near Christmas, boys were wading in the river; ladies were slowly promenading in the open air, sitting on the seats, or, in lazy elegance, half-reclining in their open carriages. The trees were still well clothed with leaves, and the grass as fresh as in June. This sunny luxuriance was in a climate two degrees north of Boston. The panorama was a brilliant one. I wish my pen could place it before the reader. Austrian staff-officers were galloping here and there, showing off their horsemanship, and the most tasteful of uniforms. Groups of gentlemen clustered about the carriages of dark-browed Italian belles, whose brilliant eyes rather commanded than solicited homage. There were worshipers, too, at the shrines of English, German, Russian, and French loveliness. My own country furnished specimens as fair as any. Each was the centre of a little out-door reception. The toilettes corresponded with the occasion—as bright and as varied as the flower-beds of the Tuileries in summer.

The scene was a fair one to look upon—the more the pity that it was not all harmony within. I had beside me a companion deeply versed in Florentine life, and, whether I was in the mood or no, Mephistophiles like, he continued to unravel in my ear its Gordian knot. Those of my readers who disapprove of any thing that savors of scandal, even though that frightful name be but a reflection of the sadder truths or ludicrous shades of society, will please skip any remarks not to their taste. For my own part, I speak of the world just as I find it. I wish it were a wiser and a happier one, but, such as it is, it is the best that we have.

"Do you see that lady," said Mephistophiles to me, "in the blue hat, with the unmistakable air of the Quartier Brèda about her? There she sits, in that elegant coupé. See how saucily those young exquisites stare at her as they pass along! Her game flies higher, but she has missed her swoop, and is going back to Paris soon.

"Just look at that carriage full of bulky English! heavy dames those, and dressed as most English women dress, so as to conceal beauty and exaggerate defect. The daughters are pretty enough, but see how unamiable they look—a thunder-cloud gathering before the sun. Turn your eyes a bit, and detect the cause. They are miserable unless they can outdo their neighbors, the Dashaways. At this moment they are undergoing the agonies of a defeat, for Lord Twaddle, with his foot condescendingly placed upon the Dashaways' carriage-step, is saying saucy things to the mother, and flirting desperately with the youngest of the girls. Nature has no charms for such persons. Their happiness is made up of bows, beaus, and badinage. Just beyond them is that fair-haired Scotch clan, who so admirably represent the pride and beauty of their country. They come as regularly as the sun to the Cascine, and hold themselves as coldly distant as the moon.

"Whose is that sweet face next to a mamma that looks worthy of such a daughter? With what becoming elegance they are dressed! They are Americans, and the girl is to inherit a fortune of a million, it is said, but she looks as retiring and unassuming as if she had never seen city life. How unlike that dark beauty near her! She's Italian, not yet sixteen, but married at fourteen. At twelve she professed herself blasée and tired of the world of fashion. Like Marie Antoinette, she should retire to the country and play at milk-maid to recruit her exhausted sensibilities.

"Here comes the Grand Duke and his family. Quite an imperial turn-out, with their outriders and mounted guard. But they mingle very unceremoniously with the crowd. They have been walking along the Arno, jostled by any one who may be unconscious of their rank, for there is nothing to distinguish them except a couple of footmen, walking out of earshot in their rear. This sort of attendance is so common, that, unless you know the royal livery, you could not tell them from any of the Fiesole nobility.

"The Florentines rarely enter the galleries. To go beyond the Cascine would be to set out on their travels through the world. One of the journals gave, not long since, a list of thirty names of persons who had passed their lives in Florence without once crossing the river from the side on which they were born to the other. Twenty minutes, as you know, is quite sufficient to take a good walker to the farthest extremity of the city. You may judge, then, of the enterprise of these descendants of the proudest and fiercest Republicans of Italy—those merchant princes, whose commerce drew the wealth of the world into their coffers. Every thing now is allowed to take as much rest as it pleases except the church-bells; their tongues keep up a perpetual clatter. Several hundred, all ding-donging at once, from four o'clock in the morning on fête-days to midnight, is a trying thing for the nerves in a small city like this. The coachmen have as little rest. If they sleep at all, it must be on their boxes. Under the paternal strictness of the Grand Duke, every thing goes on as regular as clock-work except the clocks themselves. There is as little accord between them as between Italian families. One would suppose that they had inherited the social feuds of their fabricators. They do not even agree in striking. I asked a Florentine one day why they did not set them to rights. 'What the devil does any one want to know of the time in Florence?' was his reply. He was quite right. Where there is nothing to do but to amuse one's self, there is no time but the present.

"Take notice of that group to your left. Magnificent carriages these! not those cumbersome and stately old family coaches covered with gold and paintings, but those light, tasteful affairs, which make the very horses proud of their chains. Each represents a family charged with centuries of names splendidly historical. A tinge of pride may be pardoned in the descendants of the Albizzi, Capponi, Gherardesca, Guicciardini, and the Medici, even though wilted by despotism and fashion into idle elegants. I have no sympathy for the Medici, for, if they suffer, it is by the 'lex talionis.'

"Remark how aloof the Italians keep from the Austrians! not all, but some. They do not know how to govern themselves, yet they hate those who save them that trouble. No

Austrian ever crosses their thresholds. Some noble families have even abandoned the court because there they must meet their rulers. To speak to an Austrian is to be estranged from them. One lately told me, with frank bluntness, that strangers must choose between the Austrians and Florentines; they could not be on good terms with both. When you come to know the Tuscan patois better, you will appreciate the wit and humor of the street 'gamins,' as they mock the stolid Germans. It is like pouring oil upon the wounds of those haughty patricians, for other revenge than street jibes and social isolation is beyond their power."

Among so many lions of the first magnitude, there was no cessation of curiosity. My friend had barely time to dispose of one before I probed him upon another. His memory was a perfect epitome of the life within the life about us. I picked out a couple of the most distinguished appearance. The gentleman was driving a faultless span of black horses. He was one of the finest specimens of refined manly beauty I had ever seen, perfect to a nicety in his costume, with that unexaggerated tone in both his mental and physical aspect that marks the polished man of the world. The lady beside him was his equal in these respects; pale, unanimated, and delicate even beyond the American standard of female loveliness. Their "tiger" was the model of his species. I looked in vain for a loophole for criticism, and at last triumphantly exclaimed, "There's my pattern for a family turn-out. Count D'Orsay might rival, but could not excel, the chaste style of their entire appearance. Then, too, their faces interest me prodigiously. They seem so well matched. Who are they?"

"The gentleman is noble—an old family—his ancestors have left a name in Italy. He is a perfect specimen of a Florentine lion. Our day is his night—that is to say, like the rest of the idlers, he rises at midday or after, dresses for the Cascine, thence to the Pergola, to receptions and soirées at midnight, and retires toward morning. The want of sufficient sunlight will explain, in him as with others, the extraordinary paleness of the fashionable Florentines. Their education is not, as the French say, 'très fort,' and their chief passion is for horses. With many, even with princely incomes, there is little comfort or hospitality within doors, but great show without.

"The lady you admire so greatly is a relative of an emperor. There has been some difficulty about the 'dot,' and other matters not uncommon in European circles. The cardinal archbishop who married them patched up a sort of peace, and for a while she and her husband appear together in public, while at home they live separate. But that is the case with many. You may visit a lady familiarly for a year, and not make the discovery that she has a husband. Do not make so vulgar a mistake as to suppose that every couple you see are the legitimate twain. Matrimony in Italy has a very droll signification, according to our ideas. But some allowance should be made where estates and families, but not tastes or inclinations, are united. The intervention of a friend becomes indispensable for harmony. Hence the much-talked-of 'cicisbeism,' or husband within the husband, the veritable bond, while the nominal is only a name. A lady said to me, 'What would you have us do? We must have some one to advise with, to act for us, to attend to all our little wants.' It never occurred to her that a husband was the person for those familiar offices."

"But what rôle do the husbands fill?"

"That question," said Mephistophiles, "I will reply to by quoting a little dialogue.

"'M. de ———,' said the emperor to one of his courtiers, 'they tell me that you are a cuckold. Why have you not told me?'

"'Sire,' answered M. de ———, 'because I believed it neither interested my honor nor that of your majesty.'

"Italian husbands are much of this advice. Fidelity, and even chastity, is estimated, not by the amount of attention to the external union, but by the faith preserved toward the second; or, in other words, the liaison grows to be the veritable marriage. As soon as the choice is public, it becomes hedged about with a morality which would do credit to true virtue, and is as imperative in its requisitions as are our own rules of conventional etiquette. The very fidelity of Italian women toward lovers proves their capability of correct attachments, if national customs did not force them astray. Many of these unions, with all their external familiarity, do not extend beyond friendship. They, however, are being mitigated, and 'cicisbeism' is not now universal. Don't blame too severely the warm-hearted daughters of Italy. Custom and carelessness make them indifferent to what we consider immoral. I am sorry to say that the standard of other women too often varies with every migration. Difference of latitude effects a surprising revolution in morals. Look at Mrs. ——— and Madame ———, both from countries where morality is taught with the alphabet. Yet here they manage to slip from their lawful lords, and taste the apple of variety, publicly too, and are every where well received, or else I should be silent. But in Italy society does not think it worth the trouble to cloak its vices, or, I should say, *our* customs are *your* vices."

"Do these ladies go to court?"

"Certainly. The truth is, that the silent sanction given to 'cicisbeism' makes sad breaches in the right standard of morals. Society here is extremely latitudinarian so long as certain conventionalisms are observed. As I have said, a woman is virtuous as she cleaves to her lover. To create scandal, she must indulge openly in more than one. You see this couple, and that, and dozens of others that you know about as well as I. Marriage with them is more a treaty of separation than a bond of union, or if united, the connection, owing to the intervention of a third party, too often a priest, is less to their credit than if they lived apart. I do not think that now, as formerly, parties stipulate in the marriage contract for the right of lovers, but keener eyesight than mine might be pardoned for becoming confused by the extraordinary cross-lights of this matrimonial jumble. As for children—why, legitimacy, like justice, is blindfolded—they are born, named, and no questions asked. The poor victims are ordered to marry by their parents, which they must do, just as if they were told to go to school. Ten to one they know as little of each other as they do of their confessors when first subjected to their questionings. If the acquaintance does not improve with time, it soon becomes as politely distant as that of two friends about to fight a duel. But as new social wants have been developed, their solace explains those habits which tacitly acquiesce in the fact, or expect every woman to be more intimate with her neighbor's husband than her own. This is the whole story in a nut-shell. And when you ask if Duke so and so is married, and are told yes, but he lives in one wing of the palace and the wife in the other, perhaps the one at the villa and the other in town, and that they never meet except in public, do not look incredulous. Many put even a greater distance than that between them. Yonder elegant noble, so attentive to that lady beside him, receives a handsome annuity on condition of not coming nearer to his wife than he is at present; that is to say, some hundreds of miles.

"There drive by the descendants of a king of Poland, and heirs of one of Napoleon's most gallant generals. Their palace is veritably regal. The sons and daughter are great musicians, composing and executing their own performances sufficiently well to please the fastidious ears of Italian critics. They performed at the Opera at Boulogne with great applause, and retired under a shower of bouquets. But, as they distributed the tickets gratis, perhaps the praise savored a trifle of thanks.

"That old lady, with an ocean of rouge on her cheeks, now the Princess ———, was formerly the wife of a Roman mechanic. The prince fancied her charms, and she his money and titles. A bargain was soon struck, and the carpenter's spouse became the mother of princes—and a good mother she made. At last the carpenter was good-natured enough to die, and his wife became a legitimate princess by the superfluous ceremony of marriage. It is said in society here that her son remarked to a friend on that ceremony, when asked to go elsewhere, 'Excuse me; you know I am engaged to attend my mother's marriage!'

"It is wholesome for your republican eyes to look occasionally into the morale of the titles they gaze upon so wistfully. Aristocratic vices are great levelers of patrician principles. We hold up the Socialists, with their doctrine of 'marriage is robbery,' as the great bugbears of the age. But with them it is but an empty theory, while many of the nobles who are perpetually crying 'stew-boy' to the people against the Socialists on account of their disorganizing doctrines, are actually exemplifying in their own persons the most pernicious one of all. Human nature is like that crooked stick we read about, that was constantly turning over in the vain pursuit of an easy position.

"Here drives up the Duke of ———, a dashing, wild young fellow, and fond of scrapes of all sorts. See, he does not wait to descend by the steps, but jumps over the back of his carriage. He is married to the sister of King ———, a woman possessed of many virtues and exemplary patience, though the public will have it that the wind does not always blow fair in their palace. The newspaper talk has been of a divorce, but it is nothing but talk, for they live as comfortably together as their rank will let them. She is an angel of mercy to the poor."

"Who are those handsome young fellows, driving so rapidly in those elegant dog-wagons, with those matchless black horses?"

"The first couple are Greek exquisites and princes—dwarfish Alcibiadii—their talent running chiefly to dress and horseflesh from sheer necessity of idleness. The others are the princely * * *, fast competitors in the same line, and lovers of the chase. They have an old father of upward of eighty, who knows how to keep his house and lineage in order. His possessions are scattered all the way from Sicily to Trieste. He has a deep head and purse. Napoleon made him a Councilor of State, the Pope a senator, and the Grand Duke his embassador to Naples when he sent to that court to solicit the hand of the present Grand Duchess. He accepted, conditioned upon paying the expenses of the embassy himself, and he made it a second 'field of gold.'

"Do you see that lout? He bears an honored name, and honors it so greatly as to consider it an equivalent for lack of brains. He divides his attention between the bottle and low women. But do not take him as a type of the male Florentines of good family. If they are not what the world expects, it is their misfortune rather than their fault. It is their disadvantage to be overwhelmed by the greatness of their ancestry. Commercial enterprises and industrial pursuits are interdicted to them by the inexorable laws of caste. Army and navy there are none, or next to none. The Church, to the non-religious, is rather a cloak for vice than a school of religion. There is nothing free to them—not even, as we have seen, marriage. Their country is a conquered province. Politics are forbidden fruit, with the bayonet and guillotine to hedge it round. Is it surprising, then, that they should degenerate into elegant idlers, and prefer cards to books, horses to the sciences? There are among them talents and spirit. Many fought bravely for the emancipation of Tuscany during the Revolution. They groan in heaviness of spirit at the degradation of Italy. One said to me lately that he should be proud to be an Englishman or an American, but he was ashamed to be an Italian. If they are ignorant, it is because the government supervises education and the press, so that nothing that bears not its stamp of orthodoxy shall penetrate their minds. Poor fellows! with natures fitted to make them the equals—nay, the superiors—of other races, they are crushed under a load that no humanity would be proof against. Worse than all, no ray of hope brightens their horizon."

"Who is that man with such a thin, fierce face, white hair, and long mustaches, which he is constantly twirling? He looks about him with a suspicious, uneasy glance."

"That is Field-marshal Haynau, of Hungarian notoriety. He is living here incognito. He calls himself an abused man, both by the press and his government; for, as he told a friend of mine, he never ordered women to be whipped, though the laws of Austria required it. 'They say,' he added, 'that I am a cruel man; but it is not so. I am a soldier, and have lived all my life in camps, and have the rough habits of a soldier, but I never committed any cruelty not required by my position. I have friends who love me dearly, and there is not another general as popular as I am with the army.' His friends assert that the Austrian government used him for their own purposes in Hungary, and then sacrificed him to the public opinion of Europe as a sort of scape-goat for their own sins. Others say that he is an obstinate and troublesome officer; on one occasion hanging eighteen Hungarians that the government wished to spare, and, on being reprimanded, allowing as many more to go free that they wished to have executed. However that may be, he walks and acts like a man conscious that he is under the ban of public opinion, and that it is a weightier load than he can well bear.

"But I tire you. We will pass a few more lions in review, and drive home, for it is not wholesome to be out on the Cascine after sunset. See, the old Duke de —— sets the example. He is the heir of the wiliest of diplomats, by whose code a mistake was a graver error than a fault. Did you ever see a man of his age in a better state of preservation? His toilet is a study. Strip him, and the change would be surprising. There goes, too, a lady of equal age, and one who has done you Americans a world of good by her abuse. She enjoys high consideration, in consequence, among the English. Indeed, all Americans who know her respect her talents and thank her for her criticisms. She is the famous Mrs. Trollope, now enjoying here the fruits and honors of her industrious and clever literary career.

"That family, divided between a carriage and horseback, is Charles O'Malley's, or, in other words, the wife and daughters of that prince of Irish wit and humor, Charles Lever. He sports fine horses, and is a capital fellow, as amusing in conversation as he is entertaining in books. He should go to America, to keep you serious Republicans in a roar of laughter, by way of enlivening your blood. That dreamy young man, so intimate with him, is a son of England's greatest literary lion. He is secretary to his uncle, the British embassador, and has inherited all of his father's talent.

"That stout, handsome man, leaning on his cane, is the prince of harmony, Rossini, who, with fifty thousand a year, fears that poverty is coming upon him like a strong armed man. And now for the greatest lion of all—that magnificent-looking fellow, seven feet high, with the proportions of one of Michael Angelo's statues. He is a mechanic, and for a pension of five pauls (fifty-five cents) per day, has sold his skeleton to the Academy of Medicine. They have bargained that he is not to leave Florence; but as he bids fair to live a half century more, his bones will cost them dear, and few of the present generation will see them. They call him the living skeleton, by virtue of the bond. There is one other such a giant at Pisa, a shrewder chap, who has sold his frame to two different corporations. Won't there be a rattling among the dry bones when the two powers seek to enforce possession?

"If the Italians needs must have masters, I am glad that they send them such fine-looking specimens of the warrior tribe as we find here. Their uniform does much for them, still it would be difficult to find more well-made, good-looking men elsewhere. There trots by the Prince L——, the Austrian general-in-chief, a genuine St. George. He looks like a hard foe and a dare-devil friend. A chivalrous, gallant soldier all account him. There are more reasons than grow out of politics why the jealous Italians should hate their handsome conquerors.

"You perceive that the Cascine still boasts of a respectable herd of lions, mingling here in peaceful pastime. The burgher citizens gaze admiringly upon the brilliant throng, but rarely attempt to cross the line of rank. They bring their families to see, but not to make a part of, the show. An American or Englishman, in their eyes, has not much to boast of in way of blood, but he looms up in their vision like another Nebuchadnezzar's image, all made of gold. Heretical though the metal be, he is not unwilling to worship it, and much of his extraordinary civility can be traced to the power of lucre.

"The Cascine has the power of loadstone. The needle of

fashion turns to it from every quarter of Florence, and as Tuscany has been, until recently, the home of distinguished exiles, it can boast of having sheltered within its palaces at one time more great titles, if not names, than any other pleasure-grounds of Europe. A few years since it might have claimed cousinship with Napoleon's celebrated pit full of kings. Here could be seen the Count Saint Lew, ex-King of Holland; the Prince of Montfort, ex-King of Westphalia; the Duke of Lucca, ex-King of Etruria; Madame Christophe, ex-Queen of Hayti; the Poniatowski's, descendants of the King of Poland; some sprouts from the magnificent line of the Medici; and the Prince of Syracuse, an ex-viceroy of Sicily. A tolerable crowd of dethroned heads."

With such entertaining discourse my friend enlivened our way back to town, bestowing upon me some characteristic information or piquant anecdote of each notable name or title as they proudly swept along the beautiful avenue. It was an interesting accompaniment to an agreeable picture. Such as I could remember I have given, but if my readers would enjoy it as I did, let them come and take their places in the panorama. Mephistophiles still watches over the spectacle with his good-humored cynicism, and I will bespeak for them the favor of his interpreting glance.

I had almost forgotten his last quiet probe at the social world, as the subject of his tale, in all the pride of aristocratic equipages and liveries, came up. "Those grand ladies," said he, "are daughters of a London sausage-maker. A manœuvring mother brought them here, and, by the promise of magnificent dowries, bought them titled husbands. By some extraordinary absence of mind, their Italian lords were simple enough to sign the marriage contracts without the equivalent in hand, so that they have had the pleasure not only of possessing, but supporting their wives ever since. There is no speculation more uncertain than these matrimonial mesalliances. They make a terrible hodge-podge of morals and society. If there be any difference between them and the Circassian mode of supplying the wife-market, it is that in many instances the candidates for the nuptial bed sell themselves—a much greater ignominy than if sold without their own consent. That dilapidated-looking marquis, just crossing the road on foot, married a rich old Englishwoman. The result is, that while he all but starves, and endeavors to raise a loan for his personal wants from his friends upon the dubious security of his wife's death, she rides in her coach and four, covered with jewels and velvets, reveling in the eclat of her artfully-secured title. Those who play with edged tools—you know the rest."

CHAPTER VI.

WHAT A "SIGHT-SEER" DID SEE IN ONE DAY.

If I were called upon to name the individual of the human species that unites in his or her person the greatest powers of endurance with the utmost impatience, the most unflagging activity to a body always just ready to drop from fatigue; a mind skeptical from its shallowness, yet ready to ingulf entire kingdoms in its capacious maw, and to bolt miracles and relics by scores—in short, that individual who combines in him or herself the most opposite qualities, whether of body or mind, I should unhesitatingly pronounce that individual to be the modern "sight-seer." Reader mine, has it ever fallen to thy lot to travel with one? If so, now that thy fatigues have become reminiscences, it may please thee to renew, on paper, thy self-inflicted sufferings of yore, when, impatient of home, thou rashly becamest a tourist. If not, reader, ponder and inwardly digest a day's experience of mine, lest thou, too, in the folly of thy heart, shalt say,

"John, pack my trunk; to-morrow I'm off for Italy."

"Sight-seeing," from its original purpose of information, has been perverted by these traveling pests into a frigid duty. Nothing must be allowed to escape their observation that has attained the dignity of being a "sight." They neither study, examine, nor look. "They have been there." That short sentence embraces with them equally the entire Rise and Fall of the Roman Empire, the Chinese Wall, Mohammed's Tomb, or the hair of the Virgin. It has been the fashion heretofore for lions to swallow travelers; but now travelers swallow lions by scores, in one day. So far is digestion from being impaired by this enormous meal, it but serves as a whet to the appetite for the succeeding. There is but one soft spot in their conscience. Hint to them that there is something that they have missed—be it but the ass's jaw-bone with which Samson slew the Philistines, an antediluvian salt-cellar, or an Etruscan tomb—and their remorse is fearful to behold. True, some will stoutly deny the possibility of there existing any thing that they have not seen; others will offset their loss by more marvelous sights in the neighborhood, and endeavor to overwhelm your discovery by the magnitude of their own; but it is easy to perceive in both that the wound rankles, and can only be cured by seeing for themselves also. The only object that such persons can possibly have in view must be a "catalogue," and the malicious pleasure of saying to the unsophisticated tourist who travels really "to see"—but to see and study only those objects which both gratify and instruct, believing that to see every thing is really to see nothing—"Oh! you surprise me; how could you miss it? I assure you it was worth all the rest." For my part, I should like to see every thing; but then I should desire to have both life and memory augmented to tenfold their present capacity.

The gender of these "sight-seers" is both male and female. What is the most singular, neither age, infirmity, nor other evils to which human flesh is heir, have the slightest effect in modifying this passion. Even delicacy is often discarded as inconvenient. As for health, that poor orphan must take care of itself. "To see" is the entire creed—to know, remember, or understand, are indifferent points.

The necessities of this class have created a dozen other classes—parasites of the worst and most annoying character—who effectually contrive to destroy all the comfort and pleasure the modest seeker of knowledge, or lover of association, otherwise might have. I speak of the race generally, and class them as guides, ciceroni, coachmen, donkey-drivers, venders of prints and antiquities, couriers, inn-keepers, showmen, valets, door-keepers, and beggars of every quality. All these are purse-leeches, united in a common league to defraud and extort. But the depletion of coin is the least of their evils. Better, by far, is it to fall among the savages of the American deserts, or to be surrounded with wild animals, than to be in the midst of these human wolves. The more they are fed, the worse they snarl and bite. Unsusceptible of gratitude, they are proof against generosity. Like cormorants, every thing is food for their maws; and with the baseness peculiar only to human nature, they fawn upon those they fear, and mock at those they gull.

I shall select one only out of the many similar days' experience that, thanks to the system introduced by "sight-seers," have now become the common lot of travelers on classic soil. By the time my readers have followed me through that day's labor, they will have come to the conclusion that all play and no work is not the fate of tourists who have been so unfortunate as to link their fortunes to those of a universal sight-seer.

One of these terrible beings, of the female sex—the mania with them is even worse than with the male—had taken us in charge for the day. In addition to her all-seeing and omniscious qualities, she was tormented with an insatiable desire for system, and an incurable propensity to lecture; so that we were called upon to look and listen, at the same moment, after the most orthodox manner possible, of the most skillful of all the mighty lion-hunters that yearly do the "grand tour." "Us" made a party as unfavorable as can well be conceived for the appreciation of the talents of our anomalous Nimrod.

It consisted of a young lady, who much preferred youthful beaus to old ruins; a fashionable matron, who would like to see what fashionable people went to see—but in as ladylike a manner as possible, and who much preferred the use of her own tongue to that of another; a young gentleman, to whom every thing but cards, and suppers, and talking were unmitigated bores; and your humble servant, who went because it would have been so stupid to have staid behind. The locality was Naples; the hour of starting, as soon as the coffee was swallowed; and the conveyance, a comfortable carriage, with three horses, covered with innumerable bells, that jingled merrily as we rapidly sped over the level pavements.

Our first station was Virgil's Tomb, at the entrance of the Grotto of Pausilipo. It is in a garden, midway up the hill which commands so magnificent a view of the Bay of Naples. This was, at all events, worth seeing; so was the tomb, for those whose faith has not been destroyed by antiquarians. It is a nondescript stone building, of a cylindrical shape, surmounted by a dome, with nothing to remind one of the poet except a modern inscription. We had four volunteers to show us the gate of the garden, directly before our eyes; another insisted upon being our guide on a path which as plainly led to the tomb as Broadway does to Union Square; then an owner of the lot joined in the procession; lastly, not to mention the usual assault of beggars, appeared the guardian of the tomb, with his key, to show us how empty and dark it is within—each of whom clamored for *bucksheesh* with an eagerness worthy of Bedouins.

I know nothing within the range of sights that more belies its name, and puts to flight every poetic and romantic association, than the so-called Grotto of Pausilipo. This grotto is a tunnel, half a mile long, twenty-two feet broad, and some eighty feet high, cut through the hill to form a subterranean road, by which the distance to Pozzuoli is materially shortened. It is an ancient affair, an antiquity in the days of Seneca, who thought it worth mentioning. But, in comparison with modern railroad tunnels, this ancient bore is the work of pigmies, particularly as the rock is as easily cut as ice. There is a petty chapel at the entrance, excavated out of the hill-side, the station of a dirty, savage-looking hermit, who waylays every carriage with his frightful gestures and screams for alms. The grotto is the main road to Baiæ, now, as formerly, a crowded thoroughfare for carriages, foot-passengers, and droves of animals. Every one who ventures through undergoes a fearful purgatory of unwholesome air, lamp-smoke, dust, and countless other annoyances, before emerging to daylight and a filthy suburb of Naples. The road is good, however, and soon takes one into the midst of vineyards and other vegetation.

Before reaching the Lake d'Agnano it becomes circuitous and sandy, being a by-road. This lake, like all others in the vicinity, is an old crater, which nature, with a love of change quite worthy of a woman, has emptied of fire only to fill it with water. But there is fire near by, and plenty of it too, judging from the steam cracks in the earth, and the sulphurous fumes which impregnate the atmosphere. Before reaching the lake we were snatched up by a guide, who, pointing to the lake, gravely informed us that it was a lake—next, that the bath-house was a bath-house—consigning us at the door to another, who ushered us into various rudely-built chambers, from the sides and floors of which sulphurous vapors ascended with all the force of a young Tartarus. These baths have been in use for thousands of years for the destruction of rheumatism. They have an alternate action with Vesuvius, growing hotter and more copious in their discharges as Vesuvius becomes quiet. In their rear are the remains of one of the numerous villas belonging to Lucullus.

At a short distance to the right is the "Grotta del Cane," where unhappy dogs are doomed to daily-renewed deaths for the philosophic gratification of pitiless visitors. This grotto is merely a small cavity in the hill, scarcely large enough for a man to enter, and closed by a wooden door, to which, of course, was attached its keeper. A pretty little dog, of a mongrel-spaniel look, had followed us, without much reluctance, to this cave, though seemingly aware of the fate in store for it. The master of ceremonies asserted, as was natural, that the experiment was harmless to the dog; but if a human being can not breathe with impunity carbonic acid gas until it causes convulsions, neither can a dog. The experiment is a cruel one, and we were hard-hearted enough to consent to it. The keeper held the dog by his legs, with his face toward the ground, from which issued the mephitic gases. He turned his eyes piteously toward us, and yet seemed to take a morbid pleasure in the fatal draught. In less than a minute his limbs were convulsed; in another minute life would have been extinct, but the keeper withdrew him, and laid him upon the grass in the fresh air. The recovery from this semi-death must be more painful than its previous endurance, for the poor animal gasped, and was evidently in torture. A few minutes brought him entirely to—languid, but not without some animation—for he made an attempt to frisk about. A moment after, he came to me and licked my hand.

I inwardly vowed that no dog should again be immolated for my sake. A lighted torch, held close to the ground, was immediately extinguished. It was a hopeless effort to attempt to discharge a pistol within its influence. I breathed it for a second, and became so dizzy and faint, with such a painful sensation at the stomach, that I was but too glad to withdraw, without farther experience of what the poor brute must have suffered.

A cold boiling spring, as it is termed, close by, completed, as we supposed, the sights of this lake; but another guide made his appearance, and insisted that he had charge of a curiosity worth them all. To miss nothing, we followed him. He led us to a newly-constructed grotto, opened the door, and ushered us in. This grotto covered a spring or fountain of ammoniacal gas, which is inhaled by consumptives. Following his example, we bent ourselves toward the floor, and lapped up with our hands mouthsful of this not unpleasant air. Its first effect was somewhat exhilarating, but it should be breathed only with great caution. A frog, placed on the floor, made at first desperate attempts to escape. Gradually his limbs became motionless, and in three minutes he was dead. In the half hour that we passed at this lake we had encountered five guides or guardians—disbursed among them nine francs—run through the usual gauntlet of beggars—been steeped in hot sulphur, drugged with carbonic acid vapors, and made light headed with ammoniacal gas—an experience, one would have supposed, quite sufficient for an entire day, though it proved but the initiative ceremonies of ours.

From the Lago d'Agnano we drove to Pozzuoli, along the new beach road, affording on one side fine sea-views of the Bay of Naples, and on the other an occasionally almost overpowering stench. Indeed, Pozzuoli, or Puteoli, as it once was called, derives its name from its fetid odors, which do not grow any sweeter from age.

At the entrance of this ancient town, the onslaught made upon us was terrible. Guides charged upon us in scores, catching hold of the carriage, and even seizing upon the wheels to arrest our progress. Beggars, whose entire capital consisted of broken or maimed limbs, crutches, sores disgustingly exposed to public view, and every species of natural deformity, and acquired impudence and importunity, chanted their ceaseless whining chorus in our ears. "Charity, charity! your excellencies, charity! Beautiful ladies, for the love of the holy Madonna, give us something, and the saints will bless you!" "Do you want a guide?" "Do you want a donkey?" "Here's a bronze Mercury, a veritable antique, your excellency, just dug up!" shouted a vender of antiquities, waving his clever imitation of the classic idol in the air to attract observation. "Look at the beautiful relic, your excellency!" cried another; "one dollar only," at the same moment endangering my face by a shapeless mass of metal, covered with verdigris, which he thrust almost into my eyes. Ragged and dirty urchins, but with fine faces and waggish tongues, swelled our cortège, and made the "confusion still worse confounded" by their sharp cries for the smallest coins. Mothers, still more ragged and dirty, bronzed in the sun, and hardened by poverty to reckless lying and beggary, snatched up their own or their neighbor's infants, and rushed after us in furious haste to gather their share of the spoil. To give or buy off such a horde was to make each succeeding visitor's path more perilous. It would have been a bounty on vice and violence. Having been furnished at Naples with the name of a reliable guide, we shouted for Angelo, and, almost instantaneously, as if he had sprung from the earth, Angelo was upon the box, and we under his orders. Seeing us a prize to Angelo, the besieging crowd gradually returned to their lair at the outskirts of the town, to await fresh arrivals.

"Now, Angelo," said our lady patroness, "we wish to see all the sights of Pozzuoli, Baiæ, Cumæ, Misenum, Solfaterra, and every thing else between this and—" "Hell!" our exasperated dandy added, as the prospect of the day's work began to dawn upon his already half used-up faculties. He meant "Avernus," but in his angry haste gave the plain English. "And, Angelo, return to Naples by a different route, and do not omit a single ruin or interesting object," continued she, not noticing the interruption. "Angelo," I added, "drive off all beggars and sellers of antiques; pay all ciceroni, hire all donkeys, settle for every thing yourself; and take care, as you value your own pay, that no side demands reach us." "Yes, your excellency, you shall be well served," replied Angelo, delighted at the prospect of the haul before him. I would advise all travelers in such straits as we to do the same. To be cheated by one to whom you have given a *carte blanche* is vastly more satisfactory than to be annoyed by countless impositions at every step of the way.

St. Paul rested seven days at Pozzuoli on his voyage to Rome, but I think it would be difficult for any modern saint to obtain even an hour's rest in this place since it has become a show town—a sort of galvanic grave-yard of antiques. Our first stage was the curious old temple of Jupiter Serapis, the titbit of geologists, on account of its columns, which furnish a sort of conchological chronology of the earth's movements ever since their erection. It was built more than two thousand years ago, and originally, judging from the numerous ancient baths around it, to which the water still has access—and, indeed, some are still in use—it must have been a sort of religious hydropathic establishment. When first discovered, in 1750, after its partial burial by an earthquake, it was quite perfect, and might have been made, at slight expense, the most complete and beautiful relic of antiquity. But the kings of Naples, wanting its graceful columns, colored marbles, and fine statuary for their modern buildings, have reduced this temple to the skeleton of its former state.

The next antiquity to which our attention was directed were the immense piers of the old mole, constructed so far back that nobody can now decide when, though they were indebted to the Roman emperors for repairs. They remain under the charge of Neptune ; and as nobody can fence them in, there was nothing to pay for looking at them. Caligula used them as a parting station for his temporary bridge of boats, with which he connected Baiæ with Pozzuoli.

Rejoining our carriage, we took the road to Cumæ, passing every inch of the way over classic, but very dusty and heavy soil. On our right were the remains of the villa of Cicero, about as interesting in present appearance as a dilapidated brick-kiln. Singularly enough, all that is left, that is not vague and shapeless, is a *wine-cellar.* Here the Emperor Hadrian died, and Cicero composed his Academic Questions—two facts which, in the way of reminiscence, make these ruins of more interest than most of the others that so thickly strew this coast.

The road to Cumæ took us past Lake Avernus, quite a picturesque and gentle sheet of water, with nothing at present about it to remind one of Virgil's Tartarus. However noxious it may once have been, birds not only fly across it now with impunity, but alight upon its surface, and fish find a safe home in its waters. But nature in this region performs strange freaks, often in a most unexpected manner, so that one should take heed how he indulges in skepticism as to what does not now exist as described by ancient ocular authorities. The entire coast vibrates under the influence of volcanic action. Looking down from the precipitous cliffs at Bauli, we could see the ruins of temples and villas beneath the clear waters. The temple of Jupiter Serapis had been submerged, and afterward restored to earth again by the same fiery agent. An earthquake in 1538, or more properly a volcanic eruption, created in thirty-six hours the present Monte Nuovo, a hill quite large enough, if inverted, to fill the Avernine Lake. To make room for this mountain, the earthquake swallowed up an entire village, and destroyed the greater part of the Lucrine Lake, with the descendants of those oysters so prized by Latin poets and epicures. A classical lake would make but a diminutive mill-pond in New England; but every sheet of water large enough to float a boat is dignified in Europe with the name of lake.

Angelo shortly after announced our arrival at the "Arco Felice," a colossal gateway of old Cumæ, a city so ancient as to make all others in this vicinity seem quite juvenile in contrast. It has retained its ancient appellation for three thousand years. This gateway is still in excellent preservation, and spans the old paved street which leads directly through the heart of what was once a populous and important city, but is now a shapeless mass of ruins, half hid in vegetation. Antiquarians sagely point out aqueducts, temples, baths, and various other edifices, which may be so or may not. They are now not worth the trouble of either dispute or investigation. All this side of the Bay of Naples is a cemetery of nations, the ruined cities of which lie scattered about over the soil like the disinterred bones of an old grave-yard. At Cumæ recent excavations have brought to light the tombs of *three* distinct races, built like the stories of a house one over the other, after the existence of each, in its turn, had been apparently forgotten by its successor. The topmost stratum consists of the narrow abodes of the old Romans; beneath this we find the tombs of the Greek colonists; underneath these, in some instances sixty feet below the present surface of the soil, we come to the aboriginal sepulchres, when and by whom made the world may never know. That they were a civilized and refined people, their domestic utensils, pictures, jewelry, vases, and their mode of disposing of their dead, plainly show. How singular, that all we now know of a lost race is only what the tomb discloses!

To reach the top of the Arco Felice, we were obliged to walk through the cultivated patch of ground of a peasant. He came bawling after us for toll. Angelo threw him copper, but this was not enough. He did not cease his noise until silver crossed his hand. His cabbages were planted on the very walls of Cumæ. From their summit we enjoyed a view of the distant Liternum, the retreat and death-place of Scipio Africanus, the Circean Promontory so nearly fatal to Ulysses, the Acheron, and the islands of Ponza, Ischia, and Vandolena.

Descending from the walls, which time has almost wholly hidden in a hill, we rattled over the Via Domitiana, still, in parts, as good as new, toward the Lake of Fusaro, where the King of Naples has a sort of oyster-lodge. On the way we passed by and along the River Styx, the Elysian Fields, and other localities immortalized in the verse of Virgil. The Elysian Fields reminded me of one of our prairie swamps—a fitter abode for snakes and musquitoes than for beatified shades. The Styx was black enough not to belie its fame. The ladies—excepting, of course, the patroness—voted Virgil an impostor, and the dandy declared the King of Naples's oysters to be worth a dozen Æneids. So to Fusaro we drove, and bribed the honest guardian into selling us a basket-load of the very best, not excepting those retained for the private tooth of his majesty. Some we dispatched from the shell on the spot. If royal Ferdinand had ever been on Chesapeake Bay, he would set small store by his oyster-bed. I came to the conclusion that either the Roman poets were indifferent judges of oysters, or else they had greatly degenerated from the fatness and flavor of their illustrious ancestors.

Arriving at Baiæ, Angelo deposited us and the remainder of our oysters at the door of a hut, elevated on a stone platform, over the steps of which, in large capital letters, was written, "*Grand Royal Queen Victoria's Hotel.*" This name promised something, so we entered. We were classically located, at all events. On either side of us were the ruins of the temples of Venus Genetrix, and of Mercury and Diana, built with brick, and probably once cased with marble. Several chambers were quite perfect, and contained finely-executed stucco ornaments. But their entrances and interiors were choked with earth and brambles. These ruins were the only intelligible remains of the once luxurious Baiæ, which for a thousand years retained a sort of prescriptive right to corrupt the easy virtue of the several races that succeeded each other in the lordship of this seductive soil. Baiæ was notorious, even amid the most licentious cities of Italy during the Roman and Middle Ages, for its profligacy. At present, it presents nothing more seductive than beggars, colliers, and fishing-boats. It could not even provide a dinner. We called for meat: there was none. We ran over an entire "carte" of supposed eatables. The result was, that our host of the "Grand Royal Queen Victoria's Hotel" agreed to provide us a table to eat our oysters from, a loaf of bread, a dish of maccaroni, and a bottle of wine. This was not over-satisfactory to the appetites of a party who had been already six hours hard at work, and had as many more in prospect. There was nothing else, so we fell to. The maccaroni was too hard and black for heretical throats, so we had the satisfaction of seeing Angelo swallow that instead of ourselves. The wine I mistook for vinegar, but "mine host" indignantly asserted that it was "genuine Falernian," and quite as good as any Horace ever tippled with. We all owed it a debt of gratitude; for, had it not been as potent as it proved, I believe the slimy oysters would have given us the cholera. While we were *dining*, several carriage-loads of visitors drove up. Some provident souls had brought their dinners from Naples; others came as we, with the spoils of the Fusaran Lake, and dined on them. Beggars clamored for alms and the *remains* of our meals. They said that they were hungry. We sympathized, and wondered on what the poor of Baiæ could possibly exist, when its "Grand Hotel" could furnish but bad maccaroni and stale bread. One old woman, a regular Hecate in looks, brought grass, and devoured it by handsful, to show the quality of her appetite. The fare of this female Nebuchadnezzar was only one stage worse than ours, so all we could do was to give her money, by way of encouragement to repeat her trick for the benefit of Angelo's next victims. A little boy and girl danced the tarantella after a manner that won for them many coppers, and cries for more.

From Baiæ to Bauli is a short and romantic drive, and a series of views such as the combined natural and artificial beauty of the Bay of Naples can alone present. In contrast with the other towns in this neighborhood, which grow out of and upon the ruins of temples, palaces, and imperial villas, like fungi and other vegetable excrescences from the decayed trunks of once noble trees, Bauli was cleanly and industrious. Every man, woman, and child—even the infant at the breast—begged; but they begged good-naturedly, and as a matter of course, without interrupting their work, grateful if they got any thing, and joking each other if disappointed. Mothers pointed to their children, and asked for a penny because they were so pretty. The traffic in distorted limbs and disgusting diseases had not taken root here. The population was too good-looking to be willing to sacrifice their beauty for the doubtful gains of spurious charity.

From the hill we looked down upon the foundations of the villa of Hortensius, in the water, near which Nero caused his mother, Agrippina, to be killed. The graphic description of this event by Tacitus came up vividly before me as I gazed upon the site of his demoniacal crime. For miles we wandered over the hills, every where meeting some interesting remains of antiquity, until they became tiresome from their very numbers. There were the villa of Lucullus, where Tiberius died—the subterranean chambers, dark, narrow, and more than gloomy; ghastly, like the Roman catacombs, christened "the prisons of Nero;" they are foul and terrible enough for the tender mercies of any tyrant, ancient or modern, though Nero may be guiltless of any thing in regard to them except having given them a name; and the most wonderful object of all, the immense artificial reservoir, which contained the purified water for the use of the Roman fleet at Misenum. This reservoir is excavated in the hill, the top being arched, and sustained by vast brick pillars. The whole interior is covered with cement, which is coated with incrustations of lime. It is ventilated from above, and stone steps lead down to the floor, now free from water, except what is deposited by rain. Cape Misenum commands an extensive *coup d'œil* of the Bay of Naples, the old port and naval station —now a sort of lake—and the classical shore and sites which we had traversed.

We had still much work before us, according to the plan of the lady patroness, who was resolutely bent upon condensing into one day enough for the labors of six. Accordingly, allowing only a few minutes to one of the finest prospects in Europe, she turned our heads toward Pozzuoli, giving us a different view of many of the objects already examined, besides a closer one of the artificial fish-ponds, so dear to Roman gourmands. Pliny would have us believe that the fishes in these ponds knew the voices of their keepers, and came at their call; that each responded to its name by leaping out of the water, and that the pets wore necklaces and ear-rings: his statement must have been the father of "fish-stories."

At Nero's villa, of which some brick-work alone remains, we entered his vapor-baths, which are underneath its site. The entrance is like that of an ordinary cave, but the heat soon becomes oppressive and stifling. Before we were aware of his object, a guide, stripped naked to the waist, seized a bucket and some eggs, and requested the ladies to follow him. They did for a rod or so, into a circuitous and narrow hole leading down into the bowels of the hill, and then rushed back, faint, and streaming with perspiration. Angelo said it would be imprudent for them to venture farther without they stripped also, a process to which they were not at all inclined, even to gratify their curiosity by discovering what there was so hot below. In two minutes the guide returned, reeking with steam like a leaky boiler. He had been far enough to dip up the boiling water, and brought us back the eggs cooked to a charm. We were already half boiled ourselves, and gladly hastened to the outer air to cool. Angelo had a warm battle with this salamander, who wanted twenty-five cents apiece for his eggs; but the threat of bringing no more strangers to his lair brought down his demands one half.

The Sibyl's Cave, or, as it is more poetically called, the grotto of the Cumæan Sibyl, was too tempting a titbit for the ladies to forego. Dandy and myself were content with our present experience of classical grottoes, but we were out-voted, and forced by our gallantry to accompany the ladies to this, if we may credit Virgil, avenue to the infernal regions. It was none too good to be such, judging from first impressions, as its gloomy door opened, and we followed a tribe of half-naked, muscular guides into a descending passage cut deep into the hill. Its darkness was scarcely relieved by the flaring light of torches. How deep and far we trudged after our officious guides, who encouraged us at each step to proceed, I can not say. All at once they stopped and pointed to a narrow passage, descending rapidly into the mountain, and scarcely wide enough for a man to pass through. This, they said, was the entrance to the Sibyl's chambers. As she was out, there could be no impropriety in entering, though there would have been a touch of it in the way the ladies penetrated into her sanctuary, had we been exposed to daylight. This passage, the depths of which the eye vainly sought to penetrate, was two feet deep in water. The only mode of ingress was by mounting the backs of our guides, "good horses" as they called themselves. A man with a torch preceded each. The ladies put their knees into the hands of their "horses," which were turned behind them, threw their arms with choking tightness around their necks, bowed their fair faces, destined soon to lose their fairness, close to their curly manes, and cried out, "Go ahead." As we were all alike mounted, all were on an equality of appearance, though I "guessed," as well as the darkness would permit, that the ladies, in their anxiety to preserve appearances, cut the worse figure. Splash, splash went the water; of course, the ladies screamed, and wondered where the next step would take them. The water became a little deeper, that was all; but the sides of the passage were coated with the soot of the thousands of torches that had for centuries preceded curious ladies into or down this chimney of Pluto, for to nothing else could I liken it. The soot, of course, rubbed off into their dresses—the torches sent flame and smoke into our faces. We were half choked with foul air, but still held on; indeed, to turn was impossible. At last a sort of chamber opened upon us. It was about the size of a state carriage, half full of water, and as black as Erebus. The panting guides deposited us, nearly up to our ankles in water, on a narrow stone platform, which they called the Sibyl's bed. A little farther on there was another chamber, the counterpart of this. We knew there was water there, because we felt and heard it; there were walls, because we rested against them; but, except as the torches flashed out their dubious light, we could no more see than if we had been put away mummied on a shelf in the centre of the grand pyramid. We had come thus far through smoke, soot, and water, to find ourselves buried in a small-sized tomb, deep into the earth, with an equal chance of being suffocated or drowned. The lights might go out, or the guides might clear out. Either thought—and such thoughts will come, under such circumstances—was unpleasant. I suggested the policy of a speedy retreat, as there was not sufficient inducement for additional exploration. Into such an "infernal" (I speak classically) hole had the devouring curiosity of women plunged us; and, worse than all, I afterward learned, on good authority, that no Sibyl ever dwelt there—a statement easily to be believed after a personal inspection of the apartment. In fact, the whole story is an "invention of the enemy" for the benefit of the biped horses. Daylight revealed to each other faces blacker than Othello's. I bathed mine in the much scandalized waters of Lake Avernus, and brought to light a portion of its original color. The ladies polished away with their handkerchiefs, and dropped their veils to soften the effect. We had a long walk to meet the carriage, which rapidly bore us to a new field of antiquities.

As we drove into Pozzuoli, a squad of donkeys awaited our arrival. We had in the course of the day tried almost every other mode of locomotion, and now Angelo said we must alight and mount these self-willed brutes. I refused, insisting that my two legs were quite as capable of carrying me as the donkey's four. But it was of no use. The others were mounted, and the urchin driver of the ass allotted as mine drove him after me, now causing him suddenly to stop before me, brushing by at my side, every once in a while making an offensive demonstration with his heels, until, to escape them, I was forced to stride his back. Thick and fast came the blows upon the poor creature's flanks as we hurried through the narrow and uneven lanes. Up hill and down, over rocks and gulleys, they trotted tumultuously, now tossing us against each other, then rubbing our legs against a stone wall, or threatening to leave our brains on some wayside tree; on, on we jolted, clinging in desperation to our saddles, our spines twisting, bobbing, and dodging like saplings in a whirlwind in our efforts to avoid overthrowing and being overthrown, while the impish drivers vigorously applied the lash, and frightened, by hideous yells, their Liliputian animals into still more pell-mell haste. Even donkey nature has its limits of forbearance. Dandy was mounted upon the fleetest. It had gone ahead of all the others, quite indifferent as to whether it bore us from our saddles as it scrambled furiously by, or left its rider's limbs lodged in some rocky crevice. This was quite as much as could be expected from the most ambitious donkey; but its owner, proud of its spirit, concentrated all his energies of muscle and lung into a combined blow and shout, intended to develop all its latent powers of wind and speed. His success in astonishing us was both complete and satisfactory. The donkey stopped as short as if he had been simultaneously changed into stone. Dandy, who had been enjoying the race, the only thing besides the oysters that he had enjoyed, was pitched hat-foremost over his head. In falling, he threw his arms around the animal's neck. This manœuvre saved his beaver and its contents, but brought him underneath the ass, with his face in affectionate proximity to the brute's, as if he were bent on giving him a kiss, while donkey was shaking his ears with anticipated delight. The ludicrous attitude of the two was irresistible; the young ladies merrily complimented Dandy upon his conquest, and laughed until their own equilibriums were shaken. Even madam patroness said the sight was worth one grotto, or even a cracked column.

Without farther accident we arrived at the semi-extinct crater of Solfaterra, which had seen its best days before Vesuvius was born. It is about a mile in circumference, and at present serves as a vast laboratory of alum, vitriol, and salammoniac, which are here manufactured in large quantities. Scalding fumes of sulphur still arise in places. The floor of the crater is a vast dome. Upon dropping a large stone, the noise is like that of muffled thunder or the reverberation of the bottomless pit. How deep and extensive is the cavity beneath, none but Providence can tell, but the sound gives one a nervous apprehension of the thinness of this natural roof, for it really seems as if the stone would break it through, and precipitate the visitors into its fathomless fires. It would be a curious experiment to pierce this volcanic arch, and peer into the secrets of nature beneath.

But our greatest danger was from the workmen, who clamored for money with more the air of robbers than beggars. They surrounded our animals, insisting upon performing numberless unwelcome services. To give to one was to encourage all. Angelo counseled closed fingers and frigid apathy. We got away as speedily as possible, but not without paying tribute to a well-dressed and polite individual, who represented himself as door-keeper to the volcano.

After visiting the ancient amphitheatre, the subterranean story of which is an anomaly in this species of architecture, and, thanks to the earthquakes that buried it, is now well preserved, we voted, as it was dark, that we would go to see no more ruins this day. This amphitheatre was a mere bagatelle of an edifice. It held only forty-five thousand spectators. The price of admission, I judged, was about the same now as when the imperial butcher Nero honored the games with his presence. The royal bounty of King Ferdinand to his loving courtiers is shown more by the gift of an ancient ruin than by a modern palace. The latter would bring most of them to ruin, but the former pays the better in proportion that it lacks repairs. The ancients were a liberal race. They not only made their own fortunes, but those of their remotest descendants.

The asses were to be paid, and Angelo also. The former had taken us to our carriage just outside the town, where awaited us a similar crowd to that which we had encountered in the morning. Angelo, who I mistrusted was chief of the asses himself, recommended a liberal sum. This given, the drivers wanted each about as much more for their efforts to break our necks. One had held the bridle while the beautiful "signorina" had mounted, another had picked up the fallen dandy, a third had yelled and pelted the donkeys with stones; each had some similar service to urge. As no Italian is satisfied with being once paid, we gave each a trifle more, and they showered down upon our excellencies "many happy returns of the day," to which we devoutly responded, "God forbid!"

"How much do we owe you, Angelo, Prince of Ciceroni?"

"Oh! your excellency, some gentlemen give me a dollar. and some a dollar and a half."

The smaller sum was just double his legitimate wages, and he had, to my certain knowledge, made nearly as much more out of the oyster speculation alone; but we were all in good humor at the prospect of the speedy termination of our labors, and I handed him the "dollar and a half." Angelo received it with a profusion of Neapolitan thanks, and hoped we would remember him the next time we came that way. The very next day I sent him another greenhorn, and I do not doubt that he remembers me in his prayers to this hour.

As for the horde of venders of antiquities, and beggars of all grades, we left them our good wishes and the hopes of our return. Fifteen dollars disbursed among the parasites of sight-seers in one day, in the cheapest country in Europe, was quite sufficient relief to our consciences. Besides, we yearned for our dinner. The coachman drove rapidly Naples-ward along the beach fronting the superb little island of Nisida, where Brutus was wont to pass his summer hours. We then ascended the road made by the French, leading to the city, and looking down upon the most magnificent sea and shore panorama in Europe. Beautiful is that prospect by day, and glorious by night, with Vesuvius looking like a thing of life, keeping treacherous watch over a coast it adorns but to destroy. Other bays are lovely—as Santa Catharina, Panama, and Rio de Janeiro bear witness—but in this wide and beautiful world there is but one Bay of Naples.

In thirteen hours from the time we had left the hotel we were back again. That the reader may really appreciate what we "did up," I shall catalogue our principal game: Two craters, five lakes, four ruined cities, five grottoes and vapor-baths, more or less poisonous, an amphitheatre, one ruined prison, two ditto reservoirs, one ditto gate, two ditto aqueducts and bridges, seven ditto villas, three fish-ponds, and six temples, including thirty miles carriage-ride, three ditto donkey-back, distance man-back uncertain, and some five or six miles of walking, climbing, stumbling, and subterranean exploring, besides a small piece of boating, and the paying of upward of thirty distinct fees and gratuities.

CHAPTER VII.

A DAY AT POMPEII.

WHAT traveler fails to associate with Naples a laughing sky, a beauteous soil, a smiling sea—in short, that happy combination of elements which, making up our idea of a terrestrial paradise, ever beckons us to approach and pluck its fruits of enjoyment? The ancients sought to secure this coveted happiness by the discovery of the "Fortunate Islands." Their descendants, still more eager and worldly, not contented with the prodigality of Nature in a climate more favored than Plato ever imagined, have worried science and research in the futile effort to detect the elixir of life, or discover the fountain of youth, that they might drink of the one or bathe in the other, and live forever on the earth. But there are certain secrets that Nature seems determined to keep, although constantly flattering us that she is upon the point of disclosing the coveted mysteries. Among them is the common delusion of a "good climate"—an atmospherical Eden, which is neither too hot nor too cold, too damp nor too dry, and, opening every pore to sensuous delight, we would be content to pronounce it "just right." Having tried a greater variety of climates than is the usual lot of man, I am satisfied that while all have their good points, there is none perfect. The only sure rule of enjoyment is "to make hay while the sun shines," and not to believe that because Dame Nature smiles to-day she will to-morrow. She is a coquette from principle, and often fascinates but the more speedily to disappoint.

She smiles so sweetly, however, upon Naples, when she does smile, that one is, as it were, subdued into enjoyment, in spite of human nature and its thousand ills and wayward humors. Her fine days are absolutely borrowed from Paradise. The atmosphere absolutely becomes an elixir of health and fountain of happiness. The soul is not beguiled into that dreamy languor, so fatal to exertion in the tropics, but it nerves the body to active pleasure and grateful emotions. Like the lark, one longs to soar and sing in the sparkling sunlight, receiving health and bliss in each expansion of wing. The ripe fruit, however, does not drop into the lap, but it must be plucked. Hence, in a temperature like that of Naples arises that superior happiness which results from the equal stimulus and employment of both mind and body under circumstances the most favorable, so far as God's works are concerned, for the perfect development of life—life in the sense of blissful existence, where every breath is pleasure, and every pulsation joy.

Yet Naples is sadly capricious, notwithstanding her largess of delights. She gives, but she exacts also. The scorching sirocco shrinks the pores and strangles the mind. It is a fiery furnace, in which every previous atmospherical sense of enjoyment is consumed by slow torture. The reaction in the nervous system is terrible. Africa, by one blast of her breath, revenges a thousand wrongs. I know nothing in the whole range of winds more soul-subduing, body-famishing, than the sirocco. It wilts, it shrinks, it parches, it enfeebles; it irritates, it pinches, it pricks, it tickles; it is an amalgam of melancholy and imbecility, the subtlest medium for low spirits ever let loose upon egotistical man, and yields to no exorcism save that of a shift of the weather-cock.

The eccentricities of weather tend, I believe, to make Naples what it really is, a city of paradoxes. Its subtle influences affect the national character, and give it a composite element of seeming eccentricities. One is equally eager to arrive and to leave; both emotions have their pleasurable associations. Naples, after Rome, is like a resurrection from the grave to the world. Here we find life in its active sense. London life is a dull, plodding, staid, wearisome life; forms and shams—much eating and loud speaking are its elements. New York life is a commercial whirlpool; "to get" is written on every man's brow; the weak are swallowed up, while the strong splash, and toss, and foam upon the broad current of Mammon. Paris life is a refined, sensuous emotion, selfish but courteous—a graceful flowing of the stream of pleasure toward the precipice of death. Naples life is deviltry itself. It is at once the busiest and idlest city of them all, overflowing with merriment while steeped in misery; with the most glitter it exhibits the most rags; and from beauty to ugliness there is but one step, which forms the bridge of contrast; and these external contrasts, joined to virtues and vices of equally opposite degrees, are in general concentrated in every individual inhabitant. Electrify these extremes by the active affinities of life, quickened into intensity by a climate which gives, as it were, an additional sense of pleasure or pain to every passion or emotion, and we have the veritable Neapolitan, the real child of the Sun—at once the most indolent and most active, the most vivacious and the most taciturn, the best humored and most revengeful, the most cunning and the most frank, the greatest vagabond and the best fellow—all things to all men; quick-witted, sagacious, begging, specious, hypocritical, superstitious, lying, droll, amiable, talking with double-tongue power, and gesticulating specimen of humanity extant. To complete the paradox, because Nature has been to them overbountiful, they want but little besides her sunshine.

Naples is frightfully busy; the stir in the streets is most extraordinary. Even the fleas must be endowed with extra hopping powers to get a bite, so quick and restless is this population, unless they see fit to slumber, when they partake themselves to the apathy of death. A stranger is tempted to ask, What the deuce is all this noise and shouting about? The very dust seems endued with a portion of this mercurial activity. There are no commerce, war, elections, or protracted meetings—in fact, it seems as if there were nothing to do, and yet a more vigorous doing-nothing no population can display. One would suppose that the city was each day either upon the point of being taken by storm, or had laid siege to itself. The clang of the trumpet, the rub-a-dub of the drum, and the tramp of uniformed men, regiment after regiment, are heard at every corner, while batteries of grim guns point through the squares, and rake the principal streets. Above them, below them, and around them, the Neapolitans are girt with volcanic fires, and a cordon of gunpowder and steel. Daily, in their midst, do they see the tender mercies of their government displayed by troops of their fellow-citizens, clad in galley costume, and heavily chained together in couples by their arms and legs, followed by hireling soldiers, as they are driven like cattle to their repulsive labors. These are simply criminals in law—criminals in politics are withdrawn from even the semblance of human sympathy, and in irons, starvation, and solitude, banished to unwholesome dungeons, to expiate, in protracted torture of mind and body, the crime of patriotism. From prisons blackened with the misery of ages and battered by time, through strong and thick-set iron bars, despite the terrors of a tyrant-drilled soldiery, famishing, hardened wretches stretch their gaunt arms, and, with mingled ribaldry and blasphemy, demand charity, or mock the freedom of their former associates, who, with strange fascination, sun themselves beside the walls of these sepulchres of human virtue and liberty. Elsewhere the apparatus of tyranny is masked, but in Naples it stands forth as prominent as Vesuvius, bristling with horrors like an infernal machine. Yet the Neapolitans laugh and sing, work or doze, as the impulse seizes them, as reckless of these evidences of their degradation as if they were intended solely for the inhabitants of another sphere, and not for themselves, their wives, and their little ones. Their climate is to them meat and drink, raiment and liberty. At once the results and supports of a political tyranny and religious despotism that recalls the darkest ages, they will continue to bask contentedly in the mire of ignorance and slavery until some new Massaniello fires their passions, or education awakens in them the loftier hopes and desires of humanity.

To enjoy Naples, one should not think. Its mocking joys and stores of fun come really home only in the perfect abandon of its life. To float on its current, and not to dive, is the rule for enjoyment. Yet the hour of satiety, even of pleasure, is not slow to come. A perpetual grin is fatiguing, dust is choking, and noise is stunning. Disgust is apt to poke its sardonic face through the mask of novelty, so that what one not to the manor bred and born at first found amusing, begins at last to be wearisome. Now, as in the days of the Pharaohs, the skeleton will appear unbidden at the feast. Besides, there are some ingredients in a Neapolitan crowd rather unprofitable than otherwise both to purse and morals. Pimps importune with a pertinacity peculiarly Neapolitan, reciting a tariff for every feminine charm and masculine vice ; beggars whine, extort, and turn the public walks into pathological museums for the exhibition of sores and deformity. But the most amusing and successful of the street leeches are the pickpockets. A thief in Naples is a hero. The public make way for him to escape, and close up against his pursuer. I had my

LAZZARONI AT NAPLES.

pocket picked almost as soon as I entered the street—an event which, in fifteen years' travel, had happened but once before. A friend of mine rarely was able to keep a handkerchief through a promenade. In self-defense, he took to the cheapest cotton. As he was stepping into his carriage, he missed, as usual, the article. At the same moment, he saw it thrown contemptuously toward him by one of the street gentry, who, amid the jeers of the crowd, vented his disappointment by crying out, "Who would have thought a gentleman like *him* would have carried a pocket-handkerchief like *that!*"

Then, too, one tires of seeing surfeited urchins swallow maccaroni by the unbroken fathom at the rate of a copper a dish, for the amusement of the "*forestieri*," who marvel at such gastronomic dexterity. Turning their heads, they can see lazzaroni family groups amicably engaged in furnishing each member with food from their superfluous craniological stock—a process unfortunately common, and by no means a whet to a fastidious appetite. But the cruelest sight of all is the amount of work exacted from one little horse. An Italian nowhere is by any means sensitive in his treatment of these animals. The whip is made to supply the deficiency of spirit even among gentlemen's studs. But Naples is the true purgatory of horseflesh. The horses here must possess some vital tenacity unknown elsewhere. The Neapolitans, too, contrive to infuse some of their own devil-may-care hilarity even into their beasts, dressing them up with flowers, feathers, bells, and gay trappings, so that what with the shouting, laughter, jokes, and flogging of the party he draws, the poor brute seems really to be enjoying his holiday instead of doing the labor of four horses. A Neapolitan cabriolet is a "sight" of itself. Look, dear reader! This is no rare show. A medley of priest and woman, thief and peasant, beggar and bride, characteristic Neapolitans every soul of them, with a baby screaming

NEAPOLITAN CABRIOLET.

for joy in the basket under the axle, twenty-one in all, over head and ears in frolic, with but one half-starved horse to shake them to their journey's end. They manage, too, to get a speed out of these quadruped victims that is really astonishing to pedestrians, and often puts them in no little danger of their limbs. I can compare one of these parties in full chorus only to a jovial war-whoop—one's hair stands on end as they dash by, and one laughs as if it were his last chance.

On an unimpeachable morning toward the end of April, when the weather was literally faultless, the air the breath of heaven itself, not a cloud to dim the lustre of a sky whose lucidity seemed to realize infinity, while the "Bay" slept tranquil under the balmiest of zephyrs, and the distant islands and headlands lay robed in translucency as if defying criticism—on such a day I awoke in Naples, satisfied, nay, disgusted with its chaos of sights and sounds, and cast about me for some quiet retreat where I might, if but for a few short hours, become oblivious to its soulless turmoil.

"Eureka!" The dead city flashed on my mind. I have it! To Pompeii, then, I would go, and commune with the past; not gregariously, with simpering misses, yawning dandies, or impatient women, with heads too full of the living to give place, even for a brief moment, to thoughts of the dead, but *alone*, without companion or guide, and there, in the reaction of thought and silence, refresh my mind from the vacuous tension of the capital of fooldom.

No sooner thought than executed. A few minutes found me, with rail-road speed—no great matter in this kingdom, where iron is spared and flesh only is driven—rumbling along the shores of the bay, now almost plowing up its quiet surges, then bounding high over roofs and houses, the present generations strangely mingling and overtopping the past, Resina upon Herculaneum, a gulf of two thousand years dividing the interval between them, while Grecian sepulchres, Roman tombs, mediæval lava streams, modern vineyards, deserted houses, broken walls, and towns, like ant-hills, bursting with life, were mingled at my side in strange confusion. No other rail-road possesses an interest like this. Sepulchral cities lie beneath and along its track. The waters of Naples splash its seaward embankments. On the other side lives a population as dense as that of China, and more picturesque in garb and manners than that of India. They dwell in habitations built upon the graves of their ancestors, the very earth they cultivate being the ashes of their forefathers, whom war and volcano have alternately stricken down and buried in one wide devastation, but to be quickened again into being by a vigorous nature that knows no exhaustion. Life and Death here meet in ceaseless strife. Each boasts its trophies, and each in turn triumphs. If the former exultingly displays Portici, Castellamare, Torre del Greco, and the many towns and villages that so lovingly nestle amid the vineyards of sunny Vesuvius, all teeming with joyous existence, forgetting that they are undermined by eternal fires, the latter sternly reminds you that beneath them, imprisoned in her fatal embraces, lie Herculaneum, Stabiæ, and Pompeii, once the homes of a population more numerous, more happy, and more prosperous than those which have succeeded to their dubious heritage, while above them all the treacherous volcano lifts its head, ready at Nature's signal to do again the bidding of Death. It seemed to me a moral defiance of Fate, an insult to the avenging Nemesis, thus to rudely bind together her domains with bars of iron, and to let loose the shrieking fire-horse to scatter about the cinders of dead cities in the very shadow of the fierce old crater itself. While I was speculating whether Vesuvius was a stock "bull" or "bear," and what influence it might possess at the brokers' board, the locomotive's whistle announced our arrival at the pretty little station-house of Pompeii. This is but a short distance from the disinterred town, of which nothing can be seen while without, owing to the vast mounds of ashes piled outside, forming a dike sufficiently high and strong to turn aside any ordinary lava-current.

The first object that attracted my attention was the "Diomedes Hotel," a snug little restaurant at the outer base of the dike of cinders. Shade of Lucullus, to what a base use had the old patrician gourmand's name descended! It had the merit, however, of being appropriate, if one can judge of the character of the owner by the traces of good living he left behind him. Diomedes's name has now become as widely known as Cato's. Death in the fiery shower was to him fame. Had he been gathered to his fathers in the ordinary way, we should never have heard of him; but now his wine-cellar, his kitchen, his bathing-rooms, garden, and all the appurtenances of a fine old Roman gentleman's mansion are better known and as much visited as the palace of all the Cæsars. As his name has occurred first, I will briefly say what I saw worth mentioning about his premises, which are at the other end of the city, just outside the Herculaneum Gate, and then return and enter the town in accordance with my actual route.

Diomedes's villa was three stories high. The upper one is chiefly demolished, but the lower two are quite perfect. You enter from the Via Domitiana by a doorway under a ruined portico with a very modern look, and find yourself bewildered amid a series of small but prettily-situated rooms, displaying even now the traces of that hospitable luxury which once distinguished its proprietor. The dining-room, or, as some think it, the best bed-chamber, looks out upon the garden and over the sea, which then came almost to the garden wall, although now nearly two miles distant. It had a bow front, or rather back, and fine large windows. Some of the

DIOMEDES'S VILLA.

windows of this house were glazed with a coarse, semi-opaque glass, not uncommon in Pompeii, and still manufactured abundantly in Italy. The cook, or rather his skeleton, was found at his place in the kitchen, near the stove, on which still remained a bronze "casserole," or covered skillet, and other traces of a coming meal. He evidently thought the eruption would not prove to be much of a shower, or else Roman cooks, like Roman sentinels, were required to die at their posts.

The area of the garden remains very much as it was left, with its porticoes still standing, the ruins of a fountain, fish reservoir, and the usual contrivance of columns to sustain vines, with seats, table, &c., answering to our summer-house. Just outside the seaward gate were found two skeletons, with keys, coins, and other articles of value. Conjecture, which of course has endless room for play amid the unclaimed property and nameless skeletons of this buried-alive city, ascribes to one of these human relics the name of Diomedes, who perished while selfishly deserting his family. In this, however, we may do him injustice, though circumstantial evidence is strongly against him. But the wine-cellar, still perfect, and lighted by the same narrow loop-holes, looking into the garden, which let in the fatal shower and gases, is the most interesting spot, from the fact that here were found the remains of twenty persons, including a child and baby, who had here taken refuge, with sufficient provision, as they supposed, to weather the strange storm. They were, however, speedily suffocated by the mephitic vapors while making a vain effort to escape from their fatal refuge, the falling stones and lava having closed the door upon them for eternity. The fine ashes and hot water, penetrating by the windows, formed a paste around their bodies, preserving the impressions of form, and even clothing, as perfectly as a sculptor's mould. Even the texture of the fine linen worn by the women was imprinted on this lava paste, as well as their jewels. The saddest relic of all was a portion of the blonde hair of the mother, still retaining its color and shape. In the Museo Borbonico at Naples, where all removable articles of value are carried as soon as discovered, we see the impression in lava of a female breast, matronly full and fair, and an entire female head, formed of a fine crust, so delicate that it seems as if a breath might disturb it, yet every feature is as perfect as in life, exhibiting a portrait of rare beauty and regularity. No sculptor could have taken his mould with more precision. The utmost care is taken of it, so that it will probably endure through all time as the sole artificial bust of Nature's moulding, a priceless and unique specimen of geological portraiture. Whether these remains were found or not in Diomedes's cellar, I do not know.

The wine-jars of Diomedes remain leaning in rows against the walls, as when he last took account of stock. They are filled with ashes. Beneath there is a dried substance, which connoisseurs pretend to say still retains a portion of the rich aroma of the wines that for thousands of years have given to Vesuvius its most cherished celebrity.

Diomedes, pagan though he was, must have had a more cheerful idea of death than most Christians. He built his sepulchre, still inscribed with his name, right over against his chamber windows, and scarcely two rods off, so that he never could cross his own threshold without having his grave to stare him in the face.

Near the villa of Diomedes there was another, supposed to have belonged to Cicero, and mentioned in his letters to Atticus. In it were found some fine paintings. On one of the lower stories was the following inscription: "Sea and fresh water baths of Marcus Crassus Frugius." Mr. Frugius would have to go a long way for his salt water now!

I entered Pompeii from the Salerno road, opposite the rail-road station. The usual array of guides and ciceroni lay in waiting to intercept visitors. They are a nuisance under almost any circumstances, and, being already as familiar with the localities of Pompeii as of New York, I determined, despite the rule which affixes one, like a shadow, to every visitor or party, from fear of the effects of antiquarian covetousness, to wander unattended and unharangued where I pleased—"up stairs, down stairs, and in the ladies' chamber," after the fashion of "Le Diable boiteux," on a voyage of discovery into the morals and customs of the deceased Pompeians. To effect this solitude required no little skill. I hung back until the parties preceding me were supplied, and then loitered on, straggler fashion, as if belonging to one in advance. The few remaining ciceroni eyed me suspiciously; some, spider-like, dashed toward me, but I dodged them, or bluntly told them to be off. A few rods having brought me to an unfrequented part of the town, in the rear of the Basilica, I slipped aside, and, privateer-like, gained a good offing, with a clear antiquarian horizon.

There was a luxury of sentiment in being alone in Pompeii—of having, as it were, an entire city to one's self in the broad day, that had a peculiar charm to me. I dived into cellars, I ascended dilapidated staircases, I pried into ladies' boudoirs, nay, even into their bed-chambers, stood before family altars, criticised the cook's department—in fine, explored with unblushing effrontery the domestic secrets of every household, rich or poor, plebeian or patrician, which attracted me, without a human voice to break the spell. Pompeii is not, as some term it, simply "a city of the dead." The soul is there, though the animal existence is departed. It is the ghost of past life, clear and firm in its outlines, and spirit-like in its talk—a veritable "medium" through which the classical ages can "rap" out their ideas to ours. There is, too, enough of reality and

STREET IN POMPEII.

completeness of preservation in many localities to make one step lightly, for fear he might intrude. This gives a lively delicacy of feeling to exploration totally inconsistent with the bat-filled towers and mouldy ruins of ordinary antiquity, with their break-neck gaps and tottering walls. Here every thing has the freshness of yesterday ; all is firm and clean, though incomplete. By some strange sorcery, an entire city has been unroofed ; doors and windows left invitingly open ; every mystery bared to strong sunlight; and the population, as it were, extinguished, like the snuffing out of a candle, leaving behind them the familiar tokens of warm hearts and a busy life, so like our own that we are ready at once to extend to them the fraternal grasp of human brotherhood.

The first thought that struck me was one of compliment to the departed " city fathers." Their streets were narrow, it is true—no great harm in a hot climate—but well paved with flat lava, and raised crossing-stones for foot-passengers. They possessed numerous fountains, and, above all, " side-walks," a convenience which Paris did not know before this century, and Naples is still without. They were well supplied with sewers beneath the pavement, leading to the sea. From these evidences of their superior civilization, and their love of fresh water, manifested not only by public baths, but in every private house of any pretensions, in beautiful marble fish-basins, fountains, cisterns, hot and cold baths, accompanied with Oriental-like tokens of luxurious ablutions, I concluded that the filthy habits and indecent exposures which the refined Florentines gaze upon with such indifference, even under the very windows of their stately palaces, to which are hourly wafted perfumes not of Araby the blessed, were forbidden by statute at Pompeii. If so, the modern Italians have sadly degenerated from their ancestral cleanliness.

The aqueducts supplied Pompeii with delicious water, as I

SCENE IN POMPEII.

verified by taste. Wells are rare, and the water not so good. There is one, still in use, one hundred and twenty feet deep. The names and occupations, generally in red paint, accompanied often with hieroglyphical signs, announced the proprietors or occupants of houses, which were numbered, and their trades. Indeed, a very respectable directory of Pompeii might be compiled to-day from its walls. There are also on them many advertisements of gladiatorial shows, festivals, and specimens of street wit or drawing, from which might be got up an Illustrated Pompeian News of the year A.D. 79, which would prove vastly entertaining.

These ideas suggested another. Streets, aqueducts, fountains, public buildings, and private houses—in short, all the essentials of a habitable town, are here, ready for use, and requiring not an extraordinary degree of repair. The spirit of Yankeedom moved within me. Would it not be a "good operation" to buy up Pompeii, reserve the corner lots, sell the intervening, and appropriate the temples to public schools? It is true that the "court-house" would require roofing, and the jail *enlarging*, but the amphitheatre would be a capital spot for caucuses, the public baths could be altered at slight expense into a "meeting-house," with ample vestry accommodation, and the Pantheon would make a capital hotel. The scream of the locomotive hourly startles the ears of the modern guests of Sallust's house by abruptly recalling them from their classical trance to the materialism of the nineteenth century, so that a rail-road is not wanting, and gas might be let on cheap from Vesuvius. Would his majesty of Naples become a partner in the speculation? Knowing his predilection for antiquities rather than improvements, I "rather guessed" not, and concluded to keep the "notion" to myself until a more enterprising ruler should arise in his place.

The present king is, however, doing something in the way

of repeopling the city, for he allows a few soldiers to select their residences, from the hundreds at their choice, in the different quarters of the town. A trifling outlay gives them a very comfortable mansion. They, in general, content themselves, like hermit-crabs, in taking possession of the dead shells of the plebeian sort, when they might help themselves to palaces. It looked odd to see, every now and then, the solitude of this disinterred city broken by a female face, gazing hopelessly into the deserted street, watching for something living go by. Luckily, I had with me no guide, or he would have been sure to have protested that these inhabitants, like the water in the wells, were not *ancient*, and thus dispel an illusion I had created out of them. Why could they not have been the families, nay, the very soldiers themselves, who perished, rather than desert their posts, on the morning of the twenty-fourth of August, A.D. 79? The sentinel was found, eighteen centuries later, still at his post at the Herculaneum Gate, while in their barracks in the Forum Nundinarium more than threescore of their number perished, victims to their military discipline. Such fidelity deserves perpetual recompense, and my fancy invested them in the shape of the present legionaries of Naples with the freedom of the city. It is true that the merit of four of these sufferers was involuntary. They were not only locked up in the guard-house, but fastened by their ankles into iron stocks, which were partially melted by the heat that slowly killed them. These stocks are now in the Museum, as well as beautiful specimens of armor, including several bronze helmets, one of which is richly ornamented in bas-relief with the story of the destruction of Troy. There is, however, a very curious specimen of genuine *ancient* water inclosed in a huge bronze cock of a reservoir to be seen in the Museum. Time has hermetically sealed the parts, but, upon shaking the cock, the splashing of the imprisoned liquid, now having been nearly two thousand years in solitary confinement, is clearly heard.

If I skip oddly about, the reader, curious in these matters, must have patience with me. It is a fac simile of the manner I spent this day—my pleasantest day of travel in Europe—darting from one point to another, as fancy or curiosity dictated. I had no rule. I knew by heart the treasures in the Museo Borbonico which had been rifled hence, and could, by the wand of memory, restore them to their proper localities; consequently, every site of interest became to me at once the familiar object of the century that saw our Savior. Then, too, I busied myself in conjecturing, from the hints in domestic life the Pompeians had left behind them, how they did this thing—how they did that; whether we were wiser and more refined than they; were we even more comfortable, with all our boasted civilization; if, reader mine, you have patience to follow me through all my eccentric investigations on this holiday, you will at least know something of how the home-life of the old conquerors of the world went on twenty centuries ago.

Their houses were not large, in the palatial sense of modern times. Unlike ours, too, their plain side was toward the street, and their decorations reserved for within. Doors which opened outward, and thereby endangered the faces of the passers-by, unless they heard the warning cry, were the fashion. The street windows were mere port-holes, and closed with wooden shutters, so that street effect, so far as domestic architecture was concerned, must have been meagre indeed. Art was lavish in decoration of the interior. The colors employed in painting were peculiarly bright, retaining even now a brilliancy that is astonishing. The taste was in general for strong colors and contrasts, but some were employed with a delicacy of tint and truthfulness of design that still continue to be the admiration and study of modern artists. A few of these paintings were in frames, and hung upon the walls, but in general they were painted upon the wall, after the manner of modern frescoes, and with so durable an art as to resist until now the fire and damp to which they have been exposed. Their secret of thus petrifying colors, as it were, is lost.

Among the finest of their paintings, classed by some even with the labors of Raphael, is the Parting Scene between Achilles and Briseis, which is of itself sufficient to exalt the feeling of the ancients for art to a high standard. The head of Achilles is a master-piece of expression. There are other

ACHILLES DELIVERING UP BRISEIS.

evidences, however, of their faithful delineation of sentiment and passion, accompanied by a correctness of drawing, which proves much close study, and, with other branches of art which this insignificant town of the Roman empire has disclosed, shows equally how little we have gained upon them, and how great must have been the intervening darkness, to make modern success appear so wonderful. Landscape painting was, however, much after the character of the Chinese, capricious, gaudy, and utterly regardless of the rules of perspective, though there are evidences that this branch of art was not wholly misunderstood. The specimens we now see upon the walls, however, were probably cheap efforts, to take the place of modern paper, and not intended for any higher purpose. But what they chiefly excelled in was grotesque and arabesque ornaments, in both of which they display a pleasing delicacy and invention, that we may copy, but not excel. Indeed, Raphael was indebted for the designs of his ornamental paintings in the Loggie of the Vatican to the Baths of Titus.

In the kitchen of the house of the Edile Pansa there still remain some droll pictures, coarsely executed, intended, no doubt, to refresh the memory of the cook with the titbits his master loved, and perhaps as a warning, also, in case of a failure of skill. We have a ham, bacon, head of a wild boar, a stately hog with a belt around his body, and the cook sacri-

PICTURE IN THE HOUSE OF PANSA.

ficing eatables upon an altar, with the guardian serpents beneath. Besides these, there is a Moruna fastened upon a spit. This delicate fish was said to be a venomous cross between the land and sea viper. It was, however, particularly prized by Roman epicures—we can forgive classical gourmands every thing after seasoning their dishes with asafœtida—and was kept in brackish water, and sometimes fed with refractory slaves, to give it bulk and flavor. There was, then, an unmistakable moral to Pansa's cook in this picture.

The lower floor of Pansa's house, upon the street, was divided into shops, one of which served him for the disposal of his own superfluous harvests. Some of these lordly mansions boasted an immense number of shops. One, owned by a Signora Julia Felix, had upon the outside a notice stating that it was to let—I presume at auction—between the coming sixth and eighth of August, together with *nine hundred shops*, with their terraces and upper stories. This amount of real estate in a little city like this looks startling; but, judging from the shops already exposed, the whole might be included within the capacity of Stewart's marble building on Broadway. The ancient aristocracy peddled out their merchandise from their own houses, as still continue to do the present grand signori of Italy, who, while affecting to despise commerce as ignoble, daily vend wine and oil, by the bottle or penny's worth, to every customer, from the basements of their palaces. The alms they bestow at one door are often returned to them at another, through the sales of their produce. I have my milk and butter of a marquis, who, if I sold cotton by the cargo, would consider me as unworthy of his noble society, but who, if I do nothing and patronize his dairy, considers me good enough "to go to court." This is a queer distinction for the descendants of merchants to make, but it is universal. Even an artist is considered in some degree to have the mechanical taint of the artisan, an aristocratic prejudice which even the genius of our Greenough, though on familiar terms with a Capponi, could not altogether overcome.

The interior view of the Pompeian houses from the street must have been very pretty. Unlike the modern arrangement, the ground floor was the principal part, for the ancient Campanians appear to have had a luxurious horror of staircases. Hence those that we see in private houses are contracted, and look as if intended only for slaves, on whom devolved the labor of ascending and descending. The porter's lodge was, where it is now in fashionable mansions, just inside the street-door. This looked into an open court, in the centre of which is always to be found an "*impluvium*," or large, open, shallow cistern of marble to hold rain-water—an exceedingly ingenious contrivance, one would suppose, for the generation of musquitoes. Many houses had also large subterranean reservoirs.

This outer court was surrounded with numerous small chambers, appropriated to purposes of hospitality, besides the larger reception-room, or atrium, answering to modern Italian antechambers, where callers were obliged to await the pleasure of the master of the house.

Beyond this court is to be seen another, surrounded in general by colonnades, and appropriated to the more private purposes of the family. Here we find all the domestic compartments which we usually divide over several floors. The ladies had their boudoirs and the gentlemen their libraries. There are, too, saloons of different degrees of elegance, and dining-rooms, shady and very inviting in such a climate, looking out as they did upon mosaic-paved court-yards, cooled by fountains, and the murmuring of flowing waters playing among marble statues and flower-beds, with gold fishes darting about in their artificial ponds. When space permitted, there was always a garden, shaded by vine-covered trellises supported on

ATRIUM IN THE HOUSE OF PANSA.

beautiful columns, under which the family assembled, perhaps to eat "ices"—at all events, to drink iced wine. Here, also, were the cold baths. These were taken in the open air, with a somewhat nonchalant disregard of exposure universal in warm countries. Some of the bath-tubs, of the purest white marble, are of magnificent proportions, and look as invitingly under the warm sky of to-day as when Grecian belles were wont to bathe their fair limbs therein. The hot baths were, from necessity, more retired. The farther end of the garden was frequently painted in fresco landscape, so that the passer-by in the street beheld a beautiful perspective of Corinthian columns, fountains, statues, and mosaic-paved court-yards, terminating with flowers and shrubbery, and apparently betraying a vista far beyond the reality. The effect of such a scene, combined with the graceful-flowing robes of the ancients, and their careless out-door domesticity, generated by a climate which invites freedom, must have been charmingly picturesque.

The chambers were in general mere closets, altogether too small for modern bedsteads, and lighted only by doors. In fact, the bedstead was seldom other than a raised portion of the floor, though they possessed others somewhat after the modern French pattern, as may be seen pictured on the walls. No doubt, inspired by the genial warmth of their climate, the Pompeians spread their mattresses, as they did their tables, as fancy dictated. It was an easy matter with them to take up their beds and walk. The women's apartments were separated from the men's, though the division does not appear to have been very close. Every house had its family altar or chapel, not unlike in arrangement to the domestic shrines of Romanism, substituting an idol for a crucifix or Madonna. They burned lamps, just as the Catholics do candles, as a religious sacrifice, and offered fruits and flowers, or more valuable gifts, as vows or piety dictated.

Some of the better houses had their kitchens and their offices under ground, but, in general, they were put aside where most convenient, approachable by a lane or back passage. They were all small compared with our ideas of culinary accommodation, but almost precisely like the modern Italian in their arrangements. The fire-places are precisely the same. But when we come to kitchen utensils, we perceive a degeneracy, not only in material and form, but in utility, compared with those in common use among the Pompeians, that is truly marvelous. Bronze, lined with silver, was not uncommon. I saw at the Museum pots with malleable bronze handles, which could be put in or taken out at pleasure. This art is lost. Their earthen jars have the *ring* of real metal, hard and sonorous, and so strong as to be proof against ordinary carelessness. Their pottery is grace itself, and some of the ornamental vases of antiquity are valued as high as ten thousand dollars apiece. The elegance of form and beauty of color of their glass—I refer to the finest specimens—astonished me. Modern art has never equaled the Portland vase, or rivaled the finest specimens of Naples, which seem more

CANDELABRA AND VASE.

like engraved gems than glass. Their common is like our greenish bottle-glass. They do not seem to have possessed the art of cutting, though we find pretty specimens of pressed glass, such as vases, drinking-vessels, &c.

Their chief excellence lay in their metallic work. In casseroles, water-jars, wine-coolers, pots and kettles, strainers, egg-containers, urns for hot water—in short, throughout the whole range of domestic ware, they display not only a variety equal to any modern furnishing house, but in many respects, especially in stoves, water-heaters, &c., an economy of fuel and multiplicity of uses that would win a patent even at Washington. To these merits they add a beauty of form altogether neglected by our unpoetical mechanics. Nothing, however homely in its uses, was beneath their passion for adornment. A handle of a pitcher or the leg of a pot became, as it left their hands, suggestive of something beyond its baser uses. It possessed a distinctive beauty, and told a history. Their mythology was pressed into this apparently humble service, so that stories of religion might be learned from a table service. This prodigality of art must have cost high. It expands our idea of the riches and civilization of the Roman empire to know that a petty sea-port affords such incontestable evidence of taste and wealth. If such were provincial Pompeii, what must have been imperial Rome!

LAMP AND STAND.

In the days of Titus, Pompeii was dug over and rifled of much of its buried treasure, probably by surviving inhabitants, who knew where to seek. In one instance modern excavators have discovered that their predecessors of the first century failed only by *three feet* in hitting a treasure which they evidently sought, but which was destined to reward the King of Naples nearly two thousand years afterward. Pompeii was evidently preserved by Fate to daguerreotype ancient to modern civilization, and teach us that, with all our boasted progress, we can learn much from the past. Indeed, its utensils and arts have been for the last fifty years a school of design to modern Europe, which has advanced in beauty and grace of ornament in proportion as it has gone back for models. The elegant designs of their candelabra, lamps, urns, and silver vases, are copied throughout the civilized world. I believe that more bronze and marble statues have been dug out of Pompeii than exist in the entire United States. It was said of Rome that the stone population equaled the living. It was not the comparative cheapness of art that made it so common, for excellence was rated at greater sums than now. Phidias or Praxiteles could command higher prices than can Powers or Crawford in the present age. The *living* masters of antiquity were rewarded as are only the *dead* by modern taste. Nothing but an inborn and cultivated sense of the beautiful could have produced this artistic prodigality. There is something in this acknowledgment and craving for Beauty—the unselfish, or, more properly speaking, intellectual exaltation of art above mere utility, that strikes me as a generous sentiment in a nation. It came from the hearts and purses of individuals, and was not the result of one tyrannical will, like that of Louis XIV., who willingly impoverished France that he might lodge in egotistical magnificence.

In one other respect the Pompeians, in common with antiquity, are not so deserving of commendation. What St. Paul says of the Corinthians must have been equally applicable to them. Their religion was purely a sensual one in its effect on the common mind. It stimulated rather than repressed vulgar passions by celestial examples of more than human infirmity. Hence, in conjunction with excitability of climate, sprang licentious habits and erotic ideas. The secret museum of Naples discloses a curious picture of the domestic life of the inhabitants of Magna Græcia. Common utensils, ornamental vases, and even jewelry, were manufactured into obscene shapes, which no modern lady could hear named, much less see and use, without the blush of shame and indignation. It would be a difficult point to fix upon the standard of classical modesty. It was, at all events, the antipodes of American delicacy, which coins new names to avoid expressing natural ideas, and discloses more from false shame in substitution than the natural truth could ever express, however frankly spoken. Christianity has banished forever from civilized life such evidence of its classical abasement. The pictures of antiquity, too, were not always of the most chaste description, and forms of vice were unblushingly delineated which are not so much as even to be named among men. The Neapolitan government, though not remarkable for prudery, has erased or hid these specimens of prurient art. It leaves, however, as specimens of the manners of the day, upon a few buildings, stone amulets in the shape of any thing the reader may conceive as particularly immodest, but which were once publicly worn, after the fashion of modern charms, by Pompeian ladies, as a specific against *malocchio*, or the evil eye. This superstition is still rife throughout Italy, and affords jewelers much custom. Turning a corner suddenly, I heard the strange sound of English voices, and came upon a party of that nation. A young girl, in her simplicity, was intently studying one of these mystic carvings over a doorway, while behind her sat a courier, in high enjoyment of what he considered a good joke. He gave me a wink and laugh as I went by. At the same instant a revelation seemed to spring into the mind of the maiden, and she hurried off as if a bee had stung her.

Since the visit of Pius IX. to Naples, the public museums have become wonderfully chaste. He condemned every display of classical beauty, while tolerating any amount of saintly nakedness. A Domenichino and Guido are packed away into dark closets if they display any thing less of female loveliness than court costume sanctions, while a Saint Thèrese, an arrow-spitted Sebastian, or any other Romish pet, in all their repulsive nudity of martyrdom, are allowed to disgust mortal eyes under the specious pretense of offering unction to their souls. Some of the popes have manifested a wonderfully keen scent in detecting immodesty in paintings that have escaped that imputation through centuries of visitors. It certainly looks like a weak spot in their imaginations. The obscene gallery at Naples is very properly closed to the public ; so should every work of art in which immodesty is obviously apparent. But to be sensitive over impassible marble, or even alarmed at the warm coloring of Titian, does not always imply a chaste mind. High art exalts what it touches. It can not descend to foulness. An artist of pure aim should not be held answerable for the imagination of the spectator. It is his business to purify his heart, even as the artist has purified his work, of all gross, earthly elements. Hence the prudery of the papal court, in the exuberance of the ridiculous metallic disguises they give their statuary, is any thing but suggestive of modesty. If the present pope is bent upon clothing the statuesque world, I would respectfully call his attention to the colossal bronze Neptune at Bologna, by John of the same name, which is indubitably an indecent figure. But I am sure that the simplest maiden can walk the Uffizii Gallery at Florence, in all its majesty of art, with as uncontaminated a mind as she can the reformed galleries of Rome and Naples, in their tin-leaf draperies. On the ceilings of the Uffizii, I am sorry that truth compels me to add, there actually exist real obscenities, fortunately difficult to detect amid the multitude of arabesques, but as palpably vicious as any thing Pompeian. They afford incontestable evidence of the decline of pure art, and depravity of manners resulting from the overlauded Medician rule, which, for the credit of the present age, should be obliterated.

Like the modern Italians, the Pompeians, in their eagerness for the ornamental, to which, it must be confessed, they did not always bring good taste, often overlooked the useful and essential. I doubt if there are any good carpenters, according to the American standard, in all Italy or on the Continent generally. The same deficiency in well-finished mechanical work obtained as extensively in ancient times. Nicely-adjusted locks, convenient door-handles, well-jointed carpentry, level floors—in short, the evidences of mechanical skill in the homeliest objects of domestic use, which are considered as indispensable to comfort in America, are unknown in Italy. Their lamps, with all their beauty, were smoky, inconvenient articles. Neither their streets or houses could be cleanly lighted. I do not believe that the general condition of the merely mechanical arts has improved or retrograded in Italy for twenty centuries. In masonry and stucco-work, the ancients excelled the moderns. Roman brick-work is like adamant in solidity. The Pompeian doors were usually bivalve, and turned on pivots. All the external ornaments were elegantly wrought. Bolts, keys, and handles are found of beautiful and capricious designs, but iron-work for internal use was most bunglingly made.

Modern belles have certainly some decided advantages in

the variety and beauty of objects of toilette and jewelry since Paris has developed her taste and resources for their adornment. The fair Pompeians were, however, by no means deficient in these respects, and even now, in full costume, would attract no small admiration beside the stars of the Tuileries. Their mirrors were usually of steel, and sometimes of glass, manufactured at Sidon, which was the Venice of that day in that respect. But, upon reflection, I must add, that however elegant in frame, they could by no means maintain a steady countenance beside French plate. Pins they had, but they would not sell nowadays alongside the Birmingham. In their haste to escape, the ladies left behind them many tokens of disturbed toilettes, with the usual variety of vanity-ware. Some of their rings, pins, brooches, and cameos have found modern imitators in modern art, and are as much admired in the year eighteen hundred and fifty-four of Our Lord as they were in the year one. The Pompeian jewelers have given designs to many of our choicest ornaments. They, I dare say, in their turn, stole them from Greece, which stole them from Egypt. There was no lack of cosmetics, and, for arrangement of hair, judging from female busts, our ladies have, as yet, discovered no modes more becoming than those of the classical ages. Forks are a modern invention, the Romans preferring their fingers, as they did also to recline at table, in a scantiness of clothing quite the reverse of modern ideas of a dinner toilet.

GOLD PIN.

RING.

In a rich commercial town, as Pompeii undoubtedly was, one would expect to find more treasure in coin, especially as

A SUPPER-PARTY.

paper currency was unknown, than as yet has proved the case. Occasionally a secret deposit, which has remained intact for a period long beyond the desires of the owner when he laid it by against a rainy day, rewards the modern explorer. In one house, near the Forum, the workmen were astonished by a shower of gold coins, fifty-six in number, as large and bright as new half eagles, which tumbled from a chink in the wall. These were soon after followed by a pile of silver money, consolidated by heat into one mass, and a silver spoon. But there are evidences that Pompeii was explored before the lava which covered it had cooled. It was not so deep as now by several feet, as succeeding eruptions have deposited over it successive strata. In one spot, some twelve feet above the pavements, several skeletons were found, with money, jewels, and plate, which they had succeeded in obtaining, but their avarice, prompting them to longer search, had caused them to fall victims to the mephitic gases which arose from the then smoking mass.

The roofs of Pompeii were in general flat, and of wood; consequently, they were either crushed in or set on fire by the hot stones and ashes. The accumulated soil on top of the buildings supports a young growth of trees, and is occupied by a farm. The process of disinterment is so slow—a few men and carts only, at the annual cost of less than a thousand dollars, being employed—that, at the present rate, centuries must elapse before the entire city is uncovered. In the mean while, a goodly portion of the unprotected parts must fall into irredeemable ruins. It could be easily exposed in one year, and there is no doubt that, as a speculation, if the sale of antiquities were allowed, it would be profitable to hasten operations. The parts yet unexplored—nearly three quarters of the town—promise well. Though the Neapolitan government protract their work to a degree that puts every antiquarian heart into a fever of impatience, yet what it does is thoroughly done. The streets and buildings are restored to a degree of cleanliness which would gladden the hearts of the dainty Pompeians to witness; the dilapidated parts of sufficient interest to warrant preservation are sufficiently repaired to prevent farther injury from the weather, and every work of art that can not be removed to the museum is securely roofed in and placed under guardianship. But they do not do enough. One of the best mansions should be restored to its condition as it stood previous to its enthralment. This could be done by causing the Museo Borbonico to disgorge some of its superfluous wealth of antiquity. It would not be difficult to restore the luxurious Sallust's house or Diomedes's villa to its actual condition of furniture, ornament, and arrangement, as they existed when their title-deeds were in their builders' hands. What correct ideas might we not then possess of the home-life of the Roman gentleman! The public buildings are more interesting as they are, but a perfect Roman house would be a gem of antiquity. So far from entertaining an enterprise of this sort, the King of Naples seems to regard Pompeii as a play-house for royalty. Houses which give evidence of being rich in spoil are uncovered only to a certain depth, and kept until a royal visitor arrives. The King of Naples makes up a party, and the work is finished for its amusement. I believe he presents his visitor with whatever is found; but that he is mean enough to republican sovereigns like myself, I can testify. On approaching the street where exploration was in progress, a soldier watched me as closely as if I had myself been a disinterred Pompeian preparing to serve on him notice of a writ of ejectment. There were human bones, broken amphoræ, charred wood, pottery, and other tokens of discovery lying about. They had just disclosed a massive doorway, on which the owner's name was as fresh as if written but that morning. Above was a window and burned beams. The carts were taking off the mingled charcoal and ashes, and throwing it away outside of the walls. I picked up a morsel of the charcoal no bigger than a walnut. The wood was so perfectly carbonized that it left not a particle of grit to the taste, and it was as easily dissolved in the mouth as sugar. The soldier saw my motion, rushed forward and seized the remnant I had not taken, roughly telling me that I must not so much as touch even a cinder in Pompeii. How I was to avoid that when the entire soil was ashes, he did not condescend to explain, but eyed me like a lynx, for fear I should take another taste. It may be that Pompeian charcoal has a market value at Naples. His Majesty sells the old lead and bronze, and why not the charcoal? Up to that time I had not thought of picking up a souvenir. Soon after, however, finding a pretty specimen of mosaic pavement, I put it into my pocket, and, knowing the house whence it came, I am prepared to account for the same to the lawful heirs whenever they shall call.

I took more pleasure in examining the private than the public buildings. The former told of individual life, while the latter gave only general ideas common to all nations. It was pleasant to speculate upon the supposed tastes and habits of the departed families from the traces of their every-day existence that the crater had, as it were, embalmed for all time. In one of the shops attached to Pansa's house there is a Latin cross of stucco in bas-relief. May this not indicate that the proprietor was a Nazarene, a disciple of Jesus, whom perhaps he had seen and heard while on a commercial visit to Judea? Perhaps he had received his faith from the apostle of the Gentiles when he disembarked at Puteoli! This cross is the more extraordinary, as it is in company with the usual symbols of heathen mythology, as if the convert either feared the popular opinion too much to banish them altogether from his house, or he was superstitiously inclined to try the efficacy of both opinions.

I entered one house which I am positive belonged to an old maid of the most precise order. It was a real bijou. Every thing was on a Liliputian scale. The mosaic pavements, paintings, and marble were all neatly beautiful. The garden was not much larger than a pocket-handkerchief, yet it contained statues, fountains, urns, and ornaments of great variety, all well executed and tastefully arranged. The chapel looked like a baby-house, and as if got up to play at religion. Whoever owned these premises evidently enjoyed them, and found their all of life within their diminutive precincts.

In striking contrast to this house, both for dimensions and grandeur, is that commonly called the House of the Quæstor. In extent and richness of ornament it is almost a palace, occupying a space of about one hundred feet deep by one hundred and fifty front. It was particularly rich in paintings: among them, Perseus and Andromeda, and Medea meditating the murder of her children, given with much feeling and vigor. In the garden, leaning against the wall of the colonnade, are rows of wine-jars, just as they were placed in the year 79 to receive the vintage. The columns and pilasters are coated with the most beautiful stucco, firm as stone, and highly polished, and as perfect to-day as if fresh from the finisher's hands. On one, some idler of taste has scratched, with a hard instrument, a well-executed drawing, and written beneath an inscription in Greek. Were the author to return, so delicately has Time treated his labor, that the long interval would seem to him but a yesterday.

A "custode" cultivates a portion of the garden, and has fitted up one of the many rooms of this mansion for a dwelling. He invited me in, and showed me quite a numerous collection of interesting fragments of the former luxury which reigned in this abode. There still exists a large money-chest, lined with brass and coated with iron, partially decomposed by heat. The locks, handles, and ornaments were of bronze. A quantity of gold and silver coin was found within it, but the chief part had been extracted by the primitive explorers, who calculated very nicely as to its locality. They dug into the adjoining chamber, and, finding their mistake, pierced the wall and cut into the chest, but were unable to reach all its contents. Probably it was hot work, and they were obliged to make dispatch.

In the Pompeian houses there was none of that jealous regard for personal privacy or delicacy that characterizes modern domestic architecture. This moral deficiency produced greater freedom of design and arrangement in the suite of rooms, so that their general effect was much superior to our mode of building. One of the most superior of the smaller houses is known as that of the Tragic Poet, a whimsical appellation, like many others, without much reason. The first object that meets the eye upon the threshold is a fierce dog, in mosaic, apparently in the act of springing upon the visitor. Beneath is the inscription " *Cave Canem*"—Look out for the dog. This mosaic is a substitute for the original, which has

BEWARE OF THE DOG.

been removed to Naples. The proprietor was doubtless a wag, who hit upon this Irish welcome to his friends, or else some literary lion, the Bulwer or Longfellow of his day, who thus delicately hinted his disinclination to be bored by autograph hunters and anecdote collectors. The so-called House of the Vestals, which I believe to be a decided misnomer, has the ambiguous inscription "*Salve*"—Welcome—upon its floor. Its decorations are not remarkable, as the name would imply, for chaste conception. The paintings found in the House of the Tragic Poet are singularly beautiful, as are also its wall-decorations. A profusion of jewels and female ornaments were discovered here beside some skeletons. The expense upon mosaic floors alone in this and some other houses must have been enormous, for it is not to be presumed that the art was cheaper then than now, while the execution, in general, was much superior. The material is the same as that now used in the Vatican manufactory—glass, of which there are eleven thousand different shades of colors. By it the ancients gave the minutest features and varied expressions of the human countenance with wonderful delicacy and effect. The mosaic of the Choragus instructing the Actors was found in the house of the Tragic Poet. As beautiful as this is, it is surpassed by the celebrated Battle of Issus, found in the House of the Faun. Although but a fragment of a larger picture, it represents twelve horses, twenty-two persons, and a large war-chariot of nearly life-size. It is executed with great vigor and truth, giving a portrait of Alexander and his war-horse Bucephalus, besides Darius and his guards, the whole displaying a knowledge of art in foreshortening, drawing generally, grouping, and the management of light and shade, but little inferior to the best modern works.

The House of Sallust recalls a custom which one would suppose would have been more honored in the breach than the observance. The family oratory represents the household gods, or Lares, with a serpent. These reptiles were supposed to watch over the family. Their images were to the old Romans what the cross is to the modern Italian, endowed with peculiar sanctity, and on that account frequently painted or placed on spots which were desired to be kept undefiled, but which the Anglo-Saxon much better protects by the simple notice, "Commit no nuisance." Whenever these tutelary genii did not answer the expectation of their worshipers, they were treated with as little respect as a Roman Catholic pays to his patron saint when disappointed of his miraculous intervention. They were cursed, and kicked out of doors, to make way for new. This respect for the serpent tribe led to their being kept as pets. Their presence was considered as a good omen, and they were allowed to play about the persons of their masters, and even eat from the cups at table. The ladies permitted them to coil around their necks in hot weather as a sort of animated refrigerator. They repaid this hospitality by keeping under other vermin; but, as no one killed them, they increased so rapidly as to become, like other idols, an intolerable nuisance. Nothing but the frequent fires of antiquity kept them within bounds. With this strange fondness for snakes by the most populous nation of antiquity, what becomes of our cherished idea of the natural enmity between the son of man and the serpent?

In one house was found a seated figure of Jupiter, with the "nimbus," or glory, encircling his head, which has since been borrowed by the Romanists for their crucifixes and saints. His figure is not unlike the bronze St. Peter at Rome, which enjoys the reputation of being an apostate pagan idol. Two houses possess large fountains, quite unique in their character. They are incrusted with colored glass, blue being the chief hue, and divided into pretty patterns by sea-shells, which look as if freshly gathered. The ornaments consist chiefly of aquatic plants or birds; but the effect of the whole is more odd than pleasing.

Notwithstanding that Pompeii abounded in objects of luxury, the shops were small and mean, in which respect they were not unlike those of modern Italian cities. The front was open to the street, with the exception of a broad counter of stone. The open space was closed at night by sliding shutters. Pompeii was celebrated for its preparation of a fish-pickle called *garum*, made of the entrails of mackerel soaked in brine. The best sold for twenty dollars a gallon. The cash system in general prevailed, if we may believe the weights, which were sometimes inscribed "eme"—pay; and on others, "You shall have no credit." Some of the counters still bear the traces of custom in the stains made by wet glasses. The

Romans cooled their wines in snow, and also *boiled* them—a taste which, not having survived their nation, was a medical caprice, that, like "cod-liver oil," lived out only its day, and then died. Vomits were publicly sold as preparations to dining out, the quantity as well as the quality of the viands to be consumed being a desideratum of Roman epicures. Cooked eggs, bread stamped with the baker's name and its quality, olives in oil which still burned well, money in tills, and a vast variety of manufactured articles, have been found from year to year in the shops. In some, the keepers and workmen had remained behind until the last moment, and perhaps left but to perish a little farther on. In one place we see marble partially sculptured, with the pattern lying by the block; in another shop, the resin still remained in the pot where it had been recently boiled, and the sculptor's tools were scattered over the floor. In the former there is the long, sliding mark of a trowel on fresh mortar, as if the workman had just given the outer stroke, and had fled too precipitately to complete the inner, which brings the whole to a level. A house connected with the medical faculty yielded more than forty surgical instruments, some of which, in modern science, have no use, while others are almost fac similes of those of today. I saw some apparently constructed with reference to the Cæsarean operation, which is generally supposed to be the fruit of recent surgery. The bakeries are so little injured that the corn-mills and ovens could be put into use again at once.

Just inside the Herculaneum Gate there is a post-house established by Augustus. The bones of horses and remains of carriages were found in the stables. Outside the gate is the general inn. By an inhospitable law, the only ancient municipal regulation which the King of Naples still enforces, strangers were forbidden to sleep within the city limits. The remains of a mother and four children, which she had vainly attempted to shelter from the fiery shower, were found in the court-yard. They were interlocked in mutual embrace, and, from the quantity of rich jewelry, including pearl pendants of great value, found with them, must have been of the wealthier class.

The number and magnitude of public buildings in so small a town astonishes, in particular, the American traveler, who seldom finds any thing worth noticing for architectural beauty at home in cities of much greater extent than Pompeii. But the Roman citizen found his pleasures abroad; his home was in public; he was content to sleep in an unfurnished closet, without other aperture than the door, and which he rarely entered except at night, provided the splendor of public edifices and the profusion of public amusements compensated him for his domestic deficiencies. It was, therefore, no slight penalty that Nero inflicted upon the Pompeians when he condemned them to two years' interdiction of gladiatorial games on account of a bloody fray which they had engaged in with their neighbors of Nuceria. This was in the year A.D. 59.

There are two theatres in good preservation, the comic and tragic, capable of holding about eight thousand persons, which is a large proportion out of a town of ten or twelve thousand souls. The performances were in the open air, there being no roof. Formerly the Romans stood. The state was considered in danger from encroaching effeminacy when seats were introduced in places of amusement. A greater storm of ridicule and sarcasm accompanied the first spreading of awnings to protect the audiences from the sun than did the first raising of umbrellas in the days of James I. in London, so reluctantly do we fall into even new comforts when opposed by old prejudices. We generally, in the pride of our Anglo-Saxon civilization, conceive that to have been the first appearance of umbrellas on the European stage; whereas I noticed on Grecian vases more than twenty-five hundred years old very well painted parasols and umbrellas, which certainly proves their existence in Italy as early as the foundation of Rome.

The seats of honor were near the stage. Each class increased its distance as it diminshed in rank, until the plebeian crowd filled all the upper rows of seats. *Behind* them, in the galleries, were placed the women, and near them the police ; a regulation which gives no favorable idea of the gallantry of the male, or the morals of the fair sex. Two of the chairs used by the magistrates of the theatres have been found. They are of bronze inlaid with silver, and of a finish so beautiful and accurate that it would be difficult to find any thing in modern art to surpass them.

Near the theatres is the pretty little temple of Isis, in such good preservation as to be a tell-tale of the mysteries of the Egyptian Deity. The priests were dining when the eruption took place. Several died beside their meal. One endeavored to hew his way with an axe through a solid stone wall ; another perished in the attempt to fly with treasure snatched in haste from the shrine. The oracular responses of the idol all find their clew here, so it is generally believed, in the secret stairs opening behind the niche for the statue, which gave ample space for a concealed priest to counterfeit the supposed voice of his goddess. But there was no more priestly jugglery in this pagan temple than is practiced yearly in a Christian church in Naples. The blood of St. Januarius is as much a falsehood as was the voice of Isis. Nor do I believe that her priesthood were, in general, worse in morals than those Roman friars who have continued their practices under another name. Both devoted themselves to celibacy ; both shaved their heads ; both mortified their flesh by coarse apparel, bare feet, and fasting ; and both pledged themselves to pass their vigils in devotion, and their lives in chastity. To continue the comparison, both, while sincere in their self-mortification, obtained credit and power, and both diminished in reputation as hypocrisy and avarice took the place of their ostensible virtues. The heathen priest was the parent of the modern monk.

The similarities between pagan forms and Christian rites in Italy prove that, with the common religious mind, more power lies in the ceremony than in the confession. Rites that have long been considered as necessary for salvation are slow in dying out, though reason and revelation may point to purer faiths and more consistent forms. Were a Pompeian to awake in Naples, he would find much to remind him of his old belief: altars, images, offerings, and lamps in the public streets, as he left them at Pompeii, constituting a shrine at every conspicuous corner. The sprinkling of holy water, the fonts in the churches, sacred candelabra, the burning of incense, display of sacred vessels, and the contribution-box, he was accustomed to witness in his own temples. These would create no more surprise than would the power of the priesthood and pomp of religious processions. The multiplicity of sacred images, the numerous altars, a queen of heaven, with an apparent plurality of gods, would remind him of his own populous mythology. In short, while regretting the absence of his favorite games, he would doubtless approve the disappearance of animal sacrifice, and consider the change of rites from the exterior of a noble temple, in the sight of the assembled people, to the interior of a gayly-decorated church, as a mere matter of taste, about which it was not worth while to quarrel. So long as he kept clear of doctrine, he would probably consider that the religious world was, after all, not much out of its old track.

Most of the temples are upon or in the immediate vicinity of the Civil Forum, which was the central point of business and magnificence. Here are the triumphal arches, and the statues, or rather their pedestals—for the statues are removed to Naples—of the eminent men who had deserved well of the colony. The stately temple of Jupiter occupies its northern extremity. It was in process of reparation from the ravages of the earthquake of the year 63 when overwhelmed in the destruction of 79. In it were kept the public archives. Opposite stands the Basilica, or Court of Justice, with its subterranean prison. On either side are numerous public buildings remarkable for their beauty, the whole, even in ruins, forming a rare *coup d'œil* of architectural interest. One of the finest of these buildings is the Chalcidicum, built by the priestess Eumachia, at her own expense, as a washing-place for the magisterial and priestly robes. In fact, it is an immense shallow basin of the purest white marble, furnished with scouring-blocks of the same material and an aqueduct for the supply of water, constituting probably the largest and most beautiful wash-tub in existence. The position chosen for an edifice of this character, in the centre of the town, is singular, but its beauty would justify an even more conspicuous locality. It is in such perfect repair that it could give scrubbing-room to a regiment of washwomen without other delay than to turn on the water. A portico, supported by exquisitely wrought Corinthian columns of Parian marble, surrounded this basin, but the columns have been taken away. A statue of Eumachia still remains, but it is a copy of the original, which has gone to Naples. On the same side of the Forum, toward the north, stands the Pantheon, as the building is called which was dedicated to the big gods, the aristocracy of Roman mythology. The twelve pedestals for their statues still remain, but the gods have departed both the earth and faith of mankind. The priesthood that waited upon them must have been a jolly set, judging from the paintings still remaining in their refectory, which are in every way provocative of gustatory ideas. Indeed, it is supposed that they were so rich and hospitable as to often feast their fellow-citizens, in which case they must have been the most popular of the ancient clergy. Perhaps the building was, notwithstanding its sacred character, but a superior kind of restaurant, for which its position admirably adapted it. The debris of many dinners was found in a sink in its court-yard, which shows that the appetites of the Pompeians held good to the last moment.

Passing from this building, I entered the lawyers' court by deeply-worn steps, which told of the tread of many busy feet in the days of Cicero. The stiff marble pulpit, from which so much eloquence and chicanery had issued, and before which had stood so many beating hearts, pulsating with selfish or generous interests, as the orator touched the human chords of wrong or right, wore an impressive stillness. Not even the hum of an insect disturbed the intense solitude of that sepulchre of law. Silence reigned supreme. In the intensity of the sunlight flashing upon the upright walls, and clearness of atmosphere over head, without a trace around or above me of any living thing, I began to realize the idea of the "last man." Lingering but for an instant on its marble pavement, I turned hastily away as the thought intruded, "What would all my fine sentiment be worth, supposing this to have been only an auctioneer's block?"

A Roman town without a public bath would have been as strange an occurrence as a Yankee village without a meeting-house. So long a time had elapsed without the discovery of any building of this character, that antiquarians began to doubt whether Pompeii, after all, had not contained an unwashed population, though the private baths, the River Sarno, and the sea which bathed its walls, were quite sufficient to have kept all Campania clean. In 1824, however, the present baths were opened. Though of a pigmy extent compared with the immense establishments of Rome, which were cities within themselves, yet they are vastly superior, both in size and decoration, to any of modern times. No considerations of modesty appear to have interfered with a Roman's enjoyment of promiscuous bathing. To bathe was a primary necessity—to bathe in public was an enjoyment equivalent to the Opera of modern civilization. At first men and women bathed together, or their baths were united. But even Roman license became scandalized at the results, and the sexes were separated. Emperors mingled freely in the baths with the commonest citizens.

It is said of Hadrian, that one day, seeing a veteran soldier rubbing his body against the marble for friction, he asked him why he did not employ the slaves. The soldier replied that he was too poor. The Emperor immediately presented him with two slaves and a sum sufficient to maintain them. A few days after, several old men, who had witnessed the fortune of their companion, attempted to attract the Emperor's notice by using the marble pilasters in lieu of crash towels. He, perceiving their drift, quickly set them at work rubbing each other.

The bathers were usually scraped with bronze instruments called *strigiles*, much after the fashion of currying horses. This was a rough operation, as the Emperor Augustus once discovered to his cost. Previous to bathing, the body was anointed with oil, and upon coming out of the bath, costly and delicate perfumes were lavishly used. To describe the entire operation of a complete bath of a Roman exquisite would require a volume. Every luxury of art was employed to gratify the taste, and every means which a sensuous race could invent was used to heighten physical pleasure. The resources of a more than Oriental effeminacy or barbarian energy were alternately exhausted to stimulate the system to novel emotions of languid or active enjoyment, until at last the Roman bath, with its libraries, gymnasiums, lecture and reading rooms, its museums of art, its imperial magnificence and prodigality of sensual attractions, became the focus and the grave of Roman life.

The Pompeian baths were sufficiently luxurious in their way, and are in such excellent preservation that they might be used to give the traveler not only the idea, but the fact of a classical ablution. It would be something to be able to say that one had hung up his clothes on the same peg which had held Pliny's, or rubbed his sides in the same marble tub which had held one of the family of Cicero. That they visited Pompeii, and of course the baths, is evident from an inscription on the architrave of the temple of Fortune, which says that "Marcus Tullius Cicero, son of Marcus, erected, at his own private expense, this temple to Fortuna Augusta." This temple held a statue of Cicero, with a purple-colored toga. The practice of gilding and coloring statuary was not uncommon to ancient sculptors, and in some cases may have been used with good effect. The English sculptor Gibson has sought to revive this fashion. The result is, that his experiments have succeeded in giving a waxen look to marble. The more severe rule of modern art is, that sculpture is the legitimate province of form, and not of color.

On the wall of the court of the baths is the following inscription: "On occasion of the dedication of the baths, at the expense of Cnæus Alleius Nigidius Maius, there will be the chase of wild beasts, athletic contests, sprinkling of perfumes, and an awning. Prosperity to Maius, chief of the colony."

The principal divisions of the interior are as follows. The Tepidarium, or warm chamber, a large oblong hall, with an arched ceiling, beautifully ornamented with bassi-relievi in stucco. Along the sides beneath, and supporting a rich cornice, are a range of niches, divided by sculptured Telamones,

TEPIDARIUM.

or male figures two feet high, flesh-colored, and with black hair. The baskets upon their heads and moulding above were gilt. This room is lighted by a window two feet and a half by three, formerly closed by movable panes of glass in a bronze frame. Some of these panes were found perfect. In it still remains a beautiful bronze brazier, seven feet long by two and a half wide, used for heating the apartment. The Calidarium, or hot chamber, contains a spacious marble bathing-tub raised on a pedestal of the same material. The walls are lined with hot air and steam flues. A beautiful marble basin, five feet in diameter, containing a fountain for boiling water, occupies a niche at the lower end of this apartment. The Frigidarium, or undressing room, is circular, with a dome roof, in which is a window two feet eight inches high, and three feet eight inches broad, once closed by a single pane of ground glass two fifths of an inch thick, the fragments of which lay on the floor when the room was first opened. This establishes the fact that the ancients not only had glazed windows, but manufactured large panes of glass. It contains also a spacious circular marble bath. There are few spots of more interest in Pompeii than these baths.

The amphitheatre is at the farther end of the unexplored part of the town. I wandered slowly thither, meeting on my way two beggars, who, unlike their fraternity in general, had each a gift of his own to exercise besides the accustomed whine and promise of saintly blessings. The first was lame, or pretended to be, but, starting forth from behind a doorway, he began a most extraordinary dance, on principles of his own, to the tune of an antique pipe which he played himself. He was the most like an antique faun of any living thing I had ever seen, and, consequently, was in keeping with the scene. I gave him something, and left him to finish his performance in solitude. Ascending to the upper surface of Pompeii, if the soil *above* has any right to the name of the town it has destroyed, I met another, a regular modern interloper, who jumped a Jim Crow sort of a hop to a negro melody, which he seemed to consider just the thing for a stranger. Shade of Hercules, what a profanation! I hurried past him in silence, not even bestowing the charity of a look.

Tread lightly! On a soil like this, who can tell what lies beneath? The careless feet may rudely press upon some maiden's breast, and crush an infant form. There is a pleasure in speculating over the contents of a mine of *Art* which the search for mere gold can not possess. A statue over which we unconsciously walk may prove a "nugget" of wealth to the finder, even if soulless to its beauties. The very dust beneath bears sifting. There is gold to reward the toil, and beauty to instruct the world. How much of actual treasure remains earth-bound in Italy! Not many leagues from Pompeii lies buried Alaric and the plunder of Rome. Gold and silver keep well in the grave. The treasure men lose their lives to win mocks at their brief triumphs, and lives to corrupt successive generations. The spoils of Jerusalem's temple, the seven-branched golden candlestick, for nearly fifteen centuries, with wealth untold, have rested quietly in the sands of the Tiber. Will not avarice league with art to search for what would so well reward the discovery? Were Italy half as much dug over as are the gold-fields of Australia, the product would, I believe, astonish even California success.

I reached the amphitheatre and mounted its walls. It is a baby amphitheatre compared with the Coliseum, yet nearly fifteen thousand spectators could find room within its circumference. There are twenty-four rows of stone seats and two fine corridors.

The extreme length is four hundred and thirty feet, and the greatest breadth three hundred and thirty-five, the form being oval, and the whole in fine preservation, with the exception of the frescoes which once covered the passages, and the finer portions or facings of stone-work. I have a passion for amphitheatres, but it depends upon the associations connected with their symmetry and strength. This upward springing of arch upon arch heavenward, in strong and graceful sweep, receding gradually from the arena, but mounting directly toward the sky on the exterior, combines a grandeur of force and beauty in a higher degree than any other of the architectural works of man. The Pyramid of Cheops is indeed stupendous, but, after all, it is only artificial bulk and weight in its simplest form. The Coliseum, on the contrary, is a noble triumph of art—an expansion of science and strength which stamps the character of a nation for all time. It is Rome's proudest medal to her architectural genius. Years sufficed to build it, but centuries of devastation have been unable to destroy it. I love, then, the massive walls of the amphitheatres, with their beautiful curves and lightly-poised arches, and have visited them all—Rome, Nismes, Arles, Verona, Puteoli, and Pompeii—with unfailing pleasure. The last remains most in keeping with its original design. All that is to be learned of their brutal purposes is here apparent—the arena, dens, vomitories, and passages for slain brutes or men. There would be little need of restoration should the taste for human slaughter to afford a Roman holiday revive. While they commemorate the daring genius of the conquerors of the world, they record also their brutalization and inhumanity. Can, however, the age that tolerated the Inquisition reproach the Romans for the Amphitheatre? The latter disappeared before Christianity, though not until Christian blood had soaked its arena. The former sprang from so-called Christianity, and martyred its hecatombs, in slow tortures, in the name of a merciful Savior. We need to recall such truths to teach us humility when we sit in judgment upon the Past.

The performances in these amphitheatres of a milder character stand unrivaled in our times. Elephants were trained to *dance on a tight rope* with towers and riders on their back.

and other feats equally wonderful. Their jugglery was almost upon a par with Egyptian miracles.

The extent of the disaster in the number of the dead was not so great at Pompeii as to make it exceed some of our Western steam-boat explosions, or other casualties which we have so ingeniously contrived for sending our fellow-citizens by scores, without warning, into eternity. Here the warning was ample. Those who lingered and were lost, but a few hundred in number, judging from the skeletons as yet found, were probably the aged or helpless, the thief who stopped to plunder, or the criminal whose bonds prevented his escape. Some doubtless perished, like the soldiers, from a rigid sense of duty or discipline; some from incredulity as to the reality of danger; and others from those instinctive impulses of self-denial and generosity which so often, in the hour of peril, sanctify and exalt human nature. Selfishness and despair there were too, in their most despicable and brutal forms, and philosophical curiosity, which, like Pliny's the elder, in seeking to relieve, sought also to investigate, even at the expense of his own existence. Other great calamities, which form epochs, as it were, in the successive miseries of the human race, become fainter and fainter as they recede in the vista of time, till their interest concentrates in a brief historical paragraph, which instructs us, but does not move. Pompeii, on the contrary, is a perpetual reminiscence of the actual fears, struggles, and horror which attended its final doom. The hopelessness and terrific grandeur of the morning of the 24th of August, A.D. 79, with all its agonies, crimes, and virtues, is touchingly before us. We see the deserted house, the forsaken temple, the coveted treasure, the jewel spared during eighteen centuries of death to its fair owner, the paintings, gifts of friendship and tokens of taste, and all the evidences of a domestic life as dearly prized as our own, left as if the owner had but stepped out to see a neighbor; shops filled with merchandise, but empty of customers; the labor of the mechanic interrupted, and destined never to receive the finishing stroke; kitchens that are tell-tales of domestic economy and luxurious extravagance; the narrow, tomb-like cells assigned to slaves, bespeaking a servitude worse than the modern African; in short, every thing that goes to make up active human existence, even to the forms of manhood, beauty, and infancy, impressed upon the solid lava, disclosing the very features worn until the last hour of life—all these, and more, which Pompeii has yielded up to the present generation, bring vividly back to the heart the hour and story of her fiery burial.

Retracing my steps through the modern farm, I strolled once more along the street of tombs which led in the direction of Herculaneum. The old city of the dead was but a continuation of the old city of the living; there was not even a dividing line; sepulchre and domestic roof are intermingled. This familiarity with death was common among the Romans. They entered or left their paternal cities through long lines of ancestral monuments, reminding them of glories won and honors conferred by past generations, which in time might also become their own. These tombs are no vulgar graves, but have a cheerful look of elegance, as if intended more to please the eye of the living than to secure the dead. Indeed, the Romans could have had none of the unpleasant ideas which moderns have in connection with the bodies of the departed. They feared no grave-yard odors or fearful sights of mouldering humanity, for the simple process of burning corpses secured them equally against contagion and repulsive associations. The funerals took place at night, with great pomp and the burning of torches. This practice, in all its essential particulars, is still continued at Rome, the body, richly dressed and covered with flowers, being borne on an open litter through the streets. The modern phrase, to receive the dying breath, is become a poetical expression of attendance on the dying; but among the Romans it had a practical signification. The nearest relative bent over the body of the dying person to inhale his latest breath, fondly thinking that the principle of life left the body at that instant by the mouth.

The ashes of the dead, being deposited in urns, were placed in niches in tombs, which, from their resemblance to the arrangement of dove-cotes, were called *columbaria*. The Romans literally laid away their ancestors on the shelf. This was also an economical practice, for one tomb could contain a great number of urns.

From the tombs I ascended the ancient walls to look down upon the city. In the rear of the House of the Vestals there is a high tower in fine preservation. Passing from the wall into this, I mounted to the top to enjoy the landscape. Unroofed Pompeii, with its marble columns and spacious courtyards, lay glittering in the sunlight beneath me. If it looked lovely then, what must it have appeared when its streets were a crowded mart, its port filled with Oriental ships, and its public and private houses were robed in Tyrian purple and glittering with gold? The sea was as tranquil as in the morning, with its white sails drowsily hanging over its surface. It glittered in the sinking sun as if a diamond sheet had been dropped from the Celestial City. On the farther horizon lay Ischia and the headlands of that noble bay, reposing tranquilly on the water like floating Edens. To the right was Naples and the intervening towns, with their white walls, inclosing the landscape as a setting of pearls. Over against me, in dark shadow, was the ancient Mons Lactarius, with snow still lingering in its northern crevices. At its base lies subterranean Stabiæ, with its rich villas, a Roman Brighton, buried under the same shower as Pompeii. Modern Castellamare has grown upon its site and succeeded to its reputation as a watering-place. A broad and fertile plain, barely moistened by the shrunken Sarno, unites Pompeii with Castellamare. In my rear, Vesuvius gradually swelled up from the city walls, with mingled fertility and sterility, as the lava-streams had spared or buried its cultivated base. The clear setting sunlight sent its illuminating rays into its inmost gorges, bringing them, as it were, close to me, and revealing every secret character. Above all, the diadem of that beauteous landscape, brilliant with borrowed glory, rose the crater summit, abrupt and cragged, but as powerful as a mountain of granite. A light, fleecy vapor curled gently from its mouth, and melted away lazily like the smoke of an aristocratic cigar. The entire view formed a panorama on which one could not gaze his fill.

My eyes ranged rapidly from one object to another, but at last became fixed on the cone of Vesuvius. The light, fleecy vapor was succeeded by rich masses of pure white cloud. These were puffed fast and furiously from the crater, like escaping volumes of high-pressure steam. They gradually disappeared before a light breeze which had begun to stir, but before they were wholly gone, a dense smoke, of inky blackness, arose from a somewhat nearer point of view, and mounted with great rapidity into the sky. It soon reached an elevation of, I should judge, nine thousand feet, or three times the height of Vesuvius; then bending, as it were, beneath its own weight, it flattened out at the top like a spread umbrella or the branches of an Italian pine, and cast a deep shadow upon the mountain beneath it. There were bright spots to be seen through its gloom, not star-like, but lurid. I could compare it to nothing but to the tree of evil, with its infernal fruit shot up from hell, as an omen of coming woe to men. Pluto was preparing to visit the earth amid wonders and ruin. This strange apparition slowly sunk again into the crater.

I had been so occupied with the mountain that I had quite forgotten to look toward the city. Turning, however, as the cloud gradually subsided, I saw the inhabitants gazing in awe and perplexity upon the phenomenon. While they looked, lightnings began to play through the sky. There was no thunder, though their flashes were so intense as to be clearly seen in the bright sunlight. The colossal statue of Jupiter, fronting his temple on the Forum, was shivered to pieces, and one of the Augustals, passing at the time, was crushed to death beneath the falling fragments. A cry of horror reached my ears. By an instinctive impulse, each citizen seemed to accept the omen as the death-warning to their town and race.

The stillness that succeeded to the cloud and lightnings was awful. The leaves of the trees were as still as if carved in marble. To me it appeared as if all nature was holding its breath in terror of coming annihilation. The very air seemed extinct, and all life, anticipating its doom, lay spell-bound in silence. The feeling of passive horror was too intense to last long. Action, although no one knew what to do or where to fly, became a relief. The wild animals in their cages at the amphitheatre alternately moaned, and sulked, and flew into paroxysms of fierceness. Their instincts foreboded strange dangers, and their captivity turned their fear into rage; but their keepers were too much interested in consulting their own safety to think of the brutes in their charge. Already had the amphitheatre been cleared of its spectators, who had come up from Noceria, Stabiæ, and even Herculaneum, to witness the games. They now hurried toward their homes with a feeling that Pompeii was fated to destruction.

Many of the inhabitants, believing that a recurrence of earthquakes, such as desolated Campania twelve years before, was about to take place, sought security in precipitate flight. Some took to the shipping, and, putting off at once, escaped. Others tried their chariots; but the earth now began to move to and fro, and even up and down, like the waves of the sea, so that the horses were either thrown down or paralyzed with fright. To increase the confusion, intense darkness obscured every thing. Pompeii and the whole country became like a closet shut against all light. No one knew which way to turn. The cries and struggles were terrible to hear; lost children were calling upon fond parents who were unable to help. The weak were overthrown. Women vainly implored the assistance of men. Despair at last kept the multitude still, for to move was almost certain destruction.

A fiery light suddenly glared over the strange spectacle. Snake-like flashes darted here and there, imparting a lurid glare to the woe-struck human countenances and marble walls. I felt there was immediate danger for me to remain where I was, but I was rooted to the spot by the terrible fascination of the scene. Yet all that I had beheld was as nothing compared with what followed.

The flashes of light ceased to play about the top of the mountain. Instantly a mighty crash was heard, as if the mountain had split in twain. The very sea roared with pain. Heavy thunderings muttered and rolled deep in the bowels of earth, and, passing up, burst into the air with the noise of an exploded world. The mountain was indeed rent in twain. Every building in the city trembled to its foundations; walls were split, and statues overthrown by the concussion. The tower where I was for a few seconds reeled like a drunken man, but settled again on its base without much damage. High into the air, higher even than the cloud-tree rose, shot up burning stones, flames, and ashes all fire, a terrific shower of destruction. Some of the stones were immense masses of red-hot rock, which, striking against each other in their rapid ascent, burst into myriads of pieces, scattering fire and light in all directions. Fortunately, in falling, they did not reach the city.

A new and even more horrible enemy had appeared at the same time, but which, so taken up was I with the grandeur of the exploding masses of stone, I had not immediately noticed. Through the rent in the mountain a stream of viscid, red-hot liquid rock flowed steadily out, rapidly making its way toward the sea, enlarging in depth and breadth at every foot of its progress. This, then, was the real demon of destruction to which the mountain had given birth. It swept every living thing before it. Forests, and even hills, melted at its touch, swelling the fiery flood, and disappearing slowly beneath it with a sullen plunge, amid violent explosions and dense smoke. Valleys filled up; large rocks were floated for a considerable distance in this strange river like cork on water, tossing and splashing about in fiery spray before they became lava themselves. Some sank, and were thrown high into the air again, forming as they fell thick, blood-red whirlpools, which boiled and bubbled with a fierce sluggishness, uttering the while strange bellowings and mutterings, as if the elements of nature were engaged in mortal conflict. The light from this lava-stream shed a ghastly glow over the entire country. It soon reached the cultivated grounds, and farms and villages were speedily in flames. I watched its course until it struck that shady knoll where I had so often passed the sultry summer hours with my friend Plautus in his charming villa, which in an instant was a mass of smoking ruins. The stream now turned from the direction of Pompeii and moved toward Herculaneum.

Although this danger was averted from Pompeii, another no less destructive succeeded, warning the remaining inhabitants to abandon their homes, which no longer afforded them shelter. From my elevated position I could see all that occurred, and was near enough to hear at times the voices of the multitude and recognize my friends. Showers of hot ashes, cinders, and even large stones began to fall, obscuring the remaining light, and making the sun appear as if under an eclipse. The people retreated to the public porticoes, but the burning ashes were so fine that they penetrated into the inmost chamber, and drove out all who, until that moment, had fancied that strong walls could protect them. I had noticed that Diomedes had invited many of his friends to take refuge in the cellar of his villa, which early in the day he had stored with provisions, believing that its massive walls and half-subterranean position would be proof against the volcanic storm. As the ashes began to penetrate the narrow apertures, the male portion left and made a desperate effort to reach the sea. A few succeeded, but Diomedes and a servant, bearing such treasures as he had hastily snatched up, were struck down by a shower of stones, and must have soon perished. I could hear Diomedes's cries to the last, offering his entire wealth to any one who would aid him to escape The poor women and children left in the cellar could not have long survived, as its position exposed it to the first effects of the terrible lava-hail, which was now accompanied at intervals by showers of boiling water and sulphurous masses of vapor, that struck with immediate death every living thing that inhaled it. I had some time before retreated to a chamber of the tower, which still afforded me a good view and protected me from the immediate effects of the eruption.

The showers of boiling water, fall of burning stones, avalanche of ashes, and jets of mephitic gases completed the climax of evils upon the doomed city. Those of the inhabitants that had sufficient strength no longer looked for shelter from massive walls, but rushed into the streets with pillows, domestic utensils, and even tables tied upon their heads, to protect them from the falling masses, and made for the port, where there still remained some vessels. But the sea was terribly agitated. It ebbed and flowed with great rapidity every few minutes, leaving the fish stranded upon the shores, or sweeping them up into the streets. There was now no more hope of safety on the water than on the land. The darkness also increased. Some of the magistrates ordered torches to be placed in the public way. This afforded some relief to the hopeless confusion of the flying, but individual panic had now assumed too violent a stage to be regardful of the public good. The worst passions and most selfish instincts of human nature had come into full play. Blasphemous wretches and hardened criminals, availing themselves of the chaos of all order, plundered the shrines of the gods, robbed the public treasuries, and penetrated into private houses, snatching up the deserted wealth, and stabbing the impotent owners who attempted to resist. The falling fire had set many of the wooden roofs into a blaze, so that Pompeii was thus threatened with a double conflagration. The plunder of the villains in many cases was the cause of their death, for, burdened by its weight, they but the more speedily met the fate which was due to their crimes. Slaves, too, who had long concealed the hatred which their cruel treatment inspired, turned upon their effeminate masters, mocked their tears and appeals for aid, or slew them pitilessly before the eyes of their wives and children, whom they at length abandoned to more lingering deaths. I saw the rich widow Julia, as she rose from the luxurious breakfast-table of Sallust, aided by her gallant host, attempt to escape by the Herculaneum gate. With her children she reached the portico of the inn, and there, fainting from fear and unwonted effort, clasped her offspring in her arms and calmly sat down to die. Sallust in vain attempted to rouse her to farther exertion. A shower of burning cinders, more heavy than common, drove him to flight, and buried the hapless family in their living grave. The shrieks of the poor children were appalling. But, in the general terror, who could stop to pity individual torture?

The Ædile Pansa behaved nobly. He assembled some of the centurions and their soldiers, and inspired them with firmness to act for the general good. Never was the power of Roman discipline more heroically vindicated. To the latest moment the sentinels were changed; the relieved returned to die in their barracks—those on duty, at their posts. Patrols sternly marched through the city, arresting and summarily punishing the vagabonds who were adding crime to the universal distress. But what could a few self-devoted soldiers hope to do against the powers of darkness, leagued together for the destruction of humanity? So long as there remained a voice to command them, they obeyed; when this ceased, they too sought safety in flight, but with most it was too late.

The struggles of the flying mass were frightful. Parents fled from their children; children deserted their parents; beauty appealed in vain to strength for aid. Safety, safety was the universal thought. Numbers fell and were trampled upon by the advancing crowd; before they could rise again, the hot ashes and cinders had buried them forever, and their lifeless forms were trodden into shapeless masses by flying neighbors and kindred. Yet, amid all this utter selfishness of despair, there flashed out bright examples of generous devotion that reconciled one to human nature, and proved that, even in its darkest moments, it was instinctive with nobleness and truth. I saw the slave shelter his master's child in his brawny arms at the expense of his own excoriated back, bared to the falling water and ashes. He reached a boat in safety and put off on the water. A young woman led out an aged blind man, perhaps her father, and piloted him a while slowly but surely through the encumbered streets. I soon lost sight of them. Other examples there were of tenderness and fidelity; but who could watch individual progress to the end in such a scene? A lion had escaped from the amphitheatre. He ran howling over the scorching embers, seeking companionship with men, until at length, unable to endure the falling cinders, he crept into a deserted shop, and there laid himself down to die. But the strangest spectacle was a company of Nazarenes, who, robed in white, sought not to escape from the city, but marched in procession through the streets, with torches in hand, chanting hymns to their Deity, and proclaiming in doleful voices that "the last hour of man was come."

None seemed to bestow a thought upon the infirm and feeble, but left them to perish. Cries of anguish and despair frequently arose amid the burning buildings from these deserted victims, who gazed hopelessly upon their approaching fate. Fire consumed some; gases suffocated others; many were covered with the fine volcanic dust while still gasping for breath, or were crushed by falling timbers. Whichever way I turned my eyes, new horrors appalled them. But I soon had to reflect upon my own position. Could I escape? I hurried to each window in turn. The volcanic shower increased in fury and density. Pompeii already lay half still in death. To go out was impossible—to remain was death. How I cursed my fatal curiosity! I ran around my narrow chamber like a madman. The hot cinders penetrated by the windows and fell upon my flesh. Heavens! how they slowly burned into my body, cooling themselves in my blood! I choked for air. Thirst maddened me. Water, water; but one drop to cool the fever of my tongue! I screamed, and fell senseless upon the floor.

At this moment a hand touched me, and I—awoke. "Your Excellency will be too late for the last train for Naples if you slumber longer here," said the polite guard. I slipped a coin into his hands, thanked him, stood a moment gazing upon disinterred Pompeii and the quiet volcano, to satisfy myself that, after all, it was but a dream, and, hurrying off to Naples, speedily forgot my late sufferings in a capital dinner at the Café de l'Europe, which I take the liberty to recommend as worthy of its name.

CHAPTER VIII.

THE PAPAL COURT—THE HOLY WEEK AT ROME.

THE Holy Week at Rome! What unholy reminiscences of crowding, struggling, contention; of extortion and cheating; of dirt and discomfort; in short, of all the ills attendant upon the multiplication of the population of the Holy City tenfold in proportion to its capacity of accommodation, does not this solemn Church-festival vividly recall to every traveler who has undergone its purgatorial experience, either to view its vain show, or to stir anew languid devotion in witnessing the significant facts in man's redemption which it is intended to commemorate? Rome, during this period, is the focus of Christendom. The Protestant hurries up to the Eternal City to behold the scarlet lady in all her pomp and circumstance, with the charitable object of seeing with his own eyes whether her color is not even more deeply dyed than it has been represented. The Catholic devoutly makes his pilgrimage, to lay alike his sins and offerings on her altars, and with renewed heart and faith to carry back with him the blessing and absolution of Christ's vicar on earth. Both are not unfrequently disappointed. I have known the scorning Protestant to go away the disciple of infallibility, while the simple-hearted Catholic, gradually losing himself among the mazes of doubt and hypocrisy, which, fungus-like, cluster around the claims of papacy, at last acknowledged himself a pagan, or worse, an unbeliever in all religion.

No city, both from its past and present influence on the world's history, presents more claims to interest than Rome. The many who visit it are as nothing in comparison with those who desire and can not. I shall therefore give, for the benefit of the latter class, so far as I am able, a practical view of its ceremonies and principles during that period which it has set apart to commemorate, with all its sanctity and splendor, as one of peculiar solemnity—embracing the most momentous events that ever dawned upon the human race—the death and resurrection of our Savior. What papacy thus openly spreads before the whole world must be considered as its religious standard. By its effects on its followers it can rightly be judged. To keep within the strictest limits of charitable evidence, I shall confine myself either to papal authorities or ceremonies, for it is solely upon them that it founds its high pretensions, and by them exhibits its righteousness.

Bishop England, in a little work published at Rome, entitled an "Explanation of the Ceremonies of the Holy Week," sets forth the claims and objects of the Roman Church at this particular festival. We, therefore, can not go amiss in briefly quoting from him the doctrines which he asserts to be animating principles of the practices he advocates.

"The object," he says, "of our church-ceremony is not mere idle show; such exhibitions would, in religion, be worse than a *waste* of time." "God can never be pleased by *any* homage which is not internal and spiritual." "The legitimate objects of external rites in religion are the instruction of the mind and amelioration of the heart; their object is the promotion of enlightened piety. Whatever does not tend to this is at least useless, probably mischievous. The Catholic Church is desirous of having *all her observances tested by this principle*." By this principle I beg all, whether Protestant or Catholic, to test even the few of the manifold observances that I shall be able to quote within my prescribed limits, and to frankly confess their own conclusions as to the degree in which they promote "enlightened piety."

The Pope, as we all know, claims to be the representative of Christ, with spiritual and temporal powers commensurate with divine authority. Although our Savior expressly declared his kingdom not to be of this world, yet his successor and "*visible head of the Church*" is also a "*temporal sovereign;*" and, in addition to his ecclesiastical state, surrounds himself with as brilliant a court as can exist, in which females are outwardly excluded. In judging, then, of these incompatible functions, a charitable distinction should be drawn between that which properly belongs to the one or the other. Inasmuch, however, as the temporal power had its origin in his spiritual position, and is intimately blended with it in all its phases, it will be difficult to define the line of demarkation between his duties as high-priest and sovereign. We must, therefore, take him simply as he shows himself to the adoration of the faithful.

"His *throne* is placed on the Gospel side of the altar," says Bishop England. From personal inspection, I can assure the curious reader that no imperial robes surpass those of the Holy Father in rich and curious embroidery, gold, precious stones, and general value of materials and cunning workmanship. Description would fail to illustrate the variety and pomp of costume of the Roman ecclesiastical courts. Therefore I shall present—so far as uncolored cuts can—the extent and costliness of this branch of service of the successor of Him who exalted poverty in the priesthood to the rank of a virtue.

PROCESSION

FOR EASTER SUNDAY.

Esquires,
two and two, in red serge cappas, with hoods over the shoulders, etc.
Proctors of the College,
two and two, in black stuff cappas, with silk hoods.
Procuratores of religious orders,
two and two, in the habits of their respective orders.

Ecclesiastical Chamberlains, outside the city,
two and two, in red.
Chaplains in ordinary,
in red cappas, with hoods of ermine; of whom there are
first mitre bearer,
second mitre bearer,
third mitre bearer,
one bearer of the tiara.—(Cut 8.)
Private Chaplains,
two and two, red cappas and hoods of ermine.
Consistorial Advocates,
two and two, in black or violet cassocks and hoods.
Ecclesiastical Chamberlains,
private and honorary, two and two, in red cassocks and hoods.
Choristers of the Chapel,
two and two, in violet silk cassocks, over which are surplices.—(Cut 9.)
Abbreviators of the Park.
Clerks of the Chamber,
in surplices over rochets, two and two.
Master of the sacred Palace,
in his habit of a Dominican friar.
Auditors of the Rota,
in surplices over rochets, two and two.

Three Acolyths,
in surplices over rochets,
carrying large candlesticks
with lights.
Greek Subdeacon.

Incense bearer.
Cross bearer
in tunic.—(Cut 12.)
Two porters of the red rod.
Latin Subdeacon,
in tunic.

Four Acolyths,
in surplices over rochets,
carrying candlesticks with
lights.
Greek Deacon.

Swiss guard.—(Cut 17.)

Penitentiaries of St. Peter's,
two and two, in albs and chasubles.
Mitred Abbots,
of whom only a few are entitled to a place.
BISHOPS, ARCHBISHOPS, AND PATRIARCHS,
two and two, the Latins wearing copes and mitres,
the Easterns in their proper costumes.—(Cuts 2-8.)
CARDINAL DEACONS,
in dalmatics and mitres, each accompanied by his chamberlain carrying his
square cap, and followed by his train bearer.
CARDINAL PRIESTS,
in chasubles and mitres, similarly attended.—(Cut 11.)
CARDINAL BISHOPS,
in copes and mitres, similarly attended.

Swiss guard.—(Cut 16.)

General staff, and officers of the guard of nobles.
Grand herald and grand esquire,
in court dresses.

Swiss guard.
Mace bearers.
Guard of Nobles.

Lay chamberlains.
Conservators of Rome and Prior of the magistrates of Wards,
in vestures ornamented with cloth of gold.
PRINCE ASSISTANT AT THE THRONE,
in a splendid court dress.—(Cut 10.)
GOVERNOR OF ROME,
in rochet and cappa.
Two auditors of the Rota,
to serve as train bearers.
Two principal masters of ceremony.

Swiss guard.
Mace bearers.—(Cut 19.)
Guard of Nobles.—(Cut 18.)

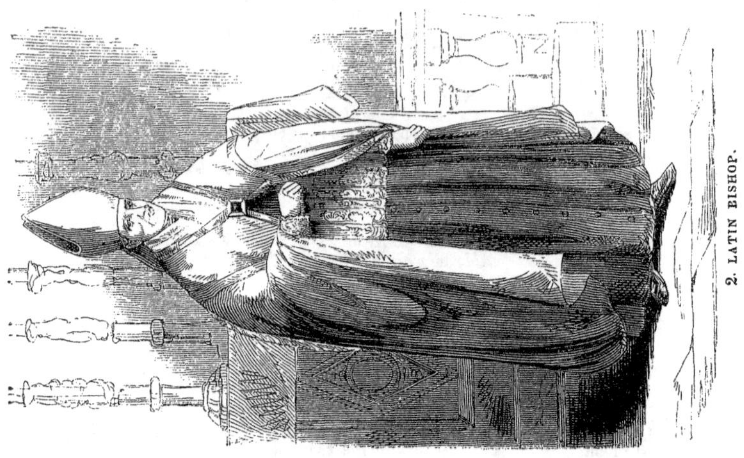

2. LATIN BISHOP.

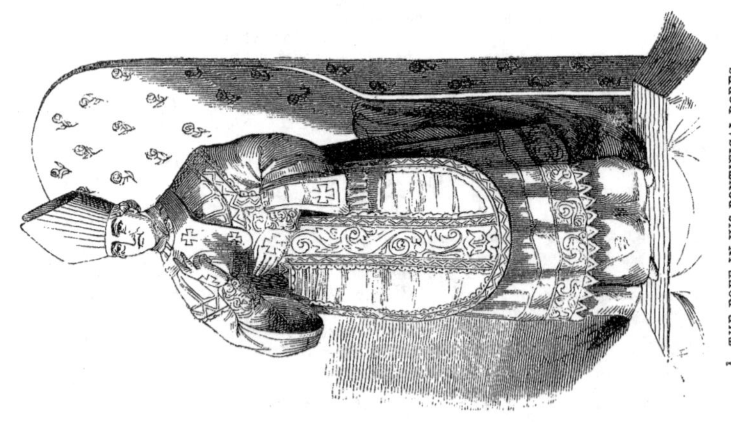

1 THE POPE IN HIS PONTIFICAL ROBES.

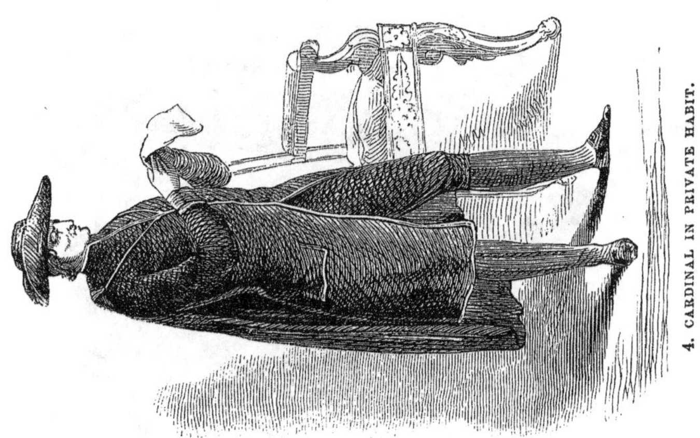

4. CARDINAL IN PRIVATE HABIT.

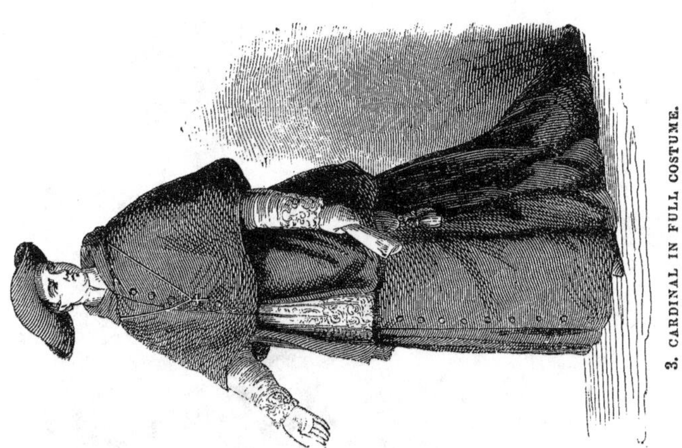

3. CARDINAL IN FULL COSTUME.

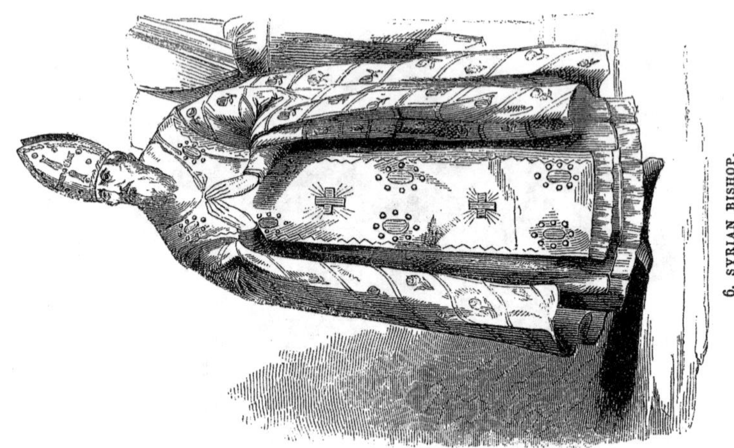

6. SYRIAN BISHOP.

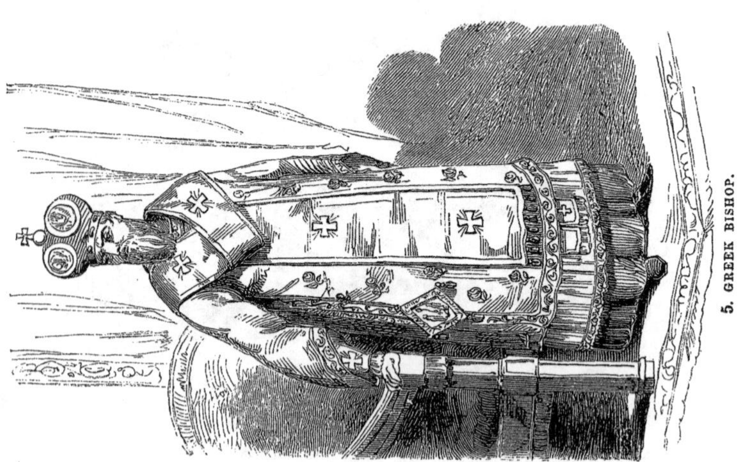

5. GREEK BISHOP.

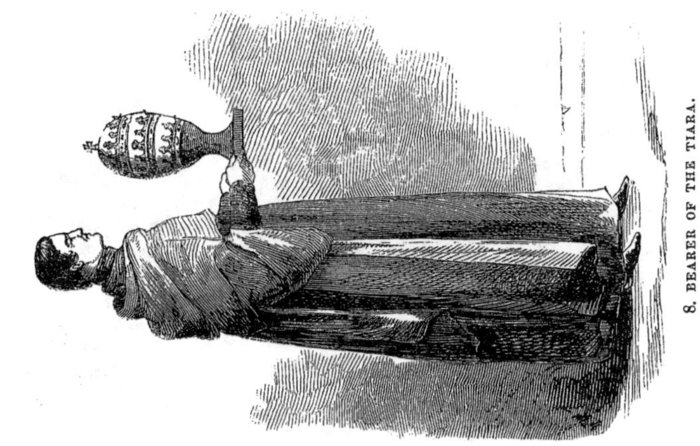

8. BEARER OF THE TIARA.

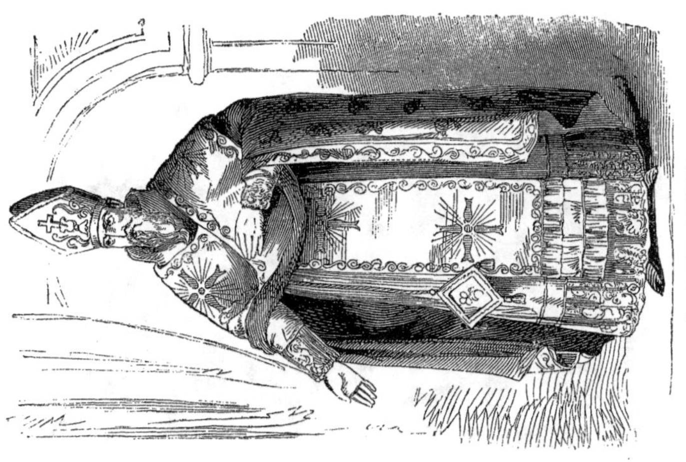

7. ARMENIAN BISHOP.

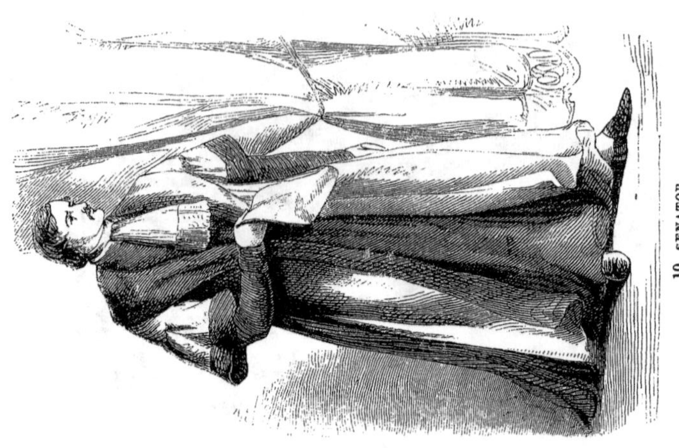

10. SENATOR.

9. CHORISTER.

12. CROSS-BEARER.

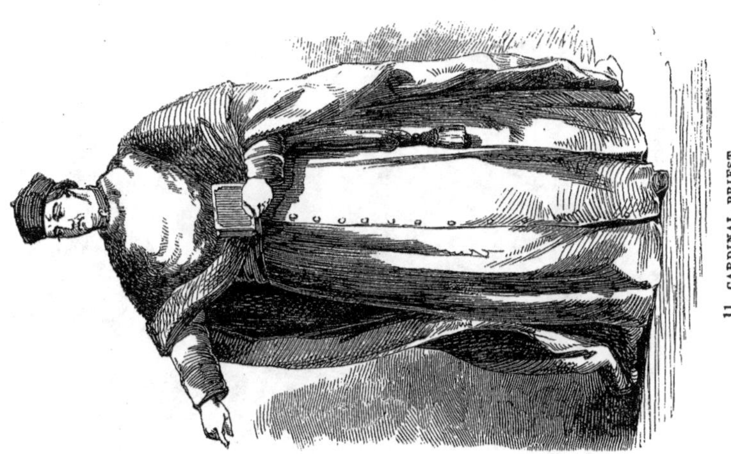

11. CARDINAL PRIEST.

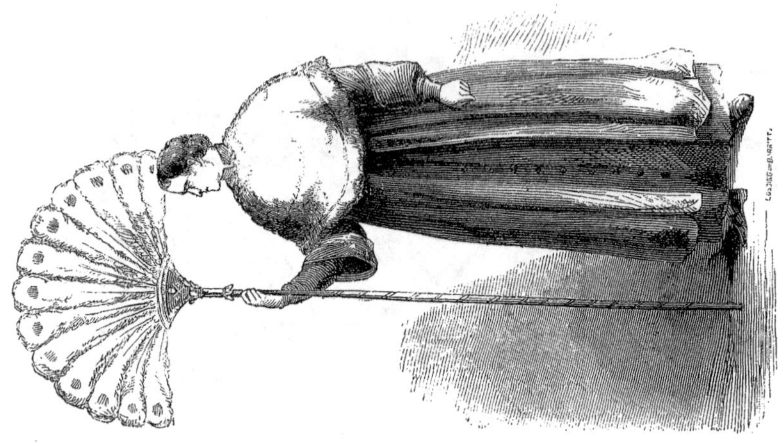

14. PRIVATE CHAMBERLAIN.

13. THE POPE.

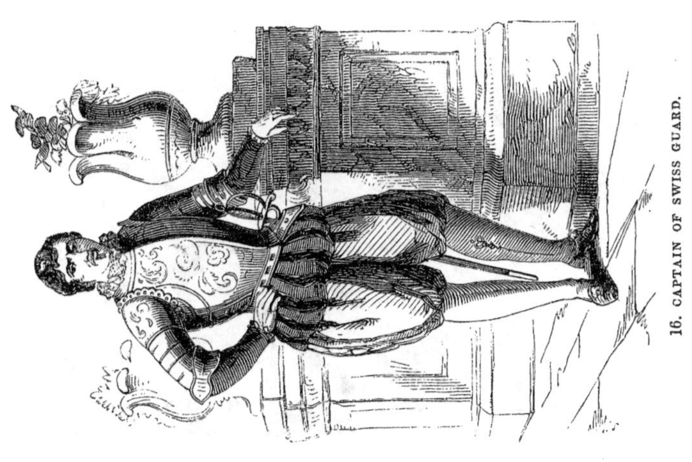

16. CAPTAIN OF SWISS GUARD.

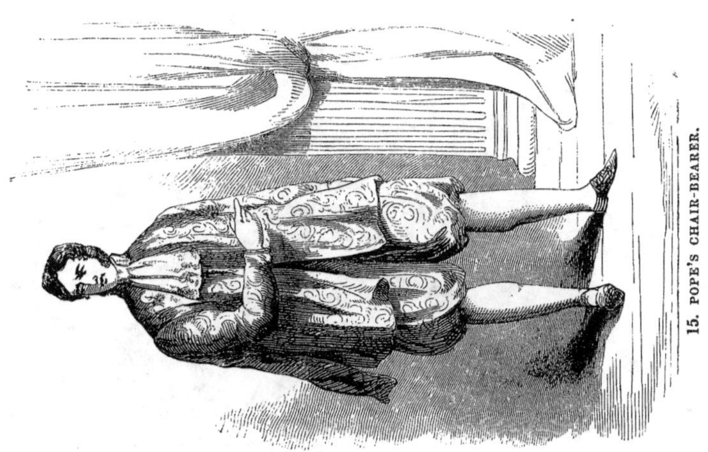

15. POPE'S CHAIR-BEARER.

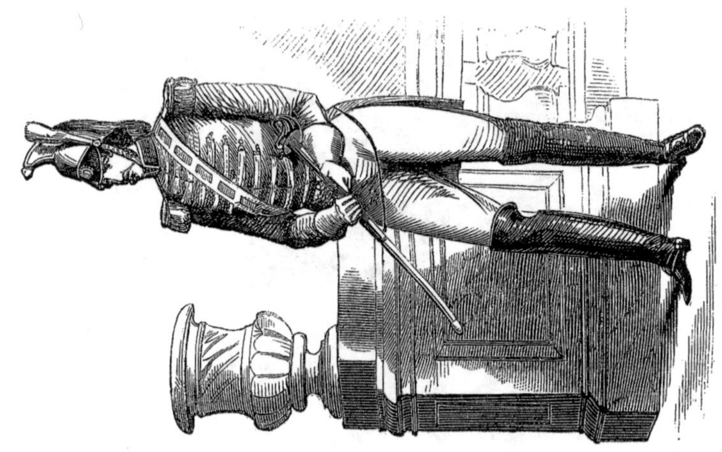

18. GUARD OF NOBLES.

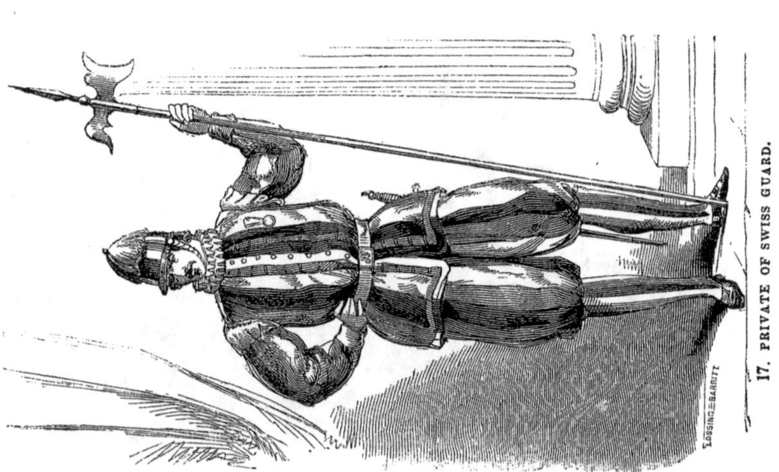

17. PRIVATE OF SWISS GUARD.

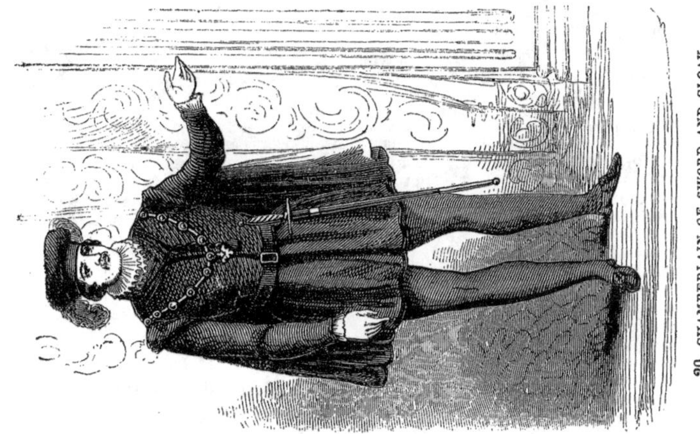

20. CHAMBERLAIN OF SWORD AND CLOAK.

19. MACE-BEARER.

CARDINAL DEACON, second assistant at the throne, *Fan* borne by a private chamberlain.	CARDINAL DEACON, for the Latin Gospel and mass.	CARDINAL DEACON, first assistant at the throne, *Fan* borne by a private chamberlain.—(Cut 14.)

THE POPE—(Cut 13)
wearing a white cope and tiara,
borne in his chair by twelve supporters—(Cut 15—*Pope's chair-bearer in livery*)—in red damask, under a canopy sustained by eight referendaries of the signature, in short violet mantles over rochets.
His holiness is surrounded by his household. Six of the Swiss guards, representing the Catholic cantons, carry large drawn swords on their shoulders.

Private chamberlain.	*Dean of the Rota,* in rochet and cappa.	Private chamberlain, of sword and cloak.—(Cut 20.)
MAJOR DOMO,	AUDITOR OF THE APOSTOLIC CAMERA,	TREASURER,

in rochets and cappas.
Prothonotaries apostolic,
Regent of the chancery and auditor of contradictions,
all in rochets and cappas, two and two.
Generals of religious orders,
two and two, in their proper habits.

On the cope of bright purple color which the Pope wears on Palm Sunday is a silver plate richly gilt, bearing, in beautiful relief, the figure of the Almighty. This was formerly of pure gold, surrounded by three knobs of costly Oriental pearls; but the cupidity of the enemies of Pius VI. overcame their fear of sacrilege, and they appropriated it to other purposes. Benvenuto Cellini, who was employed by Clement VII. to engrave this plate, says, somewhat blasphemously, though in true artistic spirit, that he endeavored to represent the "Almighty Father in a free and easy position."

His Holiness selects the cardinals, seventy in number, who form the high senate of the Church and the privy council of the Pope. They in turn elect the Pope from their own number. In costume they are a shade less brilliant than the Holy Father, wearing, when in chapel, red cassocks with gold tassels, red stockings, white ermine tippets, and red skull or square caps. On solemn occasions they add red shoes and white damask silk mitres, with other changes of raiment, telling with great effect in a procession, but tedious in description.

Throughout the whole edifice of the Roman hierarchy, costume forms a very important and conspicuous part. It is nicely graduated with decreasing splendor and diversified cut from the pope, cardinals, archbishops, and the inferior clergy, who are almost lost amid richly-laced petticoats and purple skirts, to the laughable attire of the sacristans, choristers, and the dirty and dolorous robes of the monastic orders. Each rank has its mark and number, and it must be confessed that no military display can compete, in variety and brilliancy of colors and costliness of uniform, with one got up by the Church. The nomenclature of papal costume is intelligible only to those who pass their lives in wearing it. Each article has its peculiar uses and degree of sanctity.

The etiquette of the papal court, whether in its spiritual or temporal sense, is no light service. To give an idea of the number and variety of officers attached to it, I have given a programme of the Procession for Easter Sunday as it appears in Saint Peter's previous to High Mass and the General Benediction and Excommunication. The engravings given of several of these ecclesiastical personages and their suites will bear out the assertion that no operatic or theatrical spectacle can pretend to vie with the papal court when it dons its holiday suit. Imagine the surprise of St. Peter, were he to be present, upon being told that that sleepy-looking old gentleman, so buried in gold and jewels as scarcely to be discernible, and borne under a magnificent canopy on the shoulders of twelve men clothed in the brightest scarlet, performing the pantomime of turning from one side to another his uplifted thumb and two fingers as illustrative of the blessing of the Holy Trinity, was *his* SUCCESSOR! I question whether at such a sacrilegious libel the old Adam within him would not be more signally displayed than it even was in the garden, for the zealous apostle would least of all forgive humbug. I speak only of the effect on my own mind, contrasted with what I conceive to be the proper display of that religion which consists in visiting and comforting the fatherless and widows in their affliction. There are others, as we often see, on whom the glitter of a court, or the music and architecture of a church, have greater weight than the humility and simplicity of Gospel truth. They would be loth to confess that the avenue to their minds and hearts closed with their eyes and ears; but take away the curiously wrought robes, the cunning of the artificer, the genius of the artist, the harmonies of music, and the entire combination of pomp and venerable tradition by which Rome upholds her religion, and how much of faith and conviction would be left to them?

Besides the officers who figure in the above procession, there are a legion of others attached to the court, which swell its bulk to a degree that weighs heavily upon the petty temporal dominions of the Popes, and is out of all proportion to their necessities. There are private gentlemen of the bed-chamber, and among them a secret treasurer, who purveys for the alms and amusement of the Pope. So little bodily exercise does the Roman etiquette allow to the successors of the fisherman, that his present Holiness has been ordered by his physician to play at billiards daily, to counteract his tendency to obesity.

There are one hundred and eight officers and valets, under different titles, attached to the personal service of the Pope; a modest number, when the extent of his several palaces is considered. No sovereign pays the penalty of greatness more severely than the Holy Father. His sanctity dooms him perpetually to solitary meals, except on extraordinary occasions, there being no one on earth sufficiently elevated to sit as an equal at table with him. This is the rule; but a spiritual Pope no doubt finds means occasionally to reconcile his social instincts and rank at the same time. Then, too, every dish must be previously tasted, for fear of poison; an antiquated custom, which at present no one would conceive to have any foundation in necessity. His chambers are coldly splendid. Marbles, paintings, mosaics, and gilding there are in abundance, but the whole arranged with more than the usual chilling aspect of a state palace. His private rooms, no doubt, are more comfortable, but the whole state and circumstance that surround a Pope, so far as the public eye can judge, is one which makes him, in all the relations of personal freedom and enjoyment, a being little to be envied. Each natural instinct and generous impulse is so hedged in with sacred etiquette or pusillanimous fear as to be a torture rather than a pleasure to its possessor. A bad Pope can be personally free only by being a hypocrite; a good Pope is a martyr to a rank which in its daily duties involves a constant contradiction of the simplest principles of Christianity, and is a standing reproach upon common sense.

All access to the Pope is guarded with mysterious care. He has his private chamber-men—not maids—private cooks, sweepers, and domestics of all classes. Besides these, he has his confessor, preacher, chaplains—queer necessities these for the fountain-head of religion—his porters, jesters, poultrymen, and muleteers. These all have rank and appointments in the sacred household, mingling strangely with "monsignori" the secretaries of state and other officials. The private chamberlains who wait in the ante-chambers are clergymen. In imitation of imperial courts, we find cup-bearers, masters of the wardrobe, grand esquires, private chamberlains of the *sword* and *cloak*, who wear the black-spangled dress, the most graceful of all court costumes, and a guard of nobles magnificently uniformed, a section of which attends at divine service in the Pope's *chapel* with drawn *swords*.

Each cardinal and high officer has a little court of his own. When the revenues of Christendom flowed into the papal treasury, it was not difficult to maintain this state and expense; but, now that it falls mainly on the Roman Sacristory, it becomes a burden which Christian humility might consistently seek to lighten. When there exists so numerous a corps of servants, whether of the household or Church, invention must be racked to find employment for them; consequently, we are not surprised to see that during high Church ceremonies—for instance, on Palm Sunday—it requires "a prince, an auditor of the rota, two clerks of the chamber, and two mace-bearers" to present a basin of water to the Pope, in which he washes his hands, while a cardinal dean holds the towel, a senior cardinal priest hands him the incense, which he puts into a censer held by the "senior voter of the signature." Verily, St. Peter could have written all his epistles in much less time than it would have taken him to learn the titles and employments of the household of his successors in the nineteenth century! "In the sacred functions of the altar, when the Pope assists without officiating," says Bishop England, "he selects the officers from a number of names presented by the chapters of each of the three patriarchal basilics, selecting always a *nobleman*, if his other qualifications be equal to those of his associates"—the wisdom of which choice, and its consistency with Christianity, all Republicans can not fail to perceive.

The mode of electing a Pope is curious. The conclave is the assemblage of cardinals for that purpose. They select their own place of meeting, in general choosing simply between the Vatican or Quirinal palaces.

The day after the last day of the funeral ceremonies of a deceased Pope, the mass of the Holy Ghost is repeated with great solemnity, a Latin discourse pronounced, and the procession of cardinals enters the chapel, chanting *Veni Creator.* The bulls concerning the election are read, and the cardinal dean harangues them upon the duties prescribed for the occasion. Each cardinal then takes his place in the conclave,

THE CORPSE OF THE POPE EXPOSED.

that is, retires to his cell, a small room of about twelve feet square, modestly furnished by himself, with his arms over the door. These cells are all alike, upon the same floor, and arranged in galleries. Chimneys are not permitted, warmth being communicated from the neighboring rooms. To make the isolation complete, in winter the windows are all built up, excepting a single pane. In summer the cardinals are permitted to look into the garden.

For the service of each cell there is allowed a secretary and one gentleman, who are obliged to perform the duties of domestics; but as the emoluments are great, consisting of a considerable sum before the conclave, and a distribution of ten thousand crowns by the new Pope after his election, besides certain advantages for their future career, these posts are much sought after by the younger ecclesiastics.

The conclave is allowed also the services of a sacristan, two sub-sacristans, a confessor, four masters of ceremonies, two physicians, an apothecary, three barbers, a mason, a carpenter, and twelve valets, whose livery is violet.

Before the cardinals enter into conclave, should any feel not adequate to the discipline about to be imposed upon them, he is warned to retire. Once in conclave, they are placed in solitary confinement, each in his own cell. Every avenue to the palace is strictly guarded by detachments of soldiers, and each door carefully closed. The only communication from without is by means of small revolving shelves or boxes, like the "*tours*" of foundling hospitals, through which the meals are passed, and also any official communications, but only in the presence and with the approbation of their military guardians. Vocal intercourse is permitted only at certain high apertures in the walls, in Italian, and with raised voices, so that the guards can hear and understand the conversation. The utmost precautions are taken to prevent the inmates of adjoining cells from communicating with each other. If a cardinal become ill, he is permitted to go out, but he can not re-enter his cell during the conclave.

Before the closing of the conclave, a final day is permitted

DINNER DURING THE CONCLAVE.

to the visits and conferences of the cardinals, in the hall arranged for that purpose. These interviews are according to prescribed rules.

All the expenses of the conclave are borne by the Apostolic Chamber. Among these, the meals are not the least. As nothing is done in Rome without a procession, the dinners of the cardinals are served up in the same manner. The order is as follows:

At the head, two footmen with wooden maces.

A valet with the silver.

The gentlemen in service, two by two, bare-headed.

The chief cook, with a napkin on his shoulder.

Cup-bearers and esquires.

Two footmen, carrying upon their shoulders a huge dish-warmer, containing the meats, &c.

Then follow the valets, with wine and fruit in baskets.

Upon arriving at the palace, each cardinal is visited in turn by the procession, and his dinner deposited. But, before this is done, every dish is inspected, lest some letter or message should be concealed within the viands. The bottles and glasses are required to be transparent, and the vases sufficiently shallow to show their depths. With all these precautions, however, diplomatic ingenuity at times contrives to convey hidden communications. The fruits often speak intelligibly for themselves. A truffle has served to baffle a rival combination, and destroy a choice fixed upon for the succeeding day. This species of culinary diplomacy was due, as might be expected, to an embassador of France.

There are four modes of electing the Pope: the "adoration," the "compromise," the "*scrutin*," and the "*accessit*."

The votes are deposited by the cardinals, according to certain prescribed rules, in a chalice placed upon an altar, either in the Sistine Chapel, or one of the same dimensions at the

Quirinal. They are summoned twice a day, at six in the morning and at the same hour of the evening, to deposit their votes. These are carried by themselves on golden plates. Each bulletin containing the vote is carefully sealed, and stamped with some fanciful design known only to the voter, and prepared expressly for his vote. Great care is also taken to disguise the handwriting, so that no external clew to the voter's choice can be detected. This act is preceded by an oath to choose whom they believe the most worthy, and is accompanied by sacred chants. The officers designated by lot to examine the votes, inspect them with the most minute attention and precautions, for fear of fraud. If a cardinal has obtained two thirds of the votes, they are verified by comparing the names of the voters with their chosen devices. Should two thirds of the votes be wanting to one name, the bulletins are burned, and the voting commences anew. The smoke which arises from the chimney attached to the chapel at this hour telegraphs to an expectant crowd without the failure of the vote.

Election by "adoration" is when a cardinal, in giving his vote, goes toward his candidate, proclaiming him the Head of the Church, and is followed by two thirds of the cardinals imitating his example. The "compromise" is when the uncertain suffrages are given to certain members of the conclave from which to elect a Pope. The "scrutin" is the secret ballot. The "accessit" is the last resource for a choice, but as it is seldom resorted to, and I do not clearly comprehend the process myself, I can not give it to my readers. During the examination of the votes by secret ballot, the cardinals say masses upon the six altars of the chapel.

The excessive precautions taken to insure purity of choice betray the extent to which faction and corruption must have intruded into these elections. In times past, the most scandalous scenes have preceded and accompanied the intrigues which, despite the severity of the regulations, find entrance into the holy conclave, splitting it into unholy factions. During the comparatively recent conclave which resulted in the election of Pius VI., the cardinals even proceeded to blows, and their excitement rivaled the worst scenes that have ever occurred in any democratic Congress.

ELECTION OF PIUS THE SIXTH.

After his election, the Pope selects the name by which he

wishes to be known. The Master of Ceremonies then clothes him in the papal vestments, and the cardinals, each in turn, kiss his hands and feet, the Pope giving them upon the right cheek the kiss of peace. They then chant, "Behold the high-priest, pleasing to God, and found just!" The guns of St. Angelo thunder forth a salute, every bell of the city augments the joyous clamor, and drums, trumpets, and timbrels, amid the acclamations of the people—if the election be a popular one—complete the noisy chorus.

After a special adoration in the Sistine Chapel, the Pope seats himself under a red canopy before the grand altar in St. Peter's, where he receives the adoration of the people. This finished, he is borne in grand procession to the palace which he selects for his residence. In the adoration paid to the Pope, enlightened Romanists disclaim, and with justice, no doubt, any act of personal idolatry. But while they render the same forms of homage to a man which we are taught to believe are due only to God, it will be difficult for the mass to discriminate the nice distinction they would make. Their example, at all events, is so much weight in the scale of idolatry, while their motives are far beyond the capacity of ignorant minds to comprehend.

During the interval between the death of one pope and the election of another, the papal functions are administered by an officer called the "Camerlingue," or Cardinal President, of the court of Rome. He holds one of the three keys of the treasure of the Castle of St. Angelo, the dean of the sacred college another, and the Pope the third.

The unity and policy of the papal court is undoubtedly the same in all ages, so far as concerns its claims to temporal and spiritual power. Were it not counteracted by the spirit of the age, there is no reason to believe it would not now assert its authority as distinctly and frankly as in the thirteenth century,

THE POPE BORNE TO HIS RESIDENCE.

in the mandate of Nicholas III., cited in the ninety-sixth distinction of the canon law, viz.:

"It is evident that the Roman pontiff can not be judged of man, because he is God!"

In a bull of Gregory IX., inserted in the Decretals under the title of "Pre-eminence," we read as follows:

"God has made two great lights for the firmament of the universal Church—that is to say, he has instituted two dignities: these are the pontifical authority and the royal power; but that which rules in these days, that is to say, over things spiritual, is the greater, and that which presides over things material the lesser. Therefore all should know that there is as much difference between pontiffs and kings as between the sun and moon. We say that every human creature is subjected to the sovereign pontiff, and that he can (according to the decretal of Innocent III., called the Prebends), in virtue of his full power and sovereign authority, dispose of the natural and divine right."

At this age of the world we may smile at these doctrines. But the spirit which conceived them still exists, though the power then enforced has departed. The haughty ceremonies that accompanied these assumptions of power are yet in full sway, yearly growing in imbecility, as the authority which alone could make them respected becomes more remote. That which once carried with it terrible meaning, has now degenerated into pitiful farce. Spectators now gather to Rome during holy festivals, not to worship or to acknowledge the great head of the Christian Church, but to wonder at the debasing shows proffered, and the haughty magnificence displayed by priests who found their creed on a gospel of humility and love. Should these remarks be construed as uncharitable, I can only add that where religion, as I intend showing, is metamorphosed designedly into a mere spectacle, it must expect to be subjected to the ordinary laws of criticism.

CHAPTER IX.

THE HOLY WEEK AT ROME.—PAPAL CEREMONIES.

THE grand object of the Roman Catholic Church in its observance of the Easter festival, as stated by Bishop England, is "to use the most natural and efficacious mode of so exhibiting to a redeemed race the tragic occurrences of the very catastrophe by which that redemption was effectuated, as to produce deep impressions for their religious improvement," and he hazards the following observation, that "if the multiplication of rites be superstition, then is the God of Sinai its most powerful abettor." Acting upon this view of the inspired word, the Church of Rome combines "music, scenery, action, and poetry" into a grand melodrama to excite those emotions in the minds of its disciples which it substitutes for religion, or, to use the words of its expounder, "to bring the mind to any particular frame," so that "the effect is almost irresistible."

There was a period, doubtless, in the history of Christianity, when certain religious transactions, simply given in a pictorial manner, were not without efficacy in arousing heathen minds to inquiry and interest; but, multiplied and diverted as they have since been from their original purposes, they are now presented to us more as a theatrical resource to sustain and show off priestcraft than as illustrating the truths of the Bible. Yet I would not be understood as asserting that there are no hearts moved, even in this age, to a clearer appreciation of the sublime doctrines which they are intended to illustrate by these subtle appeals to the senses and the imagination. Many

PANTHEON AT ROME.

a simple Romanist bows in adoring faith before image or relic, and arises from his devotion justified before God, as was the poor publican in the Temple who beat his breast and cried, "Have mercy upon me, a miserable sinner," while the skeptical Pharisee, who thanked Heaven that he was not as other men, left with additional sin upon his heart. The sin lies not with those who *believe*, but upon them who *deceive* those that "hunger and thirst after righteousness." If the ceremonies of the Roman Catholic Church, to which I shall allude, are the "bread of life," then is her skirt free from this great wickedness; but if, on the contrary, they confirm mankind in superstition, substituting evanescent emotion for practical piety, and shut the gates of heaven to all except those who bow before their idols and leave their gifts at her shrine, then, indeed, have the enlightened men who have upheld and sanctioned a system so much at variance with the simple precepts of the Gospel and the example of its Author incurred a weighty responsibility.

A fortnight before Easter, the church edifices are all put in mourning, the ornaments generally removed, pictures veiled, and crosses clothed in violet, in token of grief and penance. During this period, the greatest activity prevails in preparations for the coming solemnities. Each church seeks to distinguish itself above its rivals by the splendor of its decorations, its pomp, music, lights, and all those outward appliances to attract the eye, in which the Roman people for upward of two thousand years have been so curious and critical. All the communities of sisters are as busy as so many hives of bees, with the needle, embroidering, sewing, plaiting, bleaching, or repairing the linen of the altar, the damasks and velvet hangings of the churches, and the robes of the priesthood. To them, as to their isolated brothers, the monks, the coming spectacles are an event in their monotonous lives, and they enter upon the work of preparation with all the zest of secular ambition, all striving to exalt the object of their labors before God and man by the splendor of their work. Their degree of success promotes correspondingly the veneration or enthusiasm of the people toward the particular patron saint they thus delight to honor. Consequently, upon the good works of their hands hangs, in no small part, the piety of their congregations, for, as we have seen, their avowed object is to create a powerful impression upon the imagination. The Holy Week comprises the profoundest griefs and the greatest joys of the Church—including, as it does, the crucifixion and resurrection of the Savior. All that human ingenuity and expense can provide to make apparent the one and give eclat to the other, is lavished upon the ceremonies of this festival.

Rome overflows with a gaping, wondering, worshiping, or skeptical multitude. Whatever may be the creed of each individual, or whether of no creed at all, the entire mass come up to gaze upon the show. Albano, Frascati, Tivoli, and all the neighboring towns, pour in their picturesque and handsome population by tens of thousands. On a transalpine stranger, no portion of this grand gala makes a more agreeable impression than the variety and beauty of the costumes and races about Rome. Slouched-capped pilgrims, with staves, cockle-shells, and scrips, are scarcer now than a few centuries back, but enough are to be seen to complete the romantic human variety which Rome calls from the four quarters of the globe to witness the pride of her abasement. Every European country sends its representatives, and even the Republicans of America add greatly to the throng.

Rome at no time has much to boast of in the extent and cleanliness of its accommodations. It is a city a century behind all other European capitals in every public convenience except good water, in which—a legacy from imperial Rome—

it is as far ahead of them, possessing fountains and aqueducts sufficient for the wants of a million souls. The result is, that during Holy Week Rome is crowded to an extent that Paris, in its most brilliant fêtes, never realized. Prices are quadrupled; indeed, there is no limit to the demand of a Roman where the necessity is pressing. Every hotel and apartment

CAVALCADE ON PALM SUNDAY.

is crammed at prices which rival those of California when houses were scarcer than golden ingots. Alas for those tardy ones who arrive but a few days before Palm Sunday! They are to be seen anxiously driving from hotel to hotel, and from apartment to apartment, imploring to be "taken in" on any terms, paying for the carriage gold in lieu of silver, and at last content to mount some hundred steps, grimed, one would suppose, with the accumulated filth of centuries, to a dimly-lighted back room, a few feet square, containing little else but an apology for a bed, on which perhaps two or three are to take their slumbers at the rate of ten dollars per night. Such is not a rare experience. Others fare worse and pay less. Some are compelled to pass the night in their carriages. Friends of mine paid a dollar each for the use of chairs at a café until morning—a counter to sleep upon was an unexpected luxury. Others even were compelled to find quarters in towns ten or twelve miles from Rome.

A Roman shop-keeper or landlord is at all times a stolid, proud character, indifferent whether you buy, and careless whether you are accommodated. The former, at times, is too lazy to take down his own wares for a purchaser; the latter does better, but both during Holy Week are sublimely elevated above all personal considerations beyond raising their prices, to swell the stream of cash which is sure to flow in to them, like their own golden Tiber, in a flood. Above all considerations of dirt, punctuality, or even a sufficiency of food, the traveler must take his meals at hotel or café, as he can get them. The table laid, there is a rush of the first comers, who soon leave but a few cold fragments for those whose intuition could not tell them that the table-d'hôte of yesterday, at the fixed hour of seven, was to-day at four. The desperate mob at cafés is amusing. All the world being anxious to arrive at some solemn spectacle at the same moment, they are all equally anxious to breakfast in season. Pell-mell they tumble into the cafés, demanding coffee and toast in a dozen languages in one breath, carrying one forcibly back to the first breakfast scene after the polyglot confusion at the Tower of Babel. The waiter slaps on the table an unwiped cup, and a napkin that has seen a week's hard service. After waiting in an agony of impatience, for fear the Pope will bless the faithful and you be found not among them, and no coffee in sight, you angrily again summon the waiter, who comes when he can. To your emphatic remonstrance he replies, "What would you have, sir? it is Holy Week"—the stereotyped answer to every species of annoyance and extortion to which strangers are subjected during this most unholy of periods, and with which they must be comforted, for none other will be vouchsafed.

To all the principal sights of the Church there are reserved seats or positions, for which tickets are issued in the ratio of about five to one as to accommodation. These are given to the several embassadors in proportion to the number of their applications, which of course greatly exceed the number of tickets they receive for distribution. Hence arises another scramble for these permits to witness the sacred mysteries within the privileged limits. Women are required to go in black and veiled; men in a ball dress or uniform. By a strange anomaly, in all Catholic countries, the *sword* has the preference of entry to all temples of the PRINCE of PEACE. To return to the tickets. A hapless week is the Holy Week for the embassador or banker. He is besieged by notes, flattery, interest, and every weapon, feminine and masculine, to furnish the reqired billets of entry. How to gratify one, and not irritate five whom he can not provide for, is a moral problem our diplomatic Solons and financial Rothschilds are not always successful in solving. However, they do their best, and distribute the papal tickets, a different color for each day, as far as they will go.

Palm Sunday, so called from Christ's triumphal entry into Jerusalem, is the first grand day of the holy series. But preceding this there was formerly a stately cavalcade, when popes and cardinals were better riders than at present; but as it became necessary to tie some of the "eminentissimi," as the cardinals are called, on their steeds, on account of their defective horsemanship, and Pius VII., who succeeded the handsome Pius VI., being an infirm man, the custom was changed. Since then, when the procession passes into the street, the huge papal state-coach is used, in which the Pope follows the man carrying the cross, mounted on a white mule, his Holiness the meanwhile scattering his blessings over the crowd by an incessant twirl of three fingers, reminding one of the favorite Italian game of "morra." This coach, notwithstanding its color, was the special object of hate to the Red Republicans in 1848, who would have destroyed it had they not had more respect for a sacred doll called "the most holy baby," to which it was given for its daily airings.

On Palm Sunday the cardinals pay homage to his Holiness on his throne by going according to precedence, and bowing three times before the Pope—a bow for each member of the Trinity—and then kissing the border of the cope which covers his right hand. The choir commences with the Hosanna of the children, after which come appropriate prayers and chants. The Gospel finished, the second master of ceremonies gives artificial palm-branches to the sacristan, deacon, and subdeacon, who, kneeling before the pontiff, hold them up for his blessing. While the sign of the cross is made over them, a prayer is offered that God will bless all those who will carry them with right sentiments.

It would be impossible as well as unprofitable to describe

THE POPE'S CARRIAGE.

all the etiquette accompanying each religious ceremony of the Holy Week. The programme of the procession for Easter Sunday will serve to show the variety and extent of the sacred household, each member of which has not only his appropriate costume, but his specific amount of kissing, homage, and genuflexions to perform, or to fulfill some petty duty expressly created to give him something to do. No little time, and not a few learned heads, are constantly employed to regulate the numberless questions of duty and precedence, and all the nonsense of bombastic etiquette that naturally find growth in so prolific a soil of folly and absurdity. Thus the Pope reads in broad daylight, by a lighted candle, some sacred lesson which no one can hear.

The cardinals again pay homage, as each receives a palm from the Pope, by kissing the hand that gives it, the palm itself, and the right knee of the holy father. After them, in the order of the procession, follow the different hierarchal ranks down to the mitred abbots, who, with all that succeed them, kiss simply the pontiff's foot. Last of all come the military, and the foreigners of distinction at Rome who are admitted to this honor, each bearing away a palm. This, with the accompanying service, takes up a great deal of time, and is a very tiresome affair. The music of the Pope's choir is the best that Italy can provide, and the procession, seen for the first time in St. Peter's in all its elaborate pageantry, is worth perhaps all the squeezing and wrangling for room which it occasions, to say nothing of the odors arising from an unwashed, uncombed, garlic-fed Roman peasantry. Vast as is St. Peter's—so vast and massive that the same temperature is maintained during summer and winter—the smells arising from foul humanity overpower the fragrant fumes of the numberless censers, and, for days after the great festivals, leave the church in a disagreeable condition.

One of the drollest sights of the Holy Week is to see the Cardinal Grand Penitentiary from his throne dispensing absolution to the crowds that flock to him. He alone can absolve in those cases which the Pope reserves to himself, besides

KISSING THE POPE'S FOOT.

granting dispensation for contravention of civil law, illegitimate births, vows, simony, and every sin or error which, for cause good or bad, the Church takes upon herself to pardon. That pardon for every crime has its price is no fiction in the annals of Rome; not that the traffic in absolution is openly indulged or always abused, but that it is in some cases openly avowed I know, and sermons preached proclaiming the detestable doctrine, and the price attached to the greatest crimes against the law of God. Such a one was heard by a friend of mine in Spain, in which the tariff was distinctly laid down. Good priests of every persuasion will reprobate this evil; but the Church of Rome, from which it sprung, still permits a practice so fruitful in profit to her treasury. The instances of absolution witnessed by myself bore a very ludicrous aspect. A large crowd surrounded the confessional box in which the cardinal sat. Several valets preserved order, and made the

GRANTING ABSOLUTION IN ST. PETER'S.

crowd approach and disappear as rapidly as possible. Some five or six would kneel at once. He touched in silence their heads lightly, and as rapidly as one could count, with the tip of a long brass rod, and the ceremony for them was over. A woman brought up two daughters of six and four years of age. At first he declined putting the rod to their heads; but the children, who evidently had been taught to consider that some mysterious good was connected with the operation, refused to budge. The cardinal at last impatiently gave the elder the required tap; while the younger, who kept bowing and kneeling, was thrust aside unabsolved to make way for fresh sinners. Perhaps he considered her as "one of the little ones" who need no absolution from man.

The interval between Palm Sunday and Wednesday-eve is not without its catalogue of sights to the profane or pious who are moved to attend. But there are enough grand ceremonies to weary both soul and body, without giving heed to the lesser offices of the Holy Week. The great rush is to hear the three Misereres in the Sistine Chapel. The first is on Wednesday. The office is called the *tenebræ*, or darkness; though why, no one knows. At the "epistle side" of the sanctuary there is a large candlestick, surmounted by a triangle, on the ascending sides of which are stuck fourteen yellow candles, with one at the apex. There are various conjectures among the Roman Catholic writers as to what these mourning candles are intended to typify. Some say the Apostles and the Three Maries; others, the patriarchs and prophets; but the plain truth is, that as no one knows any thing about the original meaning of the ceremony, any one has the right to conjecture what he pleases. These lights are gradually put out during the office, and this extinction testifies grief.

The uses of many of the articles that find such conspicuous positions in Roman Catholic worship are an enigma to the most enlightened papists themselves. They are retained because custom has made them venerable, and they add to the show. But the reasons which ecclesiastical ingenuity invents to justify many palpable absurdities are quite worthy of the era which originated the learned discussion as to how many angels could dance at one time on a needle's point. For instance, the large fans, *flabelli*, made of peacocks' feathers, which were originally nothing but fly-brushes, are now exalted into monitors for the Pope. The brushing away of insects from the altar is considered as typical of the "*endeavor to banish the distractions of idle thoughts from the mind of him who approached to offer the holy sacrifice. Being formed of peacocks' feathers, and even now, when eyes are seen in the plumes, it admonishes the Pontiff that a general observation is fixed upon him, and shows the necessity of circumspection in his own conduct.*"

My quotations, when not otherwise mentioned, are from Bishop England's "Explanations of the Ceremonies of the Holy Week." I consider it necessary to mention this, lest some of my readers, in their simplicity, should accuse me of satirizing what I can not commend. I go to Rome to view the Papal Church, because it is there, in the city of its choice and power, that we expect to find it in its purest forms. I quote its doctrines from its own historians and clergy, so that my authorities shall be above impeachment. If either fact or faith appear too strange to be true, reader mine, make a pilgrimage of doubt to the Eternal City to relieve, through the medium of your own eyes and ears, a skepticism excusable, it must be confessed, but without foundation.

Hours before the commencement of the "Mattutino delle Tenebre," as the Italians call this impressive service, the royal staircase of the Vatican, which leads toward the Sistine Chapel, is crowded with the impatient multitude of both sexes who have the right of entry. Until the doors are opened they have

THE SISTINE CHAPEL DURING MASS.

no resource but to remain quiet, forming *queue*, as at the French theatres. But the moment the head of the mass finds itself in motion, there commences a rush and scene of confusion frightful to witness and dangerous to experience. If the salvation of each individual depended upon being first within the chapel, greater and more desperate efforts nature could not make to win that goal. It is no vulgar mob that writhes, pushes, pants, and struggles, like a knot of impaled worms, within those sacred walls. There are there the distinguished of all countries—noblemen and noble ladies—the curious traveler and the pious pilgrim—the delicate invalid, who would die despairingly without hearing those more than mortal notes; and the gallant soldier, whose brilliant uniform gives him precedence over the black veils of women and the dress-coats of men—all push forward in one selfish effort to secure the coveted position within those narrow precincts. In the *mêlée*, the stalwart Swiss guards, that endeavor to control this living torrent into something like order and respect for the sanctuary, are not unfrequently roughly borne back, and obliged to exert no slight violence to disengage themselves. They are often more rude than necessity requires, and I have heard fierce words exchanged, even during the service, between them and visitors whose tempers were not proof against their insolence and roughness. In general, however, they are assiduous to protect the weaker sex, and to keep the two sexes as distinct as possible, for the papal rule, like the Jewish, is, that they shall not mingle during these holy offices. To speak together, whatever may be the necessity, is promptly rebuked by the presiding officers. The ladies are rapidly hustled into their reserved seats. The gentlemen and the superfluous ladies remain standing, wedged firmly together, in the restricted limits below the tribune reserved for royal families and embassadors. I had literally in my arms a lovely English girl, who threatened every moment to faint from the heat and pressure, while, I am quite sure, our double weight was sustained in great part by ladies in our rear. Some do faint, and it is with the greatest difficulty that they are borne out. Dresses are torn and jewels lost as a matter of course. More serious accidents have occurred on these occasions. A gentleman had his leg broken, and a young girl was killed not long since, or rather died from the effects of the injuries she received.

From what I saw, I should say that there is no place equal to the Sistine Chapel for testing what amount of danger, inconvenience, and even rudeness, delicate females will submit to for the gratification of their curiosity. The excitement seems to develop in them a spirit of ferocity toward each other —of course, I refer only to the exceptions to their general amiability—but the curious will observe stout ladies slyly making their way by sticking pins into those in front, and slipping by as they turn to discover the aggressor; others seize hold of gentlemen, or make use of them to aid their progress, as if the idea "delicacy" had become obsolete; while one powerful French girl, who wished the situation of an Italian lady of my acquaintance in front of her, abruptly demanded it. Being respectfully declined, she, by a process well known to schoolboys, knocked the lady's legs from under her by striking her in the hollow of her knees, so that she fell as suddenly as if she had been shot. Before she could recover herself or her presence of mind, her place was gone.

The first portion of the service is the ordinary chant, a long and drowsy performance, including the Lamentations of Jeremiah, severely trying the patience of the standing spectators. As this proceeds, one by one the candles are extinguished, except that which typifies the Virgin Mary, who alone of the household of Christ is supposed, in his hour of trial, to have retained her faith unshaken. As the day declines, the gloom of the chapel, unrelieved except by the hidden lights of the choristers and the soft rays of twilight, becomes exceedingly impressive. The faces of those severely-grand Prophets, and the speaking Sibyls of Michael Angelo, look down with supernatural force from the lofty ceiling, as if from out of the firmament of heaven, while high up on the distant wall, amid the shadows of evening, the awe-struck spectator beholds the terrible outline of the avenging Judge, hurling the damned to endless woe. Beneath, amid the fires of the bottomless pit, grinning devils savagely seize their prey. The Virgin Mother pleads with the stern Son, whose mercy has now turned to justice. Saints and martyrs, bearing the instruments of their earthly tortures, are arising from their graves, and floating upward to the glory that awaits them. At this hour, and with such music subduing the soul to breathless silence, the Last Judgment stands forth as the most awful triumph of earthly art. Human strength at times faints beneath the emotions produced by the combination of such powerful appeals to the fears and sympathies. The chords of the heart and imagination vibrate in unison, and many vainly struggle to suppress their distress as the Miserere proceeds. After pauses of silence which, like utter darkness, seems as if it could be felt, a hundred accordant voices, as one, sue Heaven for pardon to a guilty world, in strains such as human ears might well conceive to arise from penitent spirits; solitary voices of wonderful sweetness and power, in alternate verses, continue the lamentation, all mingling in the last passages, when the full choir again is faintly heard in notes that die away like the expiring wail of lost humanity, but end in one final burst of choral harmony, which sends its thrill through the very soul.

Previous to the Miserere of Allegri, the Pope comes down from his throne, and kneels while two treble voices sing, "Christ was made for us obedient even unto death," and the

Lord's Prayer is silently repeated. After the singing, the Pope reads the closing prayer, and the service is concluded by the choir's imitating the confusion of nature at the death of the Redeemer, and the fear and grief of the attendant soldiers and spectators. The pathos of music is now exhausted; neither art nor sympathy could bear more.

The effect of this service varies, of course, according to individual temperament. Many do not consider it worthy of the fatigue and exertion it requires; but no one would consider Rome as visited unless he had heard the Miserere by the Pope's choir in the Sistine Chapel. It can be heard in perfection nowhere else, because there alone are those wonderful associations of art that contribute so greatly to its effect. There is no accompaniment to the voices.

Holy Thursday is the busiest day of the sacred seven. The mass is, if possible, more tedious than usual. There are endless shiftings of vestments, the yellow candles of the altar are changed for white, and the ornaments covered with white instead of purple, as indicating a less degree of mourning. The bells, and even the clocks, are all tied up until Saturday noon, or after the Resurrection, which is then announced by all the uproar they can make. The Pope blesses the incense which is used to perfume the altar, and then submits to being incensed himself by the senior cardinal priest. This is by no means a pleasant operation, if the incense be very powerful.

The officiating prelates are incensed also in their turn; a rite which strikes one as wholly pagan in its origin and application. The kissing of the robes and toes goes on as usual, but not the kiss of peace, because it is the anniversary of the betrayal of Judas. The Pope, in solemn procession, bareheaded, and with incense burning before him, deposits the body of Christ on the altar in the Sistine Chapel, which is brilliantly illuminated by six hundred wax candles for the occasion. All kneel as he passes. Why the apparent burial should precede the crucifixion is an anomaly that the Church does not explain, except so far as it gives the faithful an opportunity to worship the Holy Wafer. The devotion now displayed is one of the most impressive features of the Roman Catholic faith. No one can enter this beautiful chapel, and behold the multitudes kneeling in silent adoration before the sacrament, without feeling stirred within him the spirit of devotion. It is no graven image that they worship. They believe that before them lies the very flesh and blood of their Savior. They prostrate themselves before their God. Protestants may wonder that faith can be pushed to such a degree; but can those who thus believe do less? I am not one of those who are surprised that the ignorant Roman Catholics resent the indifference and contempt that Protestants too often show to the Holy Sacrament. They overlook neglect of courtesy toward the Pope, and even disrespect to saints and images; but want of reverence to the body of Christ strikes them as the unpardonable offense against the Holy Ghost. The doctrine of transubstantiation is the widest of all the gulfs between the two creeds. Imagine the horror of the Italian landlord when called upon for a dish of pigeons by an Englishman, who could make himself understood only by repeating the name given to the dove in religious processions, viz., *Espirito Santo*—literally, "a dish of the Holy Ghost."

As the papal benediction on Thursday extends only to the city gates, there is no great crowd to receive it. A portion of the Pope's prayer is as follows: "We ask, through the prayers and merits of the blessed Mary, ever virgin, of the blessed John the Baptist, of all the saints," &c.; after finishing which, he showers down "plenary" indulgences by the handful.

I have met very few who knew what an indulgence was. I find the general idea among Roman Catholics to be that the indulgence of the nineteenth century means shortening their time so much in Purgatory. Upon that principle, heaven becomes simply a matter of bargain with the priesthood; the wealthy realizing, no doubt, with them as much difficulty in opening the door as did the rich man spoken of by our Savior. But in the latter case it was the cares of the world that stopped his progress; in the former, it is the tariff of the Church.

The squeeze to see the washing of the feet and feeding of the pilgrims is equal to that to hear the Miserere. Thirteen priests are the selected recipients of this act of papal humility. They are all dressed in loose white gowns, with caps of the same material on their heads. The object of this custom is "to give the Pontiff the opportunity of learning and practicing a lesson of humility." The lesson of humility is studied in the following manner. A *throne* for the Pope is first placed in the hall, with the usual tokens of sovereign rank. A large retinue of nobles and ecclesiastics assist his Holiness. Two hold the Pope's train, a third bears a towel for washing his hands, while two clerks of the chamber aid him in his own ablutions, after his labors on the pilgrims. The pilgrims, alias priests, are seated on a high bench. The right foot, having been previously made most scrupulously clean, is left bare. The Pope changes his uniform for a less splendid one, and, after being duly incensed, a fine cloth, trimmed with lace, is tied upon him. Attended by his master of ceremonies and deacons, he humbly proceeds to the washing. A sub-deacon lifts the foot; the Pontiff kneels, and sprinkles it with water from a silver basin. He then rubs it with the laced cloth, kisses it, and goes on to the next. A nosegay and towel, and a gold and silver medal, are given to each pilgrim. This lesson of humility lasts about two minutes.

Another rush, and the crowd find themselves within the

"*Salla della Tavola*," where the pilgrims are fed. The Pope puts on an apron, pours water on his hands, hurriedly hands the pilgrims a few dishes, which are presented to him by

THE PILGRIMS' DINNER.

kneeling prelates, blesses them, and retires. Thus ends lesson two of humility. The dinner is a good one, and all that the pilgrims can not eat they carry away. When the Pope does not feel in the mood for the latter ceremony, he delegates it to a substitute.

The exhibition of the Cross of Fire, suspended above the tomb of St. Peter, around which burn night and day two hundred silver lamps, has been discontinued for upward of twenty years, owing to the scandalous scenes which took place among the crowd in the church, after its adoration by the Pope and crowned heads then at Rome.

On Good Friday the papal chapel presents its deepest tone of grief. It is stripped bare of carpets and ornaments. The cardinals wear purple stockings, and leave their rings behind them. The lessons are appropriate to the day; but the satisfaction which would otherwise arise in the heart at hearing the offices is wholly lost in the tedium and disgust attendant upon the insipid ceremonies which accompany them. Formerly, the clergy came barefooted; now, only the Pope and some of the superior clergy and cardinals take off their shoes during the Adoration of the Cross, from which the violet covering is removed. The Pope casts his offering, a purse of red damask trimmed with gold, into a silver basin. Then there is a procession to and from the Pauline Chapel. But the chief attractions on this day are the music and sermons at the several churches, which rival each other in their preparations for the *Tre Ore*, the three hours of agony of Christ upon the cross, lasting from twelve to three. This is a religious drama, and, when not exaggerated, by the action and grimaces of the preachers, and the tawdry scenery of the churches to represent Calvary, into a burlesque, is solemn and impressive.

The service of the *Tre Ore* is divided into seven acts, founded upon the seven supposed speeches of Christ upon the cross, at each one of which the Roman Catholics believe that a dagger entered the heart of his mother. She is called, on that

PENITENTS ON GOOD FRIDAY.

account, "Our Lady of the Seven Sorrows," and painted, as is often seen in churches and shrines, with a bloody heart on her breast, with seven daggers stuck around it.

The preacher I heard was a Jesuit, at the church of that order, the most gaudily decorated and richest in Rome. His sermon was decidedly dramatic, both in language and accessories, but much less so than one might expect from the Ro-

A ROMAN PREACHER.

man taste. The style and arguments were admirably calculated to arouse the languid devotion of his flock, who appeared fully impressed with the solemn event they had assembled to commemorate. This immense church was crowded with worshipers.

In the evening I drove to the Hospital of the *Trinitá de Pellegrine*, to witness the washing of the feet and feeding of pilgrims by the nobles of Rome. This immense building has accommodation for five thousand pilgrims, who are here gratuitously fed and lodged for three days during Holy Week. The washing and feeding here was no farce, whatever may have been the motives that induced these acts of humility. Roman gentlemen and nobles, in the garb of domestics, washed and waited upon these dirtiest of all mortals with the utmost zeal and apparent cheerfulness—the bounty being, as I was informed, so many days' indulgence to each.

In the female wards, I was told by the ladies that they saw some of the fairest and noblest of Rome's aristocracy on their knees, scrubbing away at feet that had needed ablution for many weeks previous. At supper they attended them as humbly as if they had been bred to serve, and even the loveliest among them took the filthy babies from their mothers' arms, and nursed them as tenderly as they would have nursed their own, while their hungry mothers ate.

On this evening there is a performance at some of the churches of another manner of mortifying the flesh. This is the self-flagellation of penitents, who are clad in vestments of coarse dark cloth, which completely disguises them, leaving only holes for their eyes. After an exhortation from a friar, the lights are extinguished and scourges distributed. Of course, it is impossible to tell how far the ceremony is a farce or penance. At all events, the scourging and wailing sound like earnest, while the dismal chanting of the monks does not tend to enliven the scene, which lasts about half an hour, when all depart with the satisfaction of having performed a meritorious action.

The ceremonies of Saturday attract the attention of few besides the actors. They are numerous, however, and, as a matter of curiosity, to see how far the Church of Rome carries its typical mysteries, worth noticing. The converted Jews, if any —Turks are considered a greater glory—are baptized early in the morning at St. John in Lateran. After this, an ordination of priests, in which several long hours are occupied in rites sufficiently puerile and wearisome to make one doubt the sanity of the performers. At the Sistine Chapel we have the blessing of the fire and incense, and the blessing of the paschal candle, by a deacon dressed in white, to represent the angel announcing the resurrection. This candle is of immense size, and pierced with five holes in the form of a cross, to represent the five principal wounds of our Saviour. Five grains of incense are placed in these holes, as emblematic of embalming. At this season, too, there is a general blessing and sprinkling of holy water in private houses by priests, who gratefully receive the current coin of the realm in return for their efficacious benedictions. Even the brutes come in for a share of this pious labor, but this is somewhat later, on the anniversary of their guardian Saint Anthony. After each sprinkling from the sacred brush, the priest repeats in Latin, "By the intercession of the blessed Anthony, these animals are delivered from evil, in the name of the Father, Son, and Holy Ghost. Amen!"

Easter Sunday is the grandest festival of the year. To celebrate the Resurrection, the Roman Church puts on all her pomp and pageantry. The Pope performs high mass at St. Peter's. This occurs but on two other festivals during the year, viz., Christmas, and St. Peter's and St. Paul's day. The

BLESSING ANIMALS.

order and magnitude of the procession I have already given. Those who have seen it have beheld the accumulated magnificence and solemnity of the Roman Catholic ritual. The courtly splendor of all other earthly sovereigns pales before the dazzling display of the wealth and magnificence of the successor of the poor fisherman of Judea. As soon as the

Pope appears, borne upon the shoulders of his throne-carriers, the choristers intone, in Latin, "Thou art Peter, and upon this rock I build my Church, and the gates of Hell shall not prevail against it." The deep-toned bells chime in with their welcome. In the church are drawn up the grenadiers, national guards, and soldiers of the capital, whose bands swell the notes of gratulation to the self-styled representative of the Apostle, and Christ's Vicar on Earth. For those who admit the title, this homage is appropriate; but to those whose ideas of religion are based on the humility and spirituality of the true Christian character, and the equality of men before God, this ostentation appears strangely anomalous.

One ceremony occurs during this mass which attests strongly the former depravity and present fears of the Roman court. The greatest caution is used to prevent the Holy Father from being *poisoned while he partakes of the sacrament.* The sacred vessels are carried to a credence-table, called the Pope's, on the Gospel side of the altar. During the chanting of the creed, the vessels are taken there and carefully washed. The keeper of the cellar first *drinks* some of the wine and water brought for this ablution. When the Pope goes to the altar to partake of the body and blood of Christ, the sacristan eats in his presence a portion of the bread provided, and tastes the wine, after which the Pope does not hesitate to follow his example. How strange a comment upon the doctrine of transubstantiation, to believe that poison and the actual presence of Divinity can co-exist in the same substances!

Two junior cardinal deacons stand on each side of the altar, representing the angels who were at the sepulchre. During the service the *fingers* of the Pope are *purified* with much ceremony, and when the mitre is placed on his head his entire hands are washed. He then goes to the altar and concludes the mass.

No sooner is mass finished than the immense multitude pours out of St. Peter's into the piazza in front, where the mil-

ST. PETER'S.

itary are all drawn up, to witness the ceremony of the benediction. This time it is said to extend over the entire world. On this occasion the whole French garrison were under arms, besides the Roman troops. The two made a fine military show, and to my eye furnished the greater proportion of the spectators. Even the *contadini*, the country subjects of the Pope, who are in general devoted, if not to the Pope, to the ceremonies of the Church, did not appear in their usual numbers. There were English and other foreigners by thousands. All gazed anxiously up to the balcony, where the Holy Father was to appear. After considerable delay he made his appearance, and in an audible prayer invoked the usual blessing. The soldiers knelt, in obedience to the order of their superiors. What must have been the feelings of those disciplined republicans of skeptical France, thus humiliated before an old man whose very existence in Rome was owing to their arms, it is easy to conceive. I noticed that very few of the Romans knelt, and many seemed careless about uncovering their heads. The ceremony had evidently outlived its spirit, or else Pius IX. was unloved in his own capital.

The illumination of St. Peter's and the fireworks have been too often described to require farther allusion. They are the terminating and most agreeable of the spectacles of the Holy Week. St. Peter's shines out from the surrounding darkness a colossal beacon of light; thousands of globes and stars mark its giant outline in vivid brightness, while high above all rises the illuminated cross, piercing with its bright rays the dark shadows of night. Were the heads of the Roman Church thus to illumine the moral darkness of the world, she should remain for all time as conspicuous for her piety as St. Peter's appears from artificial splendor. While thinking thus, as I gazed on the beautiful spectacle, a bright star came twinkling out of the cloudy obscurity, and took its place high and serene in the firmament, shedding its soft and lucid light in steady rays through the heavens. This was now, as in the infancy of Christianity, its true emblem. How utterly insignificant the borrowed brilliancy of the church appeared beside this single star! Could we see the nightly beauties of the universe, which Providence has made as free to the eye as air to the lungs, rarely as man exhibits his counterfeit glories, we should turn in disgust from their puny attractions, to wonder and worship at the greatness and goodness of the Author of so celestial a vision. But we gaze in rapture on our own pigmy efforts, and coldly look upon the marvels of nature as the mere truisms of physics.

I am not at all disposed to find fault with the Roman government for celebrating after this manner—I allude to the fireworks and illumination—the resurrection of our Savior. A Christian government does wisely to exalt its Author, and celebrate his mission with all possible magnificence. It keeps alive the principles of its origin, and periodically recalls to public mind the memory of events unequaled in their consequences by any others in the history of the human race. In this respect, therefore, I think the Roman Church wise; but in most others connected with the Holy Week I consider her as degrading mankind and violating the very principles to which she falsely appeals for sanction. As yet we are only upon the threshold of her profitless mummeries. I shall barely open the door to a few of the principal falsities with which she deludes the world, and leave my readers, who may differ from me in sentiment, to explore farther, if they will, for their own edification.

CHAPTER X.

THE HOLY WEEK AT ROME.—MACHINERY AND MIRACLES OF PAPACY.

The ceremonies and labors of the Holy Week, one would suppose, were sufficient for the wants of any clergy for the entire year. Not so with the Roman Church. She proclaims and enforces the observance of some seventy distinct *festas*, or sacred days, besides Sundays. Nearly a third of the year is consecrated to idleness, which vice is exalted to the rank of a virtue. I would exempt from this waste of time the periods properly belonging to divine worship, which, of course, are comprised within the duties of all men. But the Pope absolutely inculcates doing nothing on holidays, and denounces heavy penalties on the disobedient. The laboring classes, consequently, whose average daily gains are between a quarter and a half of a dollar, are compelled to abstain from all work, and take part in religious processions, or in witnessing superstitious rites of a character to confirm their own predilections. Without the physical labors which these holidays force upon the clergy, they would be almost as idle as the populace themselves. But the dressings and undressings, the genuflexions, and swinging of censers, the marching and countermarching, the collection of alms, bearing of images, carrying of candles, ringing of bells, and all the complicated and ingenious inventions of ecclesiastical brains to keep their hands from being in the service of the devil—all these find the clergy in some degree of employment, while their flocks are left to idly gape over their stereotyped displays, or find such

MONKS.

amusements as they can; in short, to do any thing but conform to the divine injunction, "Six days shalt thou labor." The Church, however, discountenances irregular pleasures, and does its best, consistently with its own example, to keep the people in a moral vein. It endeavors to reconcile idleness with goodness, and superstition with religion; unions, like all unnatural ones, prolific only in imbecility and disorder.

The weightiest objection to the absurd spectacles of the Church, sanctioned by the Pope and high clergy, is, that they cultivate credulity and ignorance among the people, and teach them to rely more upon the blessings and supernatural care of deceased saints than upon their own exertions or enterprise in providing against the ordinary contingencies of life. Hence human prudence is superseded by a puerile fatalism, equally remote from the dignified practice and sublime doctrine of Islamism. The Roman people, in particular, believe that the special business of the saints in Paradise is to watch over their daily occupations, and to interest themselves in the success of all their pursuits, good, bad, or indifferent. When an accident occurs to man, beast, or vehicle, they do not hesitate to rate their patron saint roundly and profanely for his negligence. If, on the contrary, they escape an evil, they hasten to offer a candle, or some gift in proportion to their means, to his or her shrine, as the sex may be.

Among the many ceremonies my curiosity has prompted me to witness, none more wearisome ever fell to my lot than the midnight mass of Christmas eve. Prompted by the expectation of good music, I went to the church of the "Annunciata" at Florence, at the usual hour, about ten o'clock. The body of the church was crammed with the unwashed multitude. Behind the choir were admitted the strangers and fashionables. During the dark and dismal service, gay conversation, flirting, and promenading were going on. It was more like the saloon of a theatre than the house of God. At midnight a gaudily-dressed doll was held up for the devotion of the congregation, and the ceremony was concluded.

The Roman clergy assemble five times a year in general processions. The different orders of monks, being very properly of the least consideration in the Church, march first. Thirty-seven communities appear under the banners of their

A ROMAN PROCESSION.

several saints, twenty march under the flag of the Holy Sacrament, and eight others appear under different ensigns, of which one is the banner of Death. They turn out to the number of five or six thousand, when in full ranks, of priests, monks, and clerks.

The most splendid of these processions is that of "Corpus Domini," or the Fête of God. In this, the Pope and all the civil and ecclesiastical dignitaries of Rome, and the military, take part. Embassadors, governors, senators, princes, and nobles of every degree, humbly carrying candles, appear in this

PROCESSION OF CORPUS DOMINI.

colossal cortège. The pope is borne on his pontifical litter, high above the heads of all, surrounded by his court, and carrying in his hands the holy sacrament, in vessels radiant with gold and jewels, before which the spectators prostrate themselves humbly and uncovered, as the procession slowly passes through the different quarters of Rome, on its way to and from St. Peter's.

The doctrine and abuses of relics are among the worst corruptions of the Roman Church. As they are sources of incalculable pecuniary profit, they will be among the slowest and most difficult of reformation. Doubtless the Church of Rome possesses, among its hordes of false relics, some true memorials of departed saints. It is even possible, though not probable, that St. Helena did put her in possession of some of the genuine implements used at the crucifixion. Grant this much, even, but hold her to her own doctrine in regard to them, viz., "*That in religion relics are to be held in veneration corresponding to that in which tokens of affection and memorials of endearment are preserved in well-regulated and virtuous families.*" This is right and proper.

But what use does the Church of Rome make of them? That she considers them of primary importance in her service is evident from the fact that she constitutes a congregation of relics, composed of six cardinals and four prelates, whose functions are to examine and classify the remains of ancient martyrs found in the catacombs of Rome and elsewhere. Their quarry is a large one, for already there have been taken from this necropolis the remains of one hundred and seventy thousand victims—of death surely, if not of martyrdom—most of which have passed muster as genuine relics, comforting to the faith of the living and profitable to the treasury of the Church. Unfortunately, the science of the priestly inspectors has not always been equal to their zeal, and the remains of animals have been sometimes confounded with those of the early Christians. But, as a close inspection of relics is seldom allowed, distance would lend as much spiritual efficacy to the bone of an ass as of a martyr, provided faith was equal to the sacred recognition.

St. Peter's boasts the possession of the most precious of the sacred relics. These consist of a piece of the true cross, a portion of the spear-head which pierced the side of Christ, a bit of the sponge, and the true imprint of the Savior's face upon the handkerchief of St. Veronica, which, according to Roman Catholic tradition, she lent to Christ to wipe the sweat from his brow while staggering under the weight of the cross. No good Catholic presumes to doubt the authenticity of these relics. They are exhibited to the people during Holy Week, all incased in gold and precious stones, from one of the raised galleries above the tomb of St. Peter, nearly one hundred feet above their heads, at which distance it is impossible to distinguish one object from another. Besides these, there are eleven columns from the temple of Jerusalem, and the one against which Jesus leaned when disputing with the doctors. This is carefully concealed from general sight in one of the chapels, but I contrived to get in and lean against the same spot—I must confess it, not without experiencing a sensation of pious gratification altogether remote from skepticism—so far as the iron grating with which it is jealously encircled would permit.

St. Peter's has also a chapel specially devoted to the arms, legs, fingers, heads, and other portions of saints, the list of which hangs on the outside, and is not a very attractive invitation to enter to sensitive stomachs.

There is scarcely a Roman Catholic Church in Europe that does not possess a Golgotha of relics—disgusting objects, mostly defeating their own claims to authenticity by their impossible pretensions and absurd traditions, the belief in which is far more diligently inculcated than in the saving doctrines of

ADORATION OF RELICS.

Scripture. The latter would put an end to these stupid impostures, but the former exalt the reputation of the several churches, and bring much treasure into their coffers. In fact, they are ecclesiastical museums, for which heretics pay to gratify their curiosity, and the faithful to adore, and gain the promised indulgences at the expense of their gifts left upon the altars. I have seen thousands flock around a miserable old Byzantine painting of the Virgin, of the twelfth century, scrupulously veiled in order to increase the mystery, except on certain holidays, when the public are admitted to kiss the silver railing of the altar for the purpose of devoutly leaving a sum of money with the priest for the edifying privilege. Ghastly heads and remains of martyrs, in silver or gold cases, are periodically exposed to similar adoration in the principal churches, or brought out in solemn procession on the occasion of drought or some public calamity, to induce the defunct possessor to intercede with God, or more generally the Virgin Mary, to arrest the evil. Who can view these imbecilities, and not hold the Roman clergy accountable for withholding the bread of life, and substituting pageantry and superstitions not one whit superior to the classical paganism they supplanted? It is true that the early popes, despairing to abolish altogether the heathen customs of Rome, ingrafted many of the ceremonies of the expiring ritual into their own. But their successors have allowed fifteen centuries to pass without a single endeavor to purify their religion from the corrupting influences which their predecessors deplored, and submitted to only from unavoidable necessity. Forms and names have been changed, but Rome of the nineteenth century, under a Christian pontiff and a learned clergy, in point of superstition and credulity, is as essentially pagan as in the days of Augustus. The miracles of ancient Rome, so prolific in the pages of Livy, are every whit as credible as those which figure in the annals of the Church. When devotion flags, or money fails to pour abundantly in at a certain shrine, a miracle is sure to ensue. Curiosity is excited, superstition stimulated, and the needed excitement produced. My readers will, I trust, agree with me, when they have visited a few of these idolatrous shrines, that the sooner they are swept from the earth, the better will become the temporal and eternal prospects of mankind.

In the church of the "Ara Cœli," which occupies the site of the temple of the Capitoline Jupiter, there is preserved a wretchedly-carved wooden doll, loaded with an incalculable amount of precious jewels. This doll belongs to the monks, and brings them in yearly a revenue which enriches them all. It is called the "Most Holy Baby," and the most diligent exertions are made to keep alive faith in its sovereign virtues.

THE MOST HOLY BABY.

Every stranger visits it, as a matter of course, and pays the accustomed fee; but its chief revenue is from the sick. It has a larger practice than any physician in Rome. As soon as a Roman despairs of his life or his doctor, he sends for the "Most Holy Baby," which is brought in great state. If he die, the baby has called him, which is right; if he get well, the baby has cured him, which is right also. In either case the monks receive their fee. It is so rich that it has a handsome carriage of its own. Several times a year this idol is exposed to the adoration of the crowd, no other having so great a reputation in Rome

An old marble staircase, which had seen much service in the ancient Lateran Palace, has contrived to gather to itself an astonishing reputation for sanctity. Sixtus V. was the Pope who brought it into notice. In rebuilding the palace, he discovered that it was the same staircase on which Christ descended when leaving the judgment-seat of Pilate. Henceforth it became most holy, and endowed with incalculable virtues. Sixtus inclosed it in a building opposite the church of St. John in Lateran, and provided lateral staircases for descent and for profane feet. Several thousand years' indulgence were promised to every one who made the ascent on his knees, repeating at each step Paternosters and Ave Marias. Go now when you will, and it will be found occupied by sinners, male and female, nobles and beggars, side by side, painfully winning their way to the promised indulgence. At the bottom there is always on duty a monk, who demands alms, and at the top a contribution plate beside a crucifix, into which the pilgrims deposit their offerings while reverently kissing and repeating a prayer over each wound of Christ. So great is the concourse, that wooden steps have been placed over the stones, to protect them from the pious wear. After all, the pilgrims do not touch the veritable steps, a fact which they

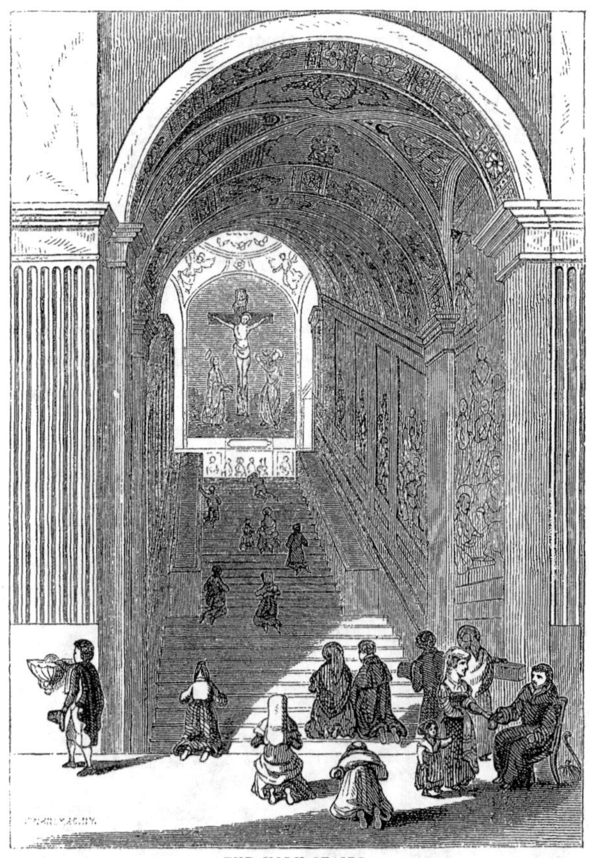

THE HOLY STAIRS.

seem entirely to overlook, but which one would suppose would detract somewhat from the promised blessings. In my forgetfulness of its sanctity, I began to ascend it on my feet, but the attendant priest requested me to desist. While I paused, some French soldiers went by with a wonderful celerity on their knees, evidently in a profane race to see who would first arrive at the top.

The Church contains a wonderful assortment of relics: the heads of St. Peter and St. Paul, as usual in jeweled cases of silver; a lock of the Virgin Mary's hair, and a fragment of one of her petticoats; some blood of Christ; the table at which he ate the Last Supper—a small affair, suitable for a café *tête-à-tête*, but never intended for thirteen, an anomaly the relic manufacturers impolitically overlooked. Then there are the rods of Moses and Aaron, with a portion of the Ark of the Covenant; the pillar off which the cock crew when Peter denied Christ, and other wonders surpassing belief.

The relics of the Virgin Mary in ecclesiastical museums are surprisingly numerous, while Joseph appears to have left no memorials behind him. At Loretto we have her entire house,

VOWS TO THE VIRGIN.

transported by angels from the Holy Land. Were all her property restored to it, one might get a tolerable insight into her domestic affairs; for we have quite a wardrobe of hers remaining, besides the cradle of the infant Jesus, preserved at the church of Santa Maria Maggiore, in total forgetfulness of the scriptural fact that the new-born babe was laid in a manger.

I will give a list of some of the most noted relics preserved at different shrines, to show what the Church of Rome exhibits instead of the simple Word of God. They exist in such profusion wherever the Roman Catholic priesthood have sway, that it is really difficult to select a collection which shall embrace the absurdities of all, as their number and variety are legion. One of the richest and most select, however, of these shrines is that of St. Mark's, at Venice. It is open at certain hours to the public for a stated fee. The wealth in precious metals and jewels lavished upon the vessels and tabernacles which contain these ghastly remains is incalculable. Were all the idle and idolatrous treasure of Italy actively employed for the benefit of the living, it would give her schools throughout her territory, or connect it by a network of railways; in either case affording education or work to her starving multitudes.

The sacristan of St. Mark's ushered me into the sanctuary where its treasures are kept. At the first glance one would suppose he had fallen into Aladdin's cave, so brightly shone the gold and silver, gleaming with rare and costly stones. Closer inspection, however, betrayed the contents of the glass vials in which most of them were preserved. There were arm and leg bones without number; fragments of morbid humanity, of every shape and variety, labeled "a piece of Saint" this or Saintess that—precious to the faith of the believing, it is devoutly to be hoped, but repulsive to doubting eyes. The taste of Roman Catholics for the morbidly horrible in death's doings is strangely general. At Notre Dame, in Paris, they showed me the spine of the late archbishop, which had been dissected from his corpse to be exhibited to his late parishioners.

The relics at St. Mark's that I particularly noticed were as follows:

The Thumb of St. Mark.

A lock of the Virgin's Hair, bright auburn, looking as if recently cut from a child's head.

Some of the Blood of Christ.

Some of the Earth soaked with it.

A piece of his Garment without a seam.

Four pieces of the True Cross, one of which belonged to the Empress Irene of Constantinople.

One Nail of the True Cross. (There is another at Paris, one at Milan, one at Rome, and the iron crown of Lombardy is said also to have been made of them.)

Two of the Thorns of the Crown.

A Rib of St. Peter.

A Rib of St. Paul.

A portion of the Skull of St. John the Baptist. (The entire head is preserved at Geneva; but duplicates of saintly remains are no more miraculous than their preservation at all, and do not appear to weaken faith in their authenticity.)

Two of the Stones used at the martyrdom of St. Stephen.

The most remarkable appeal to public credulity is to be found at Cologne, in the well-known collection of the relics of St. Ursula and her eleven thousand virgin companions, all of whom, the Church teaches her disciples to believe, were wantonly massacred by a horde of barbarians, somewhere between the years 237 and 451 of the Christian era, for refusing to submit to their embraces. "He must have an iron head," says our high authority, "who will maintain that this sublime old tradition of Cologne does not merit belief."

Be that as it may, the Church of St. Ursula exhibits to this day, in the so-called "Golden Chamber, admission fixed at thirty cents, for the benefit of the Church," one hundred and seventy skulls, inclosed in velvet cases, overlaid with silver and precious stones. These are arranged on shelves, and grin ghastly upon the spectator from their richly-decorated cases, which contrast horribly in their mock splendor with the empty eye-sockets and high cheek-bones of death. On the head of St. Ursula there is a crown of great value. The attendant monk, as he relates the legend of their death, calls upon the visitor, with great unction, to admire the glossy flaxen hair of the virgin saint, which he is allowed to handle, besides placing his fingers in the cleft skulls of those who came to their deaths by sabre strokes. Most of these skulls bear names, and are thus catalogued:

No. 2. "The Head of St. Etherius, bridegroom of St. Ursula, with the teeth well preserved."

No. 14. "Aurelius, King of Sardinia"—and a large number of bishops, dukes, priests, and soldiers, all numbered, in reckless disregard of their unvirginlike association of sex and employment.

No. 23. "St. Benedicta, Duchess, who led a cohort of the holy legion."

No. 32. "Florentia, Queen."

No. 36. "Florentia, a Princess of Negroes."

No. 50. "A small silver shrine, containing parts of Christ's *rod*."—What rod?

Nos. 55 and 57. "The right Arm and Foot of St. Ursula—her hair-net," etc.

No. 60. (The naïvete of the printed description of this is particularly funny.—"A Water-cruet used at the wedding meal at Cana, brought to Cologne by St. Bruno. An eye-witness, who has been in Cana, assures us that there are only five of these water-pots, and that the sixth he has seen in our Golden Chamber is perfectly like the five other pots." Can we wonder at the simplicity of the flocks, when such is the erudition of the shepherds?

Besides these relics there are six hundred and twelve heads, adorned with golden embroidery, in gilded glass chests.

This church is a Golgotha on a large scale. The walls inclose a solid mass of bones, symmetrically piled for the space of eighty feet in length by ten in height and two in width, which the monks joyfully point out as confirmatory of their legend. As late as the year 1642, some fourteen hundred years after the martyrdom, the liquid blood of St. Ursula was discovered, as fresh as if just shed; but the monks, probably from fear of another discovery, immediately reburied it.

It is a dismal church, full of bones, and skulls, and coffins, and all sorts of quaint pictures of monkish legends, and gloomy architecture. When I left it, darkness had overshadowed all, and my shaven and cowled guide was obliged to light a candle to pilot me out. As we passed a confessional-box, a woman suddenly arose from her knees, and a priest stepped from that silent witness of the heart's burden of grief and sin, and disappeared in the recesses of the tomb-like church. She had just finished her confession; and, with a rapid step and bowed head, passed rapidly by. But what an hour and what a place to select for penitence and absolution! The grim relics of death above, below, and on all sides. Each step disturbed the ashes and repose of a grave. Night lent additional ghastliness to the scene. A lady was with me. She pressed closely to my side, and drew a long breath of relief as we stepped over the gloomy threshold, and found ourselves once more breathing the pure air of heaven.

The most conspicuous object of adoration at Rome is a venerable bronze statue of St. Peter; a sitting figure, so ancient that it is generally asserted to be an old pagan deity, perhaps Jupiter himself, or, at all events, some eminent heathen char-

ADORATION OF THE STATUE OF ST. PETER.

acter, a consul or magistrate, but now transformed by modern cunning into the sacred image of the fisherman-saint.

This is the particular idol which the Pope loves to venerate in public; consequently, all good Catholics follow his example for their souls' sake. The motives of his Holiness possibly are pure and orthodox; but the act itself is idolatry, and, as such, becomes not only a license, but an example to the multitude. On certain festivals the Pope and high dignitaries go to St. Peter's for this purpose, pressing their lips fervently to the brazen toe, and then touching the foot with their chins and foreheads in a most devout manner, greatly to the edification of a countless multitude, who, in their zeal of imitation, rush toward it with a fury that threatens to endanger the stability of the statue itself. At all hours worshipers are seen before this image. The rich and poor, the noble and peasant, infancy and age, kneel and pray before it, never leaving without bestowing the adoring kiss, and pressing the forehead against the consecrated heel. So numerous are their embraces, that it has been found necessary to protect the toe by an additional covering from being entirely worn away. For centuries has this idolatrous worship been performed, not only unrebuked, but sanctioned and ordered by the Roman clergy as a means of salvation.

The degree of devotion which this image excites is very various. It would be amusing, were it not mournful, to witness the daily scenes enacted before it. I have seen an old woman, tottering with age, seize the foot in her hands, and kiss the toe twenty times in rapid succession with all the impetuosity and warmth of a young lover, and leave with an unmistakable expression of pious joy. Mothers press the unwilling lips of babes to the cold metal; ignorant of its efficacy, they cry and shrink from the embrace. Their older brothers and sisters kneel, and lift their tiny hands toward it, as we are taught to do when we say, "Our Father, who art in heaven." Young girls and fashionable mothers in squads approach, bow, take out their laced handkerchiefs, polish the toe clean, and then apply their lips—some devoutly, and others with a hidden laugh, as if nature repudiated the mockery. Old men prostrate themselves before the silent mass of metal as if it were the tabernacle of the "Most High." There is no mistaking their sincerity. The worship, however mistaken, gives them spiritual satisfaction, doubtless far more acceptable before Heaven than the scoffs and jibes of the cold reasoner, who, seeing no religion in this, denies the existence of a Deity altogether.

The spirit of the age extorts, even from the Roman Church in Italy, some concessions to Protestantism. She does not permit, but she shuts her eyes to the fact, that Protestants in Rome, Naples, Florence, and other capitals gather together on Sundays, in "upper chambers" or in humble chapels—to which bells are forbidden—to worship. These isolated meetings, in which religion is reduced to the standard of apostolic simplicity, carry one back to its early history, when, under the more enlightened pagan emperors, all Christians were tacitly allowed thus to meet for prayer and exhortation. Is it not strange that, after eighteen centuries, upon a nominally Christian soil, the same limited privilege only is conceded to Christians by the sovereign pontiff, the Christian head of the Church and state, as then was permitted by a Claudius or Titus, sovereigns and pontiffs of universal heathendom? The Protestants of the first century, in the fourth succeeded to the throne and power. Jupiter was cast aside forever. The Roman Church banished from the earth the grosser crimes and practices of paganism. Mankind owe her much. But she is now in her decrepitude; she is dying out. The worship of St. Peter will be cast aside, in its turn, as an obsolete idea. On its ruins there will arise a purer faith, which, in presenting to man a "Father in heaven," shall stimulate him to progress in virtue and knowledge.

In the mean time, Popery is busy preaching and proselytizing. The ignorant preacher seeks to excite the passions, and not to awaken the understanding of his hearers. The Roman

STREET PREACHING.

is theatrical even in his church. He does not hesitate to recall the crowd from Punch and Judy to the crucifix by exclaiming, as he points to the bleeding Savior, "*Ecco il vero pulcinella!*" "Behold the true Punch!" He knows how to touch the chord of their hearts, for he has made them what they are.

One of her writers spoke thus of souls in Purgatory:

"Imagine that the poor soul has his eyes upon you, and looks with anxiety to see whether you give or refuse. If it perceives that you have your hands in your pocket, it experiences a delight, which augments in proportion as your offering approaches the contribution-box; when the money is held over it, the soul jumps from the flames, and when the gift falls, the soul springs with pleasure. Oh! to procure to those that you love a moment so sweet, to make them taste these delights, if you have not money yourself, borrow of your neighbor, who, if he refuses, will be more culpable than you."

A small sum will buy, at almost any of the churches of Rome, sufficient masses to free a soul from Purgatory for from 3000 to 30,000 years; and it needs but more money to extend the time indefinitely. Hell-fire is not, however, to be bought off. The rich have no difficulty in compounding in this life for any peccadilloes or doctrines that do not affect the supremacy of the Church. The Pope issues, for a consideration, absolution in full for all past or future sins. The poor would be badly off were it not that every where friars in sackcloth, or greasy-looking individuals in long white night-gowns, piously beg through the principal streets—rattling a tin box in the ears of the passers-by—alms for the poor in Purgatory.

Of all the processions of the Roman Church, the final one, which bears its member to his last home, is the most curious and lugubrious. None but the rich can afford this display. The corpse is decked in its most brilliant attire, with its face painted to resemble life, and placed upon an open bier, which is borne through the streets of Rome, followed by as many deputations of friars and monks from the several convents as the family of the deceased can afford to hire. These fall into ranks like so many military companies, bearing crosses and candles, and chanting most dismally at the top of their voices, so that they can be heard long before they are seen. The effect at night from the glare of their torches in the face of the corpse, and the monotonous and mournful notes of the hired mourners, is unequaled by any spectacle I have ever seen of this nature, except the funeral cortèges of the South Sea Islanders, when a whole tribe lift up their voices and wail for a dead chief. There is no cry equal to that for sadness and filling the soul with melancholy. Among the savages, every act is consonant with the sad office. The tears fall to earth, but the wail rises to heaven. In Rome, the mingling of the vanities of life with the realities of death is shocking. I have seen a young female, on an open bier, her cheeks blooming with color, flowers on her head, while she was dressed as it were for a ball, and looking as fresh and rosy as if life still animated her rigid limbs, borne through the streets at night, the torches lighting up with a ghastly hue her beautiful countenance, which seemed as if it only slumbered, while the rain poured in torrents on her lifeless form. The wetted priests had ceased their chant, and hurried along at a rapid pace to finish their job. Few strangers would have supposed it a funeral, and fewer still that that lovely corpse was not a waxen image. But it was unmistakable death on one of its saddest errands.

A ROMAN FUNERAL.

CHAPTER XI.

EFFECTS OF ROMANISM ON SOCIETY.

I HAVE universally found that the difference in the relative prosperity of the inhabitants of Catholic and Protestant countries was in ratio to the degree in which the Holy Father would consider the former faithful and the latter heretical. This has indeed become a trite observation among travelers of both religions. But no less a writer than the Abbé Lamennais denies its truth, and instances for his authority the very countries which Protestants claim as their own evidence. England, Sweden, and Protestant Germany, according to him, are given over to irreligion, licentiousness, and political turmoil; while those countries that repose under the shadow of the Holy See are stable in their institutions and united in their faith. A monk of St. Bernard, in conversation with me on the extent and progress of the United States, acknowledged that we were indeed a great nation physically; but, said he, "what a pity it is you have no religion. You will soon perish."

Such is the general sentiment among rigid Catholics. They can not conceive how good morals, prosperity, a wise government, or salvation can exist independent of papal authority. To secure its supremacy, they are ever ready to trample upon those rights which we believe to be essential to human progress. Liberty of press and conscience, and the separation of civil and religious government, they consider equivalent to anarchy and atheism. The very enterprise, toleration, and freedom of thought which are developed by our political institutions, and which we fondly conceive to be the fruits of our righteousness, are, in their eyes, so many witnesses of our corruption and infidelity. With them, absolution, or centring faith and power in the Roman Church, is the "one thing needful" for humanity. This accomplished, they close their view to all farther comparison; or if by chance they look abroad, and the wide gulf between the wealth, comforts, intelligence, and energy of Catholic and Protestant states is too obvious not to be acknowledged, they class the latter among those who, in gaining the whole world, are losing their own souls.

Believing, as we do, that the possession of the good things of this earth proceeds mainly from those qualities that heap up most treasure in heaven—or, in other words, that virtue and vice, whether of the individual or nation, have their appointed rewards and punishments in this life as well as in that to come—we consider it a fair rule to judge papal rule by its fruits. In one Swiss canton we find no beggars, universal thrift, cleanliness, and enterprise; in another, beggary, poverty, dirt, and general distress. The one is Protestant, and the other Catholic.

But as Protestantism predominates in Switzerland, the contrasts are not so striking as between those Catholic countries which are exclusively the religious property of the Roman See, and England, Prussia, and the United States, where Protestantism, although enforcing toleration, sways or influences the entire population. France is in a transition state, a chaos of atheism, bigotry, and sentiment. Its shop-keepers, in mingled devotion and blasphemy, scarce knowing themselves which impulse predominates, place over their doors, "*La Grace de Dieu*" (the Grace of God), as a sign to attract custom, as may be seen in the street St. Roch, at Paris. The Spaniards call a fighting vessel the "Most Holy Trinity;" and the Romans name a bank "The Holy Ghost;" but these names are given in sincerity and solemnity. France has grown prosperous and strong in proportion as she has become tolerant and free from the control of Rome; while Italy and Spain, the beloved of the Church, are filled from one extremity to another, in proportion as they are steeped in Romanism, with indolence, superstition, beggary, and their concomitant vices. If, then, wherever Romanism is omnipotent we perceive these results, it is natural to infer that they follow the relation of cause and effect.

My inquiries relate to Italy, and chiefly to Rome. Throughout the peninsula, except where the new-born liberality of Piedmont stimulates, or the iron hand of Austria, as in Lombardy, crushes, we find *indolence* the national characteristic. The Church encourages this parent of vice by appropriating more than a quarter of the year to festivals, on which all labor is forbidden and amusements encouraged. The vacations of the schools, on this account alone, are so numerous, that the general ignorance ceases to be a wonder. Undoubtedly many of the holidays originated in the desire to relieve overtaxed labor, and recall the untaught mind to sentiments of religion; but, during so many centuries, saints have so rapidly increased as to threaten to entirely monopolize the time of the living. "Let the dead bury their dead," has a pointed moral in Italy in the present age.

Another cause of indolence are the fetters imposed on knowledge. There are numerous primary schools, it is true. Rome alone possesses three hundred and seventy-two, which receive about fourteen thousand children of both sexes. Throughout the country they exist gratuitously; but, besides the simplest elements of instruction, they, as well as the universities, are made subordinate to papacy. The instructors, in general, are priests. The Church Catechism is a text-book. All knowledge that tends to expand the mind, liberalize ideas,

AN ITALIAN HOLIDAY.

or develop physical energy unsuited to the theory of absolutism, is rigorously tabooed. Their intent is not to make citizens, but to make subjects—to train disciples, and not masters. Catholic teachers are free to receive Protestant children, but a Protestant teacher is forbidden to receive a Catholic pupil. Indeed, it is with difficulty that Protestant parents can educate their children, unless they submit to the requisitions of the priesthood. Even the Catholic principal of the best institution in Tuscany, a Frenchman, has with difficulty, by the interference of his embassador, been allowed to continue his school, because the authorities conceived that he was bringing up his pupils to be "*too manly.*" They even wished to exile him from the country.

The field of knowledge being thus limited, enterprise is proportionally so, so that the educated, who have means, become in general effeminate idlers and corrupt in morals, while the poorer sort obtain some nominal office under government at one or two shillings per day, or else try their fortunes in the few and in general despised branches of commerce left to their option, sufficiently unfettered as to admit of hope. In America we can not realize the extent of the restrictions to personal freedom, even in the commonest concerns of life, which are the lot of Italians. If you are living on the sea-shore, you are denied the use of a boat unless as a licensed fisherman. Each city has its custom-house. I have seen a carriage stopped at the gates, and a penny's worth of cake, which a little girl held in her hand to eat, taken and taxed the smallest copper coin—equal to a *mill*—for which a receipt was regularly made out and given before the carriage could enter. The poor are unmercifully fleeced at every *gabelle*, while the rich can carry loads of merchandise, unopened, in their trunks from one end of Italy to another, for a bribe of fifty cents given at each custom-house.

From Rome I have gone by land to Naples, thence through some of the northern states of Italy, and back to Florence, and never once opened a carriage-load of trunks. The gift was expected, as a matter of course ; but for the officers to do their duty, that was quite another affair. The system is seen in its greatest corruption in the Neapolitan kingdom. At every ten miles or so the traveler comes to a *dogana.* The soldiers stop the carriage. The ladies are requested to alight, and the gentlemen are ushered into an upper room, where, in solemn dignity, sit the officials, who become prolix upon the necessity of a strict examination of the baggage. Should you, in your innocence, offer the keys, they speak more to the point, and at last plainly say that it will save both trouble and expense for you to give them a fee. Otherwise they will be sure to find something contraband. If you hand a *Napoleon*, they look astonished at your meanness, and shake their heads, and say this will never do. They would do the same if it were a shilling. An Italian official must always be *twice* paid. The smallest additional gratuity settles the difficulty; and with a profusion of bows and good wishes, you think you are ready to proceed. Descending the stairs, your mistake is at once rectified. First comes the officer of the guard for his gratuity; next, the corporal; next, the soldiers, each of whom swears he has been your special guard—that is, he has invited himself to a ride on your box for a mile or so; and, lastly, the *facchini*, or porters, the most extortionate of all, who claim high pay for *not* taking your trunks off. This is all done amid a throng of beggars and thieves, who pick your pockets or steal from the carriage as opportunity offers, at the same time stunning heaven with cries for charity, or calling upon the Madonna to pass to your credit above the coppers you have distributed among them below.

A little farther on occurs a similar scene at a so-called passport-office. I have had money, with which I was paying a porter, snatched from my hand in the streets of Naples by a sentinel on duty, and no one thought it strange. Go where you will in this kingdom, and you find a similar system of organized robbery, which makes one almost regret the good old days of banditti, when novelty and excitement added zest to the adventure; but now it is barefaced extortion, disgusting wrangling, and inevitable pillage. Formerly there was a chance of escape—now none. If you refuse to pay, your baggage remains untouched, but you are not allowed to proceed. The same corruption extends through all classes, with, of course, some honorable exceptions. The King of Naples is well known as the chief of the lazzaroni. Hats, handkerchiefs, and sundries are not always safe at an Italian ball, or among even what may be considered a genteel crowd. These peccadilloes, with lying and cheating, so common among even the better classes, bespeak a defective moral education, and find their solution in great measure in the confessional, which acts as a safety-valve to the conscience, a little money or trifling penance securing indulgence or absolution, until at last habit destroys the sense of sin and shame altogether.

In France, lies are expected as a matter of course. Among the ladies they pass under the softened expression of "*broder*" (to romance); with gentlemen, more vulgarly, "*blaguer*" (to fib); but both practice the vice either to please or to add piquancy to scandalous gossip, but seldom from baser motives. They so love to exaggerate, that their daily newspapers are universally dated *a day in advance;* even *Galignani* has been compelled to follow their example, to do away with the charge that he did not give the *latest* news.

With the Italians, however, lying is a downright vice. Without the courage and gallantry of the French, they lie from fear as well as fun. One need have no greater evidence of the depravity of morals among the higher classes of Italian cities than the universal scandal, which spares no one, and at the same time announces a general corruption inconceivable in similar circles in Protestant countries, or which, if existing, would doom the offenders to social isolation. So the universal suspicion proclaims the equally-spread habit of falsehood. However much courtesy may gild social intercourse, the serpent-head of distrust is seen beneath. Jealousy is equally common; not the more honorable sentiment founded on a regard for chastity, but the meaner spirit begotten of envy. It is really extraordinary to see how ludicrously, not to say inhumanly, domestics and the lower classes will sometimes exhibit this, when one would suppose that common wants would produce common sympathies. As for the former, when it exists, it is chiefly among lovers, and not married couples, whose connubial eye is supposed to be blind. I have heard it remarked, by other ladies, of one of the chief nobility of Tuscany —a wife and mother that it would be well for the country if it possessed more of—"How strange it is that the Duchess ——— contents herself with only her husband." Such is the common sentiment. Matrimonial fidelity is the exception.

Generally speaking, Italian women are untidy, both as housekeepers and in their toilet, when not dressed for their diurnal drive. This arises from indolence and want of good home educations. Convents are the schools of Italian mothers. Slipshod at home, they loiter or doze away their time after the most approved listlessness, indifferent to every thing but appearing well on parade or at the Opera. Their households are neglected, children intrusted to servants, and their work, if any, confined to embroidery, rarely music, and sometimes a little painting or design. Their want of good taste in dress, in which, as a class, they are behind every other civilized nation, is the more strange, as they possess a natural taste for the beautiful in art. When the sex is thus unrefined in person, the mind is upon a par; so that one is not astonished to find a latitude in conversation, and an ignorance on general topics no less lamentable, but combined with an amiability and wit which, under better auspices of government and religion, would raise them to the level of their sex in more favored countries.

The general effeminacy and want of energy of the male sex would astonish any one not versed in their political history for the past two centuries. They weigh like nightmares upon the race; but, without scope for ambition, or even ordinary physical action, what else can be expected?

The care which an Italian dandy takes to preserve himself from the fresh air of heaven, to avoid all exercise, and to develop effeminate beauty, is ludicrously wonderful. There are said to be not over three days of their delicious climate in a year which are all right for an Italian. What with its being too hot or too cold, too dry or too humid, too changeable or too monotonous, the poor weather is little able to satisfy the race on which he lavishes most of his bounties. I was at a seaside watering-place last summer. The water to me, who have lived eight years within the tropics, was uncomfortably warm; but the titled Italians first prepared themselves for their sea-baths by aperient medicines and a course of warm baths, so that their systems should not undergo too great a shock.

To return to schools and ecclesiastical education. One of its chief principles tends to perpetuate a canker which is gnawing at the vitals of Italy. The Church honors beggary in its bosom by sustaining numerous communities of idle monks, who live on the charity and industry of the public. It teaches through all its lessons, even as an article of faith, that alms expiate sins, and that it is necessary to give continually and abundantly to win heaven. Her charity is not of doctrine; she holds none in store for those who deny her faith—they are inevitably damned; but in good works and alms-giving she is lavish, because by them she buys salvation for herself. This abuse of the doctrine of charity is twofold. It makes heaven a matter of barter, and teaches the poor to believe that it is only necessary to wear rags, and live in filth and idleness, for the wealthy to become their debtors; while the excess of good works of the Church provides them with a bed in a hospital when ill, a snug retreat when old, and the gifts of the rich at all times.

"By the sweat of thy brow shalt thou earn thy bread," was the early mandate of Heaven, carrying with it a blessing. The spur of want is, however, the only sure provocative to labor. In Polynesia, and those climates where Providence, as it were, houses and feeds man gratis, the human race remains stationary, never rising above the incipient stages of civilization. What Providence has seen fit to do for certain races of savages, limiting at once their sphere and their supply, Rome, from the days of the Gracchi through its long decadence, sought to do for its turbulent population. But that which God did in wisdom man imitated in folly. The Romans looked upon the state as a parent bound to provide for its offspring. From daily bread, they soon learned to demand their daily oil and wine; then money; and, finally, spectacles and amusements—all gratis. The consequence was, that Rome trained its citizens into a mongrel race of beggars and robbers, resolved to live without labor. They succeeded, but Rome fell; for the curse of idleness was upon it.

The Church succeeded the Empire. To destroy its legacy of corruption was no easy task, but one to which Christianity was equal, had she not herself bowed to idols. Under her imperial patrons she conquered, but did not reform. True, individual virtue, and occasionally able and upright rulers, did much to counteract the prominent heathen vices, which slowly disappeared before the principles of the Gospel; but with all their power they were inadequate, in the hands of papacy, to cleanse the foulest fountain of them all.

The modern Italians—I refer to the lower orders in cities and the great highways, not to the peasantry of the interior, than whom a more kindly, frank, and appreciatory race does not exist—like the ancient Romans, remain a race with outstretched hands. They are beggars. Beggary has become an hereditary vice. Shame, if it ever existed, has long since forsaken the practice. With unblushing falsehood, it is to be seen in the palace and in the hovel, in all its cunning degrees, from the throne of St. Peter's to the veriest wretch that coils his scabby limbs under its shadow. The Church is responsible for much of this, not from design, but from its mistaken doc-

ITALIAN MENDICANTS.

trine, that the greater blessing attends the *giver* than the *worker*. It honors *idleness*, sanctifies the spread palm, and thus impedes *labor*. Sixtus V. labored diligently to arrest this evil. He established work-houses, forbade mendicity under the severest penalties, and sought by energetic measures to extirpate the pest, but in vain. After brief intervals of apparent reform, it reappeared as vicious as ever. The popes forgot that, while weeding with one finger, they were bountifully sowing tares with an open hand. The Romans, of all Italians, have in consequence the most profound aversion to labor. They are listless and silent even in their amusements, varied only by occasional flashes of passion or the excitement of the Carnival.

The rich give abundantly and with indiscriminating generosity, but as frequently from policy or ostentation. Like the old patricians with their clients, they gather about them a numerous horde of idle dependents or professional beggars, who, content in the abasement of receiving gratis their daily subsistence, have ceased to envy the enormous possessions of their lords. Nearly three fifths of the real estate within the walls of Rome belong to less than one hundred families; the remaining two fifths to the hospitals and convents. Consequently, not one in a thousand of the inhabitants of Rome has any fixed property. The Church and government, including the few noble families able to support their state, own all Rome—a state of things sufficient in itself to kill enterprise, and keep the city as it is, a century behind even the other capitals of Italy.

Each city has its characteristic type of beggars, though none is without specimens of all, as they are a wandering race, and move to where charities are most abundant. Rome, however, is the capital of beggardom. In Venice they ply their art in gondolas. In Florence they dress in filthy rags, whine piteously, expose infants, and train bright-eyed young girls to waylay strangers, demanding alms with a pertinacity proof against all repulse, though liable to the penalties of the law; in fact, throughout Tuscany they are the dirtiest and most beggarly set of beggars Italy can show. At the entrance of Vassieux's reading-room, a white-haired old man, bent with age, his clothes hanging together by scanty stitches, is to be seen sitting in one position, and always in the same spot: for years he has been thus; he never speaks, but, as the visitors pass, meekly bows his head—silent if he receives a copper, and equally silent if disappointed. His dumb appeal is not without its fruits. A more expressive image of venerable patience, poverty, and humility the imagination never conceived; and yet, I presume, the old dodge, like Beppo, the legless, roguish king of beggars at Rome, is rich, and able to dower his daughters, if he have any.

In Naples they beg for the fun of it; bright-eyed, merry boys, full of life and activity, or lazzaroni, up to a thousand tricks to excite compassion and gain the trifling sum that will feed them for a week, while for a bed, stone steps or a basket are sufficiently comfortable. But at Naples they are all ready to do any thing but actual labor to unloose your purse-strings; they will lie, cheat, or steal, as temptation offers, and, if it please you, dance, sing, ingulf macaroni, and play the jackanapes after the drollest fashion possible. There is fun and mischief in their begging which half disguises its viciousness.

The begging monks form a class, *sui generis*, under the especial patronage of the Church. They are the greatest eyesores of the community, being in general men of almost brutalized appearance, unctuous and ignorant, and of corresponding habits.

Beggary in Italy is elevated to the rank of an occupation. Men and women are born and die beggars, as their parents before them. This class appears the more numerous, because they have the art of multiplying themselves, as it were, interminably. They are the carrion crows of benevolence, stripping it to its very bones, and scenting their game afar off. There is no end to their disguises and ailments. Proteus-like, they change their rags and diseases to suit every phase of charity. With an ubiquity that savors of marvelousness, they are here, there, and every where at the same instant; now lame, then dropsical, all at once minus an eye, arm, or leg, covered with sores, rheumatic, crippled by age or famished by hunger; surrounded by nursing, starving children; assuming every shape of disease or deformity, with crutches and all the outward appeals to sympathy, they excite terror and disgust as often as charity. There is no disguising their barefaced imposition. If their imperfections are real, the eighteen hospitals of Rome are ample for their relief. But they are like Bedouins in their habits, and prefer the plunder of the public to the legitimate relief of their wants. They are to be seen chiefly on the steps of the churches, when not begging, swearing, card-playing, quarreling, or sleeping from morning to night; *where* they then retire to, no decent mortal may know.

In contrast with these are the genteel beggars; counts and countesses, veiled ladies in black, who haunt theatres; others in gayer costumes, who track you to your homes; all begging under some pretext or other, and grateful for half a dollar, when, from their appearance, you feel ashamed to offer the man an eagle. I have had a well-dressed gentleman approach me in the street, bow with great courtesy, apologize for interrupting me, and then go on to inform me that he was of the higher classes, but had lost his money, and would be thankful for a "*mezzo baiocco*," *half cent!* Ladies, too, so grateful as to kiss your hands for half a dime! The degradation in such cases is too deep for the poverty to be wholly genuine.

The system of asking is universal. At certain palaces where

GENTEEL BEGGAR.

you may have dined, the servants demand of you a fee. Mechanics, tradesmen even, all who serve you in one way or other, with few exceptions, ask for something additional, grateful if they get it, and nevertheless ready to try again if they fail. In the country, on the usual routes of travelers, this nuisance is universal. Children follow the carriage for miles clamoring for coppers, and, if refused, salute your ear with a curse, and "May you break your neck! may the apoplexy seize you!" or some equally welcome catastrophe, winding up with some demoniacal sign indicative of bad luck. I have always noticed that Italians never failed to counteract the spell by some cabalistic movement of the fingers, known only to the initiated.

The usual reference is to the Madonna for your welfare, though all the saints in the calendar are in turn invoked. Sometimes, especially with the Romans and Neapolitans, there is a touch of flattery, or a dubious wish expressed in their demands, extremely naïve, and not always creditable to the morals of either party; as, for instance, "May your handsome Excellency be fortunate in your amours."

Aside from the parasitical and fictitious misery of Italy, there exists a vast amount of real, which even the colossal proportions of Roman Catholic charity are not sufficient to relieve. The mass of the people, in ordinary times, are but scantily supplied with even the most indifferent and least nourishing qualities of food; consequently, in times of scarcity, they are reduced to a condition bordering on absolute starvation. Their chief diet is coarse bread, beans, and chestnuts. Any thing better partakes of the character of luxuries. The faintness or want of strength resulting from so meagre a diet is relieved by the stimulus of large draughts of the light wines of the country—in general, mixtures deleterious to the health, though not very intoxicating. Indeed, one cause of the apparent sobriety of the peasantry is said to be their inability to swallow enough to make them tipsy, though there are men among them that will drain a gallon flask at a sitting. They drink sufficiently, however, to excite crime and disorders. Their temperance may be considered rather a passive than active virtue; though, as men will seek artificial stimulants, it would be an advantage to the United States could light wines be substituted for strong liquors.

The effects of general want and poverty are shown among the Italians generally, and especially the Tuscans, in their short stature, heavy, lifeless look, and almost haggard appearance; the *tout ensemble* of dress and mien betokening a dispirited, badly-fed, and worse-governed race. Their numerous holidays prevent their being overworked; but the pale, spiritless faces, bent figures, and misshapen shoulders of the laboring women painfully tell their lack of generous diet and healthful employments. I never walk the streets of Florence without feeling pained at the sight of so much silent misery that, callous as it were to its own wants, passes humbly and painfully by, seemingly without pleasure in the past or hope for the future. It really appears wrong to dress well and walk erect and joyful in the consciousness of health and the blessings of Providence, not to speak of the ostentation of the rich, in contrast with the blight which has fallen so heavily upon the lives of so many of our fellow-beings, through centuries of oppression and miseducation.

It is difficult to procure reliable statistics in Italy, but the few which I feel authorized to give will show not only the extent of poverty, but the extent of charity also in this land. Indeed, so numerous and so richly endowed are the "palaces" for the destitute, as the poor-houses and hospitals may truly be called, that, in view of the general beggary and destitution, we can not come to other conclusion than that they overdo their own charitable design. Too much assistance has made the population lazy and improvident. They rely more upon public charity than private enterprise; consequently, reform must commence with them.

In 1798 there were thirty thousand poor, or one fifth of the population of Rome, on the lists of the curates of the several parishes. Under the administration of the French up to 1814, the proportion had been diminished to one ninth. Since that period it has been on the increase.

There are in Rome nineteen hospitals for the treatment of diseases. One of them, Saint Roch, is for the reception of pregnant women who wish to be confined in secret. In eight public hospitals the average number of sick daily is about fourteen hundred, who cost nineteen cents a day each. For every five patients there are two assistants or nurses, at the daily wages of thirty-three cents each, so that nearly one half of the revenues of the hospitals is expended on the well, who, of course, are greatly interested in multiplying them.

The hospital of the Holy Ghost receives all bastards without question. They cost Rome yearly fifty thousand dollars. There are, besides, some fourteen semi-convents, where young girls are gratuitously received and educated. They never leave these retreats except to marry or become nuns. If the former, they receive a dowry of thirty-five dollars; if the latter, fifty dollars, so much is celibacy in Rome held in honor above matrimony. As an anomaly, however, in this doctrine, there exist at Rome, and in Italy generally, *dotal* institutions, which annually provide a considerable number of poor girls with sufficient dowries to tempt offers of marriage. The lottery is also a recognized institution of the Church, or, more properly speaking, of its charity. Benoit XIV. ordered that at each drawing five maidens should receive their dowries from as many winning numbers; hence the fortunate damsels are known, not by their Christian names, but as Miss 79, or Miss 1025, as the prize numbers may prove. The hospitals succor annually about five thousand poor, at an expense of two hundred thousand dollars.

The Pope has various resources for his public and private benevolence. The Apostolic Aumony provides him with about five hundred dollars per month for general benevolence. The Datary, whence briefs and bulls are issued, a sort of ecclesiastical chancellary, which employs about one thousand persons, and receives immense sums from the sale of dispensations, indulgences, and the usual paper traffic of Rome, produces the Pope about thirty thousand dollars. An acquaintance of mine paid to this institution two thousand francs for the privilege to marry his deceased wife's sister. Shops for the sale of dispensations from fasting, and all the numerous requirements of the Church of Rome, to say nothing of more criminal indulgences, are common. The lottery produces fifty thousand dollars; the bureau of briefs and other offices some six thousand more, so that the Pope, unless prodigal, need never be empty-handed.

Venice, which once counted nine hundred rich and noble families, now contains scarcely twelve in comfortable circumstances. Some thirty others live obscurely in corners or lofts of their dilapidated palaces, depending upon the scanty rents received from strangers. At one period, more than two thirds of its population, or seventy thousand souls, required public aid. Milan, to the stranger, presents neither beggars nor poverty; its aspect is gay and brilliant, but this is owing rather to the severe measures of the Austrian police to prevent mendicity than to real prosperity. Its asylums are on the same scale of palatial splendor as in other parts of Italy. As in Sardinia, the poor are removed from sight, and placed in buildings decorated with columns, mosaics, spacious halls and courts, rivaling in architecture the stately palaces of their rulers; which cold magnificence, associated often with forced labor, they would gladly exchange for a gipsy life of privation in the open sunshine. Two thousand eight hundred individuals, according to a Milanese writer, are daily succored by the houses of industry of St. Vincent and St. Marc alone, at a net annual expense of eighty thousand dollars. The same establishments at Venice are more prosperous, costing the city but about five thousand dollars, and even producing a saving, if the cleaning and lighting of the streets, with which they are charged, be comprised.

Mendicity in the beautiful and rich Etruria has been very appropriately termed by Doctor Purchetti an "unarmed brigandage." Its insolence and pertinacity, coupled with the healthful and robust appearance of the majority who demand, rather than ask alms, have won for it this character. Even in Florence, where alone it is forbidden by law, it often stalks the streets apparently unmolested, though it frequently assumes the disguise of traffic to blind the eyes of the police. Unlike other parts of Italy, it seldom descends to wanton exposure of ulcered or crippled limbs, or other disgusting corporeal modes of exciting compassion, but boldly says it is hungry, and simply exclaims, "Give me a quattrino." Florence and Arezzo alone have organized houses for the unoccupied poor. Elsewhere they are at the mercy of, or prey unmolested upon, individual benevolence. All strangers arriving at Leghorn are taxed nearly one dollar a head for the poor. But their "palace" is occupied by Austrian soldiers, while, in rags and vermin, they are allowed to infest the streets with more the air of nobles than of beggars. Such sights are not grateful to the eyes of a court; consequently, when the Grand Duke goes to the baths of Lucca or elsewhere, the police are active in clearing the roads of a class of his subjects which reflect no credit on his government. After his departure, they make up their temporary losses by harassing strangers with twofold energy. In the capital, however, the severity of the law, which inflicts imprisonment or fines for the first offenses, and perpetual imprisonment, with forced labor, for renewed transgressions, serves in some degree to abate the nuisance.

Formerly there were three hundred churches and convents in the little city of Florence, owning the larger part of its real estate. Thanks to the enlightened Ferdinand and the French, the greater part of these abodes of idleness were suppressed. Even now, however, the Church owns a large proportion of the city. The numerous heraldic devices of the lamb and cross, to be seen on so many of the houses and palaces of the city, indicate the wealth of the Cathedral alone. At present there are seventeen convents of men and fourteen of females, besides seven houses of refuge for young girls under the charge of nuns. Of hospitals of all kinds there are eight or ten; that of Santa Maria Nuova, founded in 1287, being one of the finest and best organized in Europe, and succoring annually more than three thousand sick of both sexes.

In this hospital is to be seen the museum of the late Professor Segato, who discovered the process of petrifying animal substances, so that, while they retained their natural colors and shapes, they became as hard as stone. The Church, as usual, interfered with his art, on the ground that it was contrary to the scriptural doctrine of "into dust shalt thou return." Consequently, unable to prosecute the discoveries farther, he soon after died, leaving to the world this unique museum as the evidence of his success, and to tantalize science with regrets for the lost secret.

It comprises every portion of the human body transformed to stone, destined to endure as long as the world itself, if not ground to pieces by violence. There are two tables, one finished and polished, the other incomplete, made of mosaics formed by sections of human bones, brain, lungs, blood-vessels, intestines, and muscles, as firm as marble, showing the internal structure of each, but resembling colored stones. Without an explanation, every visitor would presume them to have come from some stone mosaic manufactory, for they are symmetrically arranged in squares, with the great variety of colors nicely graduated. Different portions of the human body, exhibiting the internal anatomy, are so perfectly petrified as to form perfect objects of study for the medical student. Even morbid anatomy was subjected with entire success to this process. Animals of all kinds, reptiles, chickens in and out of the egg—in short, nothing that had warm blood was capable of resisting his petrifying touch. The beauty of his art was that it preserved the life-like appearance and color of the animal; hence, for anatomical and natural history museums, his discovery was invaluable. The student had before him the real object of his study, perfect as in life, without any of the inconveniencies and imperfections attending waxen representations and stuffed or spirit-preserved specimens. The Roman Church, above all others, did wrong to discourage the art. Next to medical colleges, it is the largest dealer in dead men's bones. What an improvement it would have been, instead of exhibiting a knee-pan in a vial, or a dried skull in a gold case, to have held up for adoration an entire saint as fresh as in life. All skepticism in relics would then disappear, for, however easy it may be to substitute one bone for another, there could be no possibility of destroying personal identity. The stone saint would be the actual image of the live saint; no daguerreotype could be half so exact; and when not in use, could be quietly laid by on the shelf, as is frequently done in life.

What a gallery of great men might not be bodily perpetuated to the world by this art! Who would not now like to see the real Homer, Socrates, or Cæsar, not in cold marble, but looking as if they merely slept, their actual flesh and blood stiff and erect before us? The sculptor would have abandoned his art in despair. I can not say that I should look complacently on the process as applied to one's own family. Perhaps the relations of Homer, Socrates, and Cæsar would have had similar objections, and have preferred the funeral pile to the adamantine embalmment. There is, however, in this museum the head of a young girl, with long flaxen hair of remarkable beauty, as soft and tress-like as in life. Belonging to this head is a virgin bosom, snow-white, and of a perfection of form that nature seldom equals, and art never surpasses. Powers's Greek Slave or the Venus de Medici could exchange busts with this maiden without loss, so exquisite are its proportions and so pure its outlines. Here, then, exists a figure which women will envy and men admire through all time, as cold and hard as flint, yet warming the feelings with love and pity for the fate of one so young and beautiful. All that is known of her is that she was found dead with others under the roof of a church that fell in, and Segato possessed himself of her corpse.

Hospitals for foundlings appear to be a peculiar charity of Roman Catholic countries. They indicate both great distress and a low scale of morality. Increasing as they must, from the facilities they afford to illegitimacy and concubinage, evils scarcely less than those they seek to remedy, Protestants should be cautious in imitating them. Indeed, in countries of their origin they are defended only as a choice between the infanticide and abandonment which it is their peculiar province to prevent and relieve. Both legitimate and illegitimate infants find a home in these asylums to the number of several thousands annually. When of sufficient age, they are placed in the families of the peasants, who receive a trifling sum for their maintenance, which ceases when the children are able to earn something for themselves. If the girls marry, they are entitled to a dowry of about thirty dollars, but after they have left the hospital and are at service, they frequently continue to obtain this sum without the necessary condition, through others to whom they furnish their papers for that purpose. In 1825 there were 10,194 infants received into the several foundling hospitals of Tuscany. The number increased to 12,494 in 1834, owing, in part, to the increase of the population. In 1841 the family of the Royal Hospital of Innocents of Florence alone numbered 7511, a large number of whom are legitimate children, abandoned from cause of poverty by their parents. They can, however, at any time reclaim them by reimbursing the hospital for the expenses incurred. A considerable number, one in sixteen, are thus withdrawn, but, with all the care and kindness bestowed upon those who remain, their lot is a hard one. I had a domestic once who knew nothing more of her childhood than that she was found in the streets and placed in one of these hospitals, where, after receiving the usual fare and education for a number of years, she was sent out into the world to gain her own subsistence. She knew neither parent nor relative—in fact, was perfectly alone, united to society only by the indissoluble chain of servitude; for what hope has one of these public orphans to contract ties of family, when even noble-born maidens without dowries are compelled to pine in solitude or seek religious consolation in cloisters? She was humble and grateful, but sad; feeling deeply her forlorn situation, aggravated as it was by a pulmonary complaint, which threatened soon to terminate her sorrows in life, and unite her with Lazarus in Abraham's bosom. I know not who are most to be pitied, the parent driven by shame or poverty to violate the purest instincts of human nature, or their offspring, fatherless and motherless, knowing no kin, nursed during infancy by hirelings, or else confined within the walls of a charitable institution, deprived of the sacred joys of a home, until bone and muscle are sufficiently grown for them to take their places as "the drawers of water and hewers of stone" for their more fortunate brethren. Vice brings with it another punishment. Whoever has noticed these orphans will have perceived that they appear like an inferior race of humanity compared with the civilized European type. Their faces and forms seem as if run in one mould, with dull, unintellectual, almost imbecile expressions, and short, stubby figures, like those of well-fed swine. After looking at these children, I ceased to wonder at the stunted, haggard, lifeless population so often seen in the streets.

Naples, in its "Albergo dei Poveri," possesses one of the most sumptuous poor-houses in existence ; one immense establishment, accommodating upward of three thousand paupers of both sexes, in which there are not only work-shops for the fabrication of silks, cotton, laces, the cutting of coral, and other trades, but also schools of music, design, arithmetic, and other branches of knowledge, besides a printing-office, type-foundry, and other arts, so as to afford suitable employments and instruction for all capacities. Notwithstanding this model establishment and numerous others, whose annual revenues amount to nearly two millions and five hundred thousand dollars, Naples is infested with an idle, begging population, to reform which would require all the energy of well-directed liberal institutions, or else a severity which even its heartless despotism dare not exercise.

There is an important distinction between Roman Catholic and Protestant benevolence in modes of action. Both are comprehensive, self-denying, laborious, and unwearied. The former, however, partakes of the parade and ostentation of the

Church which controls and directs its operations. It delights in uniforms, chantings, torch-lights, and masquerading. When it visits the sick or buries the dead, it puts on its robes of office. With all its apparent humility, it blazons forth its good deeds to the world by a state and trappings that announce its errand, and proclaim its subserviency to the Holy See. To relieve is the secondary, to proselyte is the primary object of its creed. Its various associations form the militia of popery, and, owing to their real virtues, they are the most successful of its soldiers in extending its conquests. No one can meet the Roman "Brethren of the Dead," whose office is to bury the deserted victims of contagion, see the mournful costume of the Florentine "Brethren of Pity" in their more comprehensive errands of mercy, or watch the noiseless steps of the French "Sisters of Charity," as they glide, like ministering angels, to the hearthstones of poverty or the bedsides of the sick and dying, without feeling his heart respond to the sublime doctrine of the universal brotherhood of man, and involuntarily reverencing that form of Christianity which thus manifests its benevolence to the world. But is there not more real sublimity in the silent, humble walk of Protestant benevolence—the doing good in secret—than in all the mighty machinery of Rome? The one takes hold of the sentiment, and exalts the imagination; it proclaims its work and demands its tribute. The other also has in its ranks Sisters of Charity and Brethren of Mercy as devoted and unwearied as any in the ranks of Rome. But they go forth on their daily rounds of Christian love unheralded by chants, and undisguised in the robes of state; less known to the public than if, in their spiritual pride, they doffed their usual habiliments to bury themselves and their good works in those lugubrious costumes with which Romanism conceals all but the eyes, for fear that the right hand shall know what the left doeth, while at the same time they bid the world to do them reverence.

Protestantism washes no pilgrims' feet, and feeds no paupers in the pride of charity amid the splendors of a dominant hierarchy. It makes no theatrical exhibition of its benevolence, though its English form delights too much in good dinners. Its benevolence flows not at the command of a human "Holy Father," directed by one fallible will toward one infallible purpose, but is the offspring of individual hearts, concentrated by love, for the simple purpose of visiting "the widows and fatherless in their affliction."

Men see not the Protestant Brethren of Mercy as they pass by, for they are like other men; neither do women kneel on stony pavements when the Protestant clergyman carries hope to the dying, for his presence is not pompously announced by a long train of priestlings in gaudy robes, with the tinkling of bells, and the armed soldiers, who guard the Roman minister as he bears the body and blood of the Prince of Peace on his way to absolve dying sinners; nor do our Sisters of Charity wear other garb than that in which they so faithfully perform their duties as Christian mothers.

Protestant benevolence appeals directly to "Our Father in Heaven" to sustain and direct its energies; it acknowledges its accountability to the public, from which it derives its material aid; and in all points it seeks to dispense its bounties as Providence extends its blessings, silently and effectively, to all who hunger and thirst. Both are the children of Christianity. Which does it most honor, and partakes largest of its spirit, the records of eternity alone may decide. Would that, while both remain on earth, their rivalry were solely in provoking each other to good deeds!

Roman Catholic cities, in their primary aspect, present a higher appearance of public morality than Protestant capitals. But few public women are met in their streets; drunkenness seems rare; and there is a general quiet and lethargy, the exact reverse of the bustle and enterprise of those towns that acknowledge Protestantism. Nowhere is this parallel more strikingly shown than between Geneva and Lucerne, Florence and New York, or Rome and London. This external morality is readily explained.

While the grosser forms of prostitution are not so openly exhibited in papal cities as in Protestant, the distinction between virtue and vice is much less rigorously drawn. The Roman clergy are able to repress it outwardly, but it extends inwardly. Society in general is corrupt, while the streets are comparatively pure. The forced celibacy of the priesthood ever has produced, and will continue to, while it exists, a vast amount of hidden concubinage. The religious restraints and expenses of marriage produce more that is open, while the general laxity of public opinion tolerates corrupt unions that in England and the United States would bring upon the offenders the penalties of law and expulsion from society. Possibly there are fewer public prostitutes in strictly Roman Catholic towns than in Protestant, but as an offset, the morals of their women are looser, and afford wider scope for intrigue, so that licentiousness is not concentrated, as in general with us, to a class of degraded females, and reduced to the baser condition of traffic. Our streets, too, are freed from a nuisance which no traveler escapes from in Italy. Pimps dog his steps every where, and though he may escape the sight of loose women, he is constantly haunted by the obscene importunities of their beastly male agents.

Intoxication is rarer, because strong liquors are not so available. There is, however, more general drinking, and perhaps, in the mass, more aggregate vice and misery from this cause than in America. In Italy all drink ; teetotalism is unknown. If we possess a confirmed race of drunkards, they do not understand the principle of temperance ; so that while they fail to show as many repulsive specimens of this vice as we, they exhibit more general misery and degradation.

AN ITALIAN WINE-SHOP.

The average morality of the Italian races, in other respects, I consider as beneath the American. Why is it that the lower story of every house and palace is fortified by iron gratings and massive doors, so as to resemble more a prison than private dwellings, if it be not from the general sense of insecurity to property? Petty dishonesty, pilferings, and what may be comprehended under the general term of knavery, extend to degrees of society whose social position would apparently place them above all risk of taint. The servility which panders to vice and clutches at gain, through ignominy or disregard of self-respect, is painfully apparent. Female servants kiss the hands of their masters, and obsequiousness is the chief recommendation in domestics. There is much kindly feeling in the relation of servant and master in Italy, it is true, to the credit of both parties; but the *gulf* between the two is an impassable one—its boundaries are those of perpetual caste.

Italians are not educated *up* to the Protestant standard of *truth* and *honor*. As beggary with the lower classes carries with it no shame, so falsehood among the higher would not be deemed a vice. The multiplicity of newspapers in the United States prevents any crime from being long hid. Every thing which in any way interests the public is spread before it, from one extremity of the Union to the other, with the rapidity of thought. In consequence, all our evil deeds are dragged to light, and every day develops, as it were, some new crime. At the first glance it would appear as if we were a peculiarly criminal race; but when we consider that the newspapers reflect as a looking-glass the moral condition of a population of twenty-five millions, our surprise is rather at the paucity than the extent of crime. Italy presents nothing of the kind. Its population is not one of readers. Journals are small, scarce, and restricted to only what jealous governments permit to be known. They are but an indifferent clew to the moral condition of Italians. Crimes may be common or rare, and nothing be heard of them away from their immediate circle. Still, I do not believe that the Italians are given to the cold-blooded atrocities which figure not unfrequently in the criminal calen-

BRIGANDS—ARMED AND UNARMED.

dars of England and America. At all events, we rarely hear of coolly-planned murders for the sake of booty; and yet brigands and assassinations figure largely in Italian tales. The Italian kills in warm blood, or in his profession of a "bravo." He uses his knife, particularly the Roman, as an Anglo-Saxon does his fists. It is his national weapon, and the idea of courage is particularly connected with a prompt thrust in revenge of real or fancied wrong. The Italian is like the Indian in respect to his mode of retribution. He seeks it in the way in which he himself is safest; and what Northern minds would consider as base and cowardly, he considers as courageous and justifiable. All who have read the appeals of Mazzini to his countrymen will not fail to perceive that he relies chiefly on treachery and assassination—a wholesale repetition of the Sicilian vespers—to bring about a revolution. The criminal statistics of Rome would show that he does not appeal to their skill in the use of their national weapon without reason.

During the last century, the average of murders in Rome, with a population of one hundred and fifty thousand souls, was five or six a day, and on one occasion fourteen. While occupied by the French, there were in a single day one hundred and twenty assassinations; and as late as 1828 they averaged one daily. A chapel of the Madonna in the church of the Augustins is hung about with knives, dirks, and other murderous instruments, suspended there by their owners, at the order of their confessor, as a condition of absolution and evidence of pardon of their crimes.

The streets of Rome are not safe at the later hours of night, even now, for any one who has aught about him to tempt the cupidity of its highwaymen. Roman friends of mine are accustomed to place their watches in their boots when out late at night. Every housekeeper will tell you the risks they run in not keeping the strictest watch over their premises; and any one's experience in visiting Italian families will convince him that they have more confidence in their portcullis doors and massive gratings than in either the honesty of their countrymen or the guardianship of the police. It is customary, when a visitor calls, to reconnoitre, either through a loop-hole or an upper window, so as to ascertain his quality and business before withdrawing the bolt. Fear and suspicion are manifested to great extent in the domestic arrangements of Italians, and with reason, for in no country is there more sympathy felt for the bandit. As he protects the poor, he is considered more as their champion than a criminal. The ranks of highwaymen are often recruited from the disaffected toward the government, whose oppressions force them, as it were, into open hostility. Hence they partake in part of the character of patriots; and, even with the aid of French and Austrian troops, Italy finds it no easy task to keep her roads and cities safe for the traveler. Judge, then, what would be the condition of the country were its five hundred thousand bayonets reduced to the number that compose the army of the United States!

The chiefs of the Roman brigands, from their audacity and the extent of their crimes, have ranked with the vulgar as heroes. The Roman government, unable to cope with them, has, after they had glutted themselves with plunder, pardoned and pensioned them to keep the peace.

One of the most noted was Gasparone, who began his career by killing his confessor for refusing to absolve him for a robbery. Yet so scrupulous was he in the performance of those religious rites that ignorant Romanism substitutes for spiritual worship, that he acquired with the country people a reputation for sanctity, particularly for his devotion to Saint Anthony, and his careful abstinence from murders on Sundays and Church festivals.

Another, Gobertino by name, killed during his career, with his *own hand*, nine hundred and sixty-four adults and six *infants;* regretting only on his death-bed that he had not been able to make up the number to a thousand. Aronzo Albagna massacred his entire family, including his father, mother, two brothers, and sister. America and England may contain criminals capable of rivaling these exploits, but it is certain that

ITALIAN BRIGANDS.

the opportunity never would be allowed them. It is rare in either country that a villain gets beyond his first great crime.

My object in presenting this unfavorable summary of Italian character is to show to what extent, in comparison with Protestantism, I consider Romanism to be responsible for it, both for what it has actually done and what it has failed to do. If such are the results where Romanism is supreme, are not other nations in which it seeks to find sway warranted in viewing it, both in a political and moral sense, with a jealous eye? If there be in the institutions of Protestant countries any superiority over those of Roman Catholic, it is owing to the purer faith, greater knowledge, and more elevated view of human rights which they have developed. Protestantism is progressive. It looks both to the temporal and eternal welfare of the individual. What it claims for itself it allows to others, asking deference only to civil law, while creeds are left intact. It seeks to convert the understanding, and not to terrify the nerves and lull them into a false repose.

Romanism, on the contrary, is the opposite of all this. She forbids liberty of speech and freedom of the press. She refuses the appeal to the Bible. Intolerance is her constant principle. By one weapon or another, by being all things to all men, by persuasion when possible, by force when she has the power, she seeks to bind all nations to her spiritual despotism. Romanism and republicanism are antagonistic powers. When together, one or the other must succumb. In the United States, thus far, Protestantism has succeeded in extracting the sting from her enemy. There are only two powers equal to cope with her: democracy on the one hand, strong in its own rights, and enlightened as to its true mission to elevate mankind by the gradual spread of liberty sanctified by religion and knowledge; on the other, a despotism capable of controlling elements as powerful as its own. In England and America it is kept within restricted limits by the superior power of an enlightened public opinion. In France it has again become restless and aggressive; not content with equality, it seeks supremacy. Whether the infidelity of France will be able to retain the toleration it has permitted to all sects in the contest with the subtleties and fanaticism of popery, remains to be seen. The policy for Romanism is to demand for itself all that it refuses to another: the golden rule has no place in its creed. Protestantism asks nothing more than that all sects should be placed on an equal basis, and left to find their way to the hearts of men through the paths of knowledge and truth. In doing this, she disarms herself of weapons that Romanism unscrupulously uses to her injury. They do not meet on equal terms except on Protestant grounds. When the Pope rules, the tongue is tied and the limbs fettered if they do not acknowledge his supremacy. It is a mistake to suppose that the attacks of popery are confined to Protestant countries. Her power has been checked repeatedly by Catholic princes, and equally against them she wages endless war on every point that crosses her selfish interests. Venice was free and powerful while she was tolerant and uncompromising to the demands of Rome; Florence populous and prosperous until her rulers became priests and her interests confided to Rome. All free communities that have trusted to her for salvation have fallen by her arts. There is no hope for Italy while popery exists as a dominant creed. It opposes an insurmountable barrier to freedom and knowledge. None are more painfully convinced of this than enlightened Italians themselves. Piedmont is now a rising state, but every step of her progress is one of contest with the Pope. In Spain, popery refuses a Christian burial to a Protestant. In Germany and France she calls marriages concubinage when not sanctified before her altars with gifts to her priests. But I have already pursued this topic sufficiently far to bear my witness against the giant cause of the darkness and ignorance that overspread so large a portion of our globe.

One topic which enlists the sympathies of liberty every where still remains. Will Italy ever become a united, free country, or must she ever remain, in the words of Metternich, merely a geographical idea? Nature evidently intended her for a unity. This, however, has never been accomplished.

Rome founded her dominion over isolated cities and kingdoms; she melted them in the crucible of her power, but did not cast them out a united state. Romans, not Italians, ruled the world. When Rome fell, Italy resumed her previous condition of rival communities engaged in ceaseless contests. Commerce and war developed wealth and energy. Italy became great from the genius and arts of her hostile sons. She contained within herself all the elements of the first power on earth but union. Her commercial cities were each worth the ransom of kingdoms. They conquered territories and spread their power abroad, while neglecting to insure it at home. All paid homage to Rome as their spiritual head. Then was the time for a patriot Pope to have healed their dissensions and united them as one people. But no! The Popes were alive only to the extension of their own petty temporal sovereignties. They esteemed it a higher honor to rule over a few cities, wasted with fire and sword at their command, than to be the saviors of Italy. To this end they sowed fresh dissensions; they repeatedly leagued with transalpine enemies; they exterminated liberty, and finally became the chief among the many sad causes which have contributed to make Italy what we now find her—the mere foot-ball of European policy.

Besides popery, Italy is held down by twofold bonds. First, the policy of France and Austria is to prevent a rival power, such as she would be if free and united, from holding a rank on the shores of the Mediterranean. Secondly, and by far the greater obstacle, is the spirit of disunion among her own sons. So long have they been accustomed to look upon cities as countries, that each citizen considers his neighbor of another city as a stranger—their country is embraced within the limits of their city walls. The bitter recollections of former feuds and rivalries are still active. Venice hates Milan—Leghorn, Florence—Pisa both; in short, the nearer are towns, the more cordial is the hatred that exists between them. Patriotism is purely local. During 1848, the Livornese wished to plunder Florence, and would have preferred turning their arms against their countrymen rather than against their common enemy. The little, poverty-struck Lucca, now merged into Tuscany, mourns its court, and resents as an injury its absorption into a greater and more powerful state. The feeling between the numerous states into which Italy is divided is far more cordial than between the cities of each state. Genoa is restless under the sway of Piedmont, and exalts in her imagination the departed glories of the Ligurian Republic. Venice dreams still of her old doges, and the power and commerce that have forever forsaken her wave-washed palaces. The peasantry of Lombardy prefer Austrian rule to Italian, and fired upon the patriots in 1848 who marched to their relief. Those of Tuscany cling likewise to their bondage. They say, We would rather have one "padrone" than many. The Grand Duke has a right to be our master, because his family have always ruled us; so we had rather have him than new masters. The unlettered Italian mind has no conception of political liberty. It is a condition it never dreamed of. Despotism may be created in an hour, but republicanism is of slow growth. Those who hope to regenerate Italy in a day are putting faith in dreams.

Is there, then, no hope of Italy? Many shrewd observers say no. I differ from them. True, I believe that the vices of Italy are as great as I have represented them to be. But there is also, in her varied population, as much innate talent, genius, and natural goodness of heart as exists in any country. Even more; for nowhere else, unless among the Greek races, do we find greater intellectual vitality, if I may so term it, and sensitiveness to the purely sensuous enjoyments of nature. Romanism has indeed wilted all that it has touched, but the germ still exists. Remove the causes, and the evils will disappear. In the simple-hearted inhabitants that people her mountain valleys she has resources of mind and soul that need but the talisman of cultivation to flood with new life her cities and her fields. Her towns still shelter learning, science, and virtue. Her industry is indeed crushed, and her commerce annihilated; but the same race that once won the markets of the world still exist, emulous of the fame of their fathers. New Savonarolas, Michael Angelos, and Rienzis will arise. The race of great hearts and lofty minds is not extinct. We say that nations die out. Is it so? A name may die out, but humanity never. It is a common saying that the races of Europe are in their decline, as if races of human beings, by a physical law, arose to a certain climax, and then degenerated to mere brutes again. If this theory were true, what creates the greatness of the United States, for Americans are but transplanted Europeans? In America the citizen creates the government, in Europe the government creates the subject. This simple fact explains the gulf between them. The European thrives just in proportion as his government permits. The Italians are but what their rulers have made them. Change their rulers, and there is hope. Unfetter the mind, and it will develop new channels of thought and enterprise. Mental stagnation was never intended by Providence as the condition of beings created in his own image. I will not theorize as to the immediate agencies by which Italy can be united and regenerated, for that concerns more particularly her own sons; but that she can be, and through her own instrumentality, aided by the sympathy and experience of other nations who have passed through their agony of travail, I both firmly believe and devoutly hope.

CHAPTER XII.

ROME THAT WAS AND IS.

In no city is the gulf between the Past and Present so wide as in Rome. With this name, associations swell high and strong in the voyager, as, launched upon the wilderness of the Campagna, he slowly traverses its solitudes, with St. Peter's dome as a colossal beacon in the mid-heavens, to direct his eyes toward the site, not of the Rome of to-day, but of the spectre of the past, which, despite reason, will haunt his imagination. The Campagna is a befitting frame, not to his mental picture, but to the moral reality which awaits his eyes in the city of the popes as inheritors of the city of the Cæsars. From whichsoever side we approach Rome, the same treeless, broken, dark soil, naked hills, and wasted country meet the view. Villages there are none. Broken masses of ruins, shapeless and nameless, rise at intervals over its surface like surge-worn rocks on wintry shores. Deserted, tottering towers, once the abode of mediæval violence, in ghost-like rigidity, cast melancholy shadows over the plain. Long lines of spectral fences lose themselves in the horizon. Far above them, majestic, sad, and lonely, here in solitary arches, there linked in stone embrace, continuous lines disappearing in perspective threads, the imperial aqueducts lift their graceful forms. Broken masses of light, fringed by stone-cast shadows, stream through the tall archways like rays of olden thought, or as though eternity opened its eyes upon time. Along their diminishing lines the sight wanders on until lost in space. By them alone the view escapes from their bed of desolation to the distant, island-like hills, smiling with life and crowned with verdure, where towns and villas, sparkling with opal tints as the sun flashes upon their white walls, heighten even more by contrast the sterility of the Campagna.

In the natural wildness of prairie-land there are a sweetness and freshness in the breath of nature that rejoices the blood. Its virtues are simple, sincere, and soul-speaking. Green space beneath, besprinkled with a gem-like wild Flora, a horizon set with the dense vegetation of virgin forests, and the pearly expanse of the clear sky above, make up a landscape smile that none but a bad heart can look upon with a cold eye. Not so the Roman Campagna! Here Nature has lost her purity. The landscape is withered and shrunken by age and crime. Every trace of innocent beauty and primitive vigor has been uprooted. Instead of rejoicing the inner life and tempting the natural man to sport upon its surface, and to essay its productive energies for his profit, it repels by a countenance furrowed with selfish thought, and an anatomy racked by pain and exhausted by futile effort. The curse of Cain lies upon its unwholesome bosom. None but the Roman Bedouin, the disease-stricken husbandman, or the skin-clad shepherd cleave to it. Poverty binds them with fetters, unloosed except by the angel of death, to their heavy tasks and scanty harvests upon its poisoned soil. Such evidences of life as it yields are but witnesses to its desolation. Stunted trees, repulsive shrubs, fever-breeding streams, pools reeking with sulphurous smells, rain-plowed ravines, bald hills, and verdure-stripped plains, over which fly startled game, and on which ruminate melancholy sheep and fierce cattle, with here and there a patriarchal tree, branch-torn and all but leafless, emblematic of man struggling against misery—these are the external features of the Campagna. Across it in various directions, like shrunken veins, wind the dreary roads that connect Rome with the civilized world, imparting to her, however, but a faint current of life. It is all she has. Were that stream withdrawn, Rome and the Campagna would soon become one common home for the fox and wild-fowl. The natural atmosphere of both is death, moral and physical. And yet at times there pours over the Campagna from the setting sun a golden, purple light, that vails it with a beauty more of heaven than earth, as if to show that hope never deserts nature. Even the Campagna can repent and be saved. Once human vitality gave it animation and joy; nature clad it in gay colors and verdant robes; it was populous, civilized, and redeemed by industry. The sites of cities and villas proclaim its former wealth. Antiquity, therefore, found it a smiling wilderness. Modern enterprise in vain tries its restoration. The luxurious villa soon becomes a damp and repulsive ruin. Farms, if any, exhibit the misery of the husbandman and not the richness of the soil. Despair, disease, and poverty brood over the scene. The Campagna is now a fit setting for modern Rome; an expanse over which the eye moodily broods as it recalls the past, or hurriedly glances as it gladly escapes to the hilly country beyond—its use a game-ground or field for puerile fox-hunts by English Nimrods and Roman imitators, whose horses quake at far lesser gulfs than that into which their ancestral Curtius so heroically plunged. But repentance to the Campagna will never be born of a Roman hierarchy. The ecclesiastical cancer has eaten too deep into humanity for other cure than amputation. The same scope and vigor of enterprise that once peopled the Campagna can alone redeem it. But "physician heal thyself" can never be hoped of priest-throttled Rome. As is the Campagna to the natural eye, so is the spiritual welfare of every country overshadowed by this church colossus. Man and nature are redeemed only in the degree they escape its bondage.

The character of a city may be read in its environs. See how the exuberance of the domestic life of London escapes into suburban homes, rays of wealth, taste, and joy from the great sun of commercial civilization! Paris, too, brilliant and buoyant with life to its uttermost circulation; Dresden, a dark gem in a light setting; Vienna, a grand dame in full toilet, surrounded by a stately progeny of her own bone and blood; New York, a focus of enterprise and riches, giving birth yearly to rival cities; Boston, queen-like, with her train embroidered with towns and villages, the whole scene the fairest edition of pictorial Christianity, wedded to knowledge and prosperity, the world has yet issued. In these and kindred towns we have but to glance at the exterior to detect the healthful beat of the public heart, sending life-giving streams in every direction. We approach these great central organizations through avenues of life. Not so with Rome! The path to her lies over the plain of death. What the sluggish and muddy lagoons of Venice, when drained by the tide, festering in the hot sun, and traversed only by snake-like channels, in the beds of which squirm slimy eels amid tangled sea-weed, are to that city, the Campagna is to Rome. But the ocean daily bathes Venice with its waters, and proffers its tribute, as of old, to its grateful mistress. An artery of modernism, the railroad, saved her from utter desolation. Rome is an isolated wreck amid the sea of the Campagna, clinging convulsively to the rock on which she foundered.

What is the rock on which she has twice shipwrecked her fortunes? Absolute power! In asserting universal dominion, she has lost the power of self-preservation. As in her imperial dotage she became the spoil and contempt of barbarians, so now, in her ecclesiastical decrepitude, she is the beggar of Christendom, whining where she dare not threaten, her pride equaled only by her poverty.

The physical aspect of modern Rome, especially as seen from the Pincian, is noble. Its sea of roofs is broken by an archipelago of domes, on the right of which rises St. Peter's, the leviathan of them all, giving to the city a grand atmospherical outline, in keeping with the stateliness of the neighboring hills. Against the horizon spectral pines stand stiff and solemn. Toward the west, where the Tiber escapes from broken walls and ruined arches, the Campagna, in great swells of earth, rolls onward until it loses itself under the waves of the Mediterranean. The eye instinctively follows the path of the setting sun in its journey through space, luxuriating in the golden robe of many colors with which it mantles the Eternal City, as if, in giving it a glimpse of the heavenly Jerusalem, it bade it repent and wear that garment of glory forever.

Modern Rome is born of the Church. I will not penetrate beyond the skin to show its constitution. Such life, cleanliness, and comfort as it possesses have been forced upon it by the exigencies of pilgrims to its shrines of arts rather than to its altars. Real Rome is dirty, comfortless, and torpid; the home of beggars, indolence, and superstition. This is the true city of the Church; the city of the travelers is another work. Withdraw them, and you have the city of the popes—a carcass picked by ravens. The scavenger-birds are sleek and lively, but they thrive upon the flesh of their victims. True, there are palaces, museums, and churches; hospitals and alms-houses; colleges and libraries; treasures of knowledge and miracles of art; mighty souvenirs of intellect, wealth, pride, and devotion. The spoils of Imperial Rome are the livelihood of Papal Rome. But the Church takes no real delight in these things. Her heart is with her mouldy bones; her holy anatomies; fragments of saints; ghastly elbow-joints and sepulchral curls; Christ's cradles, Virgin's petticoats, rusty iron from martyrs' crosses; drops of blood that defy time to coagulate; Passover tables; holy stairways; columns sanctified by the suffering of the Savior, handkerchiefs by his bloody sweat; the toys of an age of darkness metamorphosed into the idols of an age of light; *bambinos*, holy dolls, tawdry and bejeweled, so hideous in their ugliness that an infant would start from them in affright, yet daily slobbered over with sinners' kisses to win the papal paradise, and made richer than any Crœsus through superstitious hope to escape hell by buying heaven; heathen idols transformed into modern gods, before whom more prayers are said than rise to Heaven from all the closets of Christendom—such are the real treasures of modern Rome. Her soul is in them. She prefers the millinery and acting of her ritual, the multiplication of her holidays, the robing of her priests and the tawdry decoration of her altars, the propagation of a new dogma and the discovery of a new relic, to all that science, art, and progress are doing elsewhere for humanity.

In 1854, this century of so-called intelligence, the Holy Father, "with the aid of the Holy Ghost," as he claims, has added to the Roman mythology a woman-god, "the most holy Virgin Mary, Mother of God," to whom the faithful are to pray. Despite the experience of Adam, the Roman Church puts its trust in a woman, born of man. Can the imbecility of dogmatism go farther! The woman, of whom Christ said at his first miracle, "Woman, what have I to do with thee?" I object not to softening the heart of man by elevating Mary to the type of the perfect being of her sex, and thus making her, by association, a humanizing element of religion; but the substitution of the Virgin as a direct object of worship in place of God, as is the increasing practice of Romanism, is as positive an act of idolatry as any for which Canaan was cursed. The wheels of papal Christendom are turning backward. She is in her dotage, and must give way, in her turn, to greater light. In Rome alone can we see the full working of her mind-destroying system. Elsewhere she is checked or modified by civil institutions.

I have before me a circular, issued during Lent of this year (1855), giving a list of English sermons to be preached in Rome. At the bottom it reads, "The HOLY FATHER has graciously granted SEVEN YEARS' INDULGENCE to be gained by attending each one of the sermons, and a PLENARY INDULGENCE by attending them all, with the usual conditions annexed of confession, holy communion, and praying for His intention, the extirpation of all heresies, and the exaltation of Holy Church." "These indulgences are applicable to the souls in Purgatory."

Such gibberish is gravely uttered by the spiritual head of Christendom nearly two thousand years after the "Word was made flesh," that it might be intelligible to mankind. What hope has truth in the keeping of a hierarchy?

Were the absurdities and inanities of the Roman ritual confined to Rome, one would pity and forget. But living in Rome, and seeing it as the great heart from which, through the powerful arteries of superstition and faith, the great paralyzing dogmas of papacy go forth to stagnate the blood of Christendom, hanging like a black pall over intellectual progress, a gloom shrouds the spirit and weighs upon the understanding. Every where the spectre of this great lie lifts its head. No feast is without the skeleton. Hence one weighty reason of the moral depression that afflicts so many visitors at Rome. They feel the effects without tracing the cause. Physical nature sympathizes, as we see in the Campagna, with the lack of the vitality of truth, without which neither individual nor nation can escape the curse of wasted talents.

The architecture of modern Rome, as a whole, is in keeping with its theology—either pompous, coldly rich, and incongruously magnificent, as in St. Peter's and its sister churches, or deformed, inconsistent, overloaded with inappropriate ornament, made up of stolen classical wealth and debased modern ornamentation, as in the general medley of styles of the later churches. Externally, meagre or pretentious; internally, having widely departed from primitive simplicity and sincerity, it revels in tawdry decorations and theatrically contrived effects, offensive to the cultivated eye, though dazzling, perhaps, to the rude imagination. Worship in Rome has been resolved into external ceremonies, from which their ancient significance has long since fled. The senses, and not the heart, are attracted; the passions, and not the intellect, are the levers of papal power.

In domestic architecture there are but two types—the renaissant palatial, haughty and imposing, and the common, poor, mean, and repulsive, yielding long, narrow, grimed streets, the sham of civilization without the substance. These two styles stare at each other in mutual hate, and both, with few exceptions, have upon them a common deposit of ancestral dirt, that tells of general poverty and untidiness

The Corso is an anomaly in Rome. It is a noble street—a connecting link between Rome and modern civilization. There are noble avenues stretching over its seven hills in all directions, focusing the eye upon Egyptian obelisks, vast basilicas, colossal statuary, and generous fountains. The series of architectural coups d'œil are varied and wonderful. But the city lacks in this respect individuality. Its external character is not its own. As in antiquity a conquered world was pilfered of its arts and wealth to adorn Rome, so in modern times, Christendom for centuries has poured its tribute into her lap, to recreate what the barbarians devastated. Imperial Rome has proved an exhaustless granary for papal Rome. The present city dates but little more than three centuries back. It is a medley of wilderness and crowded streets; of buried and disinterred ruins; of mutilated or restored classical art, monuments, statues, bridges, temples, columns, severed aqueducts, and forums—the wrecks of pagan empire transformed into trophies of Christian rule. That, however, most proudly shows itself in the universal cross and keys of St. Peter, and in the barbarous, preposterous, and grotesque variations which, born of the Michael Angelique style, directed by monks, have made the Church architecture of the modern city at once the most pretending and the most abominable of the civilized world.

Of the domestic architecture of the city of the Cæsars, except the palaces of the patricians, we have no relics. Confused piles of rubbish overgrown by vineyards, here and there a broken shaft and mutilated capital peering through the soil, alone mark the sites of the homes of the Roman populace. Their houses were high, divided into floors as now, and in size, distribution, and general appearance—except, perhaps, some modern advantage in way of glazed windows, though the Romans used glass for this purpose—no doubt they looked then much the same as the common houses do now. Rude doorways, rough pavements, narrow and dark passages, leg-wearying stone staircases, windows pervious to every blast, shutters sun-cracked and rickety, humble doors with the locks of a Bastille, accumulations of dirt that bespeak long familiarity, festoons of washed linen hung to dry from front windows—in fine, every thing which in manufacture and custom can be condensed into the English sentence utter shiftlessness, are the facts of a Roman household. With water in such abundance that, with the eyes shut, the play of fountains seems to the senses a perpetual rain, yet no domestic interiors the world over have probably so slight an acquaintance with that purifying element. Delicious water it is too, much too good to be wasted on a dirt-loving population.

Roman habits remain as unchanged as their habitations. Modern requirements have, to some extent, forced improvements upon Rome ; consequently, we have gas, paved streets, good drains, and, as a whole, no doubt a more cleanly and convenient city than Augustus could boast. Heliogabalus, on one occasion, on a bet, collected in Rome ten thousand pounds of cobwebs. He failed, however, in exterminating spiders, as their works still show. Vespasian laid a tax on a certain nameless public habit of the citizens in the streets, which obtains as freely to this day, though less in Rome than in Florence, to the disgust of cleanly minds every where. Hopeless of reforming their beastly customs, the Emperor sought to make them subservient to the scavenger's work. The money raised was employed in cleaning the streets of rotting carcasses, and the bodies of those killed by lightning, or who had committed suicide without just cause. These were left to rot in the public ways. Such sanitary facts are seldom put in conjunction with the Golden House of Nero. Hence the imagination, no doubt, often depresses new to the exaltation of old Rome, whereas, in municipal cleanliness, the former has the advantage.

Between Constantine and Julius Second there is a wide gap in the external history of Rome. The Cæsars have stamped their features indelibly upon the Seven Hills. We look in vain, however, for the monuments of the mediæval interval, that age of violence, dissension, and ruin. A few Tuscan towers, some restored mosaics and frescoes, relics of primitive churches incorporated into new, scattered bits of Lombard sculptures and shafts to be traced in house walls in the Transtevere, the so-called house of Rienzi, and two massive, dismantled brick towers of the eleventh century, and we have all in Rome that carries the mind into this deep gulf of time. Every other city in Italy is alive with mediæval associations. The buildings, arts, and customs of that age still overshadow the present. In Florence especially is this the case. The homes of Dante, Michael Angelo, and Galileo, the palaces of her Medician despots and her republican Gonfalonieri, the very roofs which sheltered her Guelph and Ghibelline factions—in short, all that gave character to Florence in this epoch, still remain to familiarize the present with the past. Every street has its tradition. In Rome, no! Rienzi's name is the sole link that associates mediæval history with a local habitation. Even this is apocryphal. The names of Colonna, Orsini, Savelli, Marcelli, Maximi, and other historical reputations, live in Rome in modern buildings and streets. They were the destroyers of old Rome, leaving nothing behind them but the regret that they ever existed. Consequently, at the present day, we must see in Rome either the remains of the Imperial city, linking our thoughts to associations of its universal empire, or the ecclesiastical city, compounded of religious dogmas and classical relics, arrogating to itself the spiritual guidance of the world.

Cosmopolitan in its claims, it is cosmopolitan in its making up. Obelisks of Egypt; statues of Phidias; master-pieces from Greece; precious works from all climes; the noble arched buildings of her own origin, mingled with the genius of Raphael, Michael Angelo, and Bramante; the tasteless works of Bernini; Canova's superior art; artists and designs from beyond the Alps; contributions from universal Christendom fused together in the papal crucible, distinct and widely apart in their elements, yet forming that solemn, strange, fascinating whole we call Rome.

The "Niobe of nations" has played the chief part in the history of civilization. Twice has she filled the rôle of progress. Her ambition of universal political dominion brought mankind into legally-constructed and governmental communities, of which she was the heart. Men learned to be governed by law after being subdued by the sword. Civilization and order followed her banners. Unlike modern Rome, she did not proselyte. Religions she left free, or received them into her own prolific mythology. Thus she gave more than she took. The ancient world was never more peaceful and prosperous than when reposing beneath the shadow of Rome. Her government and material civilization being superior to others of that age, they succumbed; but she depended too much upon her material power, which was corrupt in principle, sensual, and selfish. The imagination recalls only the indomitable virtue of the republic, and the grandeur and civilizing principles of the imperial sway. In Rome, therefore, the mind, by the contrasting feebleness of the present government, its ragged magnificence, and futile claims to dominion, is irresistibly thrown back to the great past, which looms up so vast in the horizon of history. Mighty events, rather than great souls, haunt the memory with their spectral shadows. The Past lives while the Present swoons. Even the crimes and spectacles of the old city, from their very scale, become attractive in contrast with the dwarfish efforts of the modern. It is difficult to sleep quietly where every stone has a tongue, and the very air is peopled with the shapes of olden life, sincere and strong, in its contrasting lights of vice and virtue. There is too much vitality of association for sensitive nerves. This, joined to an atmospherical torpor, arising from poisonous exhalations, as well as the constant mental conflict between reality and vision, the actual feebleness of papal rule in contrast with its claims to infallibility, its acts warring with its principles, produce an intellectual excitement in many minds unfavorable to health. Extremes meet in Rome. To some it is a renewal of the lease of life; while to others, every breath they inhale savors of death. Two classes alone of strangers can enjoy Rome. Artists who live only in their ideal world, or visitors who turn Rome into a watering-place. Frivolity is a weed that thrives on every soil. One other race finds here its natural atmosphere. In fact, it creates it. Priests have made modern Rome. It is a labyrinth of churches, convents, monasteries, and colleges, the clew to which is a feeble old man, embalmed in ceremonies and swaddled in sacred robes. Poor old Adamite! the prisoner of Christendom—a mistaken sacrifice to that "love which casteth out all fear!"

Rome filled her second rôle of progress when, in early Christianity and the Middle Ages, society being ingulfed in the material wreck of the imperial sway, a strong arm was needed to enforce strong principles, and unite mankind under one faith. The Church fulfilled this mission. She spread Christianity over Europe. By her system, it was done perhaps speedier and more thoroughly than it could have been done by any other. Papacy, therefore, has performed its mission. Selfish as all human power has shown itself, it now says, "Perish progress, spread idolatry, retrograde the world, but let me live the Absolute!"

Papacy is still strong, because it allies itself to the selfish passions and fears of mankind. Until the spirit is released from external bondage, Rome will continue to be the nightmare on Progress.

CHAPTER XIII.

A DREAM OF VENICE.

STEAM bore us whizzing along from Padua toward Venice. It was near dusk. Without the cars, the rain poured in torrents. Within, cigar smoke poisoned still more the scanty air, and stifled our breaths. Preferring a wetting to suffocation, I opened a window and thrust my head into the damp atmosphere. At the north lay the horizon boundary of the Alps, looming up vast and mysterious in the distance, entirely shrouded at times in purple mist; then, as the rain gradually ceased, rolling off its vaporous garments, and presenting its craggy summits in all their solemn grandeur against the departing twilight. On either side lay canals and morasses, water-filled and water-soaked to the brim. It was difficult to reconcile the firm, elastic gliding of the cars with their apparently watery support. As we emerged from the last boundary which marked the termination of this amphibious soil, and shot out, as it were, upon the clear lagoon, with its refreshing salt breeze, the dash of ocean water before, behind, and all around, while the narrow causeway over which we slid was almost hidden from sight, it became even more difficult to feel that we owed our progress to iron and stone. Over our heads lay suspended a canopy of vapor. About our faces blew the night wind. The sea moaned listlessly at our feet. Just discernible in the rear lay the long, low, sad coastline. In front, toward which we were reaching with steam-speed, as if we had suddenly been launched from substance into space, rose dim tall forms, irregular opaque masses, interspersed with bright lights. As we drew near, they took habitable shape—high towers, massive domes, huge walls sleeping upon the water! There was an unreal sense in all this that to the stranger gave the whole the idea of a phantom ride and a phantom city. Nevertheless, it was Venice, in fame and solidity unsurpassed by any sister town.

Each city in which Time has harvested rich associations has a character as defined as that of the distinguished individual. Thought in relation to it becomes one. We speed to its welcome as to that of an acquaintance, investing its material substance with ideas of mingled good and evil, lofty aspiration and base action—in short, the mingled virtues and vices of its peculiar humanity. It becomes to us a great whole—the Man city, that we wish to know in person, its past and present united and individualized.

The three cities which most powerfully appeal to the human heart in this respect are Jerusalem, Rome, and Venice, each the centre of ideas that have powerfully affected the human race. Jerusalem lifts us toward heaven. In Rome we see the civilizer and tyrant, the sepulchre of religion and freedom, a nightmare among nations. Venice, the fallen queen of commerce, that for a thousand years held the throne of the seas. No other human marts can rival these in soul-emotions, and stir within us more powerfully associative sympathies. Pity it is that on approaching each, jarring notes are ever struck upon the chord of our mental illusion, breaking the magic harmony of the past by the vulgar necessities of the present.

Externally, at a distance and nigh to, no city more bravely wears its crown of romance than Venice. Internally, nowhere is the illusion of sovereignty more thoroughly dispelled. Yet Venice, both from her site upon the waters and the associations of her name, still remains Venice, and will continue to instruct and interest long after the last marble of her palaces shall have sunk beneath their ocean beds.

The rudest shock to the imagination is received upon the threshold of the city, at the station, an unromantic shed of a building, into the farther offices of which the stranger is unceremoniously thrust, to be inspected by the police, and confronted with all the annoyances of the modern passport system, if possible made more diabolical from being Austrianized. Having safely weathered this Scylla, his nose, eyes, and complexion being decided to be his own and no one's else, his mission to Venice a legitimate one, the usual coins slid into itching palms to prevent a worn coat being converted into merchandise contraband to a "free port," he is told to "step out," whereupon he finds himself upon Charybdis, in the shape of a pigmy stone quay, surrounded by a rapacious crowd screaming, "Take an omnibus, sir?" Seizing upon him and his baggage, he is bodily injected into a prosaic-looking boat, half house, half skiff, which, to his amazement, he finds dubbed "omnibus." Shades of the Doges, forgive them! an omnibus in Venice! So it is, but it goes by paddles and human muscles, and, upon the whole, is not a bad contrivance for locomotion in dirty canals.

The night was dark, the rain had recommenced, the wind was high, the waves as strong as scanty sea-room would permit, when, confounded by the confusion of the mingled police and custom-house examinations within, and blinded by the mist and lights without, I found myself, with several ladies, shut up, at ten o'clock at night, in an "omnibus" on the Grand Canal. There was neither room to sit upright nor to stretch out. We were cramped into a sugar-box closed tight, and set afloat on troubled waters. The omnibus rocked and bobbed about, now scraping against a pier, now bumping against a brother omnibus, the men shouting, the women-folks screaming "We shall be drowned!" and thus, amid darkness, noise, and discomfort, after a half-hour's novel navigation, we found ourselves suddenly arrested at the steps of a grand mansion. A large door was thrown open, the prow of the "omnibus" was run over the threshold, the waves dashed in upon the marble pavement, we sprang out, and found ourselves on the water-floor of a "grand hotel." Up, up we mounted, a hundred stone steps or more, over polished marble staircases, until we were installed in the centre of the hotel life, under the eaves. A room looking over the Grand Canal, toward the Lido, was assigned to me. Huge, rickety wooden shutters protected the interior from the outer air. I managed to throw one open. Far beneath, the distance magnified by the darkness, I could hear the waves swashing against the foundations of the palace. Opposite and on either side, each building echoed to similar sounds. An occasional light glanced over the fretful waters, brightening their tiny crests. Above and about me, the winds howled dismally through Gothic corridors and arched window-ways, every rusty hinge creaking a harsh accompaniment. A confused scene of rocking masts and tangled rigging, sighing in the gale, lay before me. The wind came in salt and angry from the ocean. Clouds swept by heavily and hastily. The ladies had complained of feeling sea-sick in the "omnibus." I felt qualmish in the upper story of the massive hotel, which seemed to sway with all the moving things about it. There was a ship-feeling of unsteadiness to every thing, or something worse, for it seemed as if we were far out to sea, floating by uncertain magic, stone on water, destined by the sudden return of Nature to her usual laws to be instantaneously ingulfed. With such fancies I passed my first and restless night at Venice, in doubtful and unrefreshing slumbers.

The morning, however, dawned brightly. Venice, with its

streets of water, busy with gondolas in the early sunlight, carried out the illusion of the previous night of a floating city, but now nestling like a sea-bird quietly on the ocean. There is an indescribable charm in the novelty, as it were, of living on the bosom of so restless an element without seeing land, as is the case in some positions, yet surrounded by all the security and comforts of the firm shore. The buildings, rising directly from the water, seem to have no other foundation than its treacherous surface ; hence the contrast between the solidity of the one resting upon the liquidity of the other, without the intermediate agency of earth, to the novice causes a sensation of dreamy uncertainty, as if the whole scene was visionary rather than real. The common experiences of travelers are all reversed. Consequently Venice, irrespective of its history, merely from the peculiarity of its site and the general varying of the perpendicular in its architectural lines, must always retain a charm peculiarly its own.

This is increased by the absence of two of the common nuisances of the shore. Here we have neither dust nor noise. There is no difficulty in threading one's way *on foot* all over Venice by means of its labyrinthine lanes, broken continually by pigmy squares or piazzas, in the centre of which is usually located a small reservoir, surmounted by elaborately-carved well-tops in stone. These constantly remind one of the first great necessity of a city built on the brine, viz., fresh water. No animals intrude upon the streets of Venice. A citizen may pass his lifetime among them, and never see horse or ox. To him the commonest cattle of the farm-yard are as much a curiosity as the elephant or leopard. He may, indeed, have some conception of a lion from that of St. Mark's, which, in paint and stone, stares at him every where from triumphal columns and public walls. But the glorious standard of his republic is now a mocking emblem, and he turns from it with a tear in his eye and a curse on his lips. Should he conceive of the real lion, he would doubtless imagine it with wings like his own.

To me there is an unfailing source of pleasure in rambling through the intricate streets of Venice. A city in which one meets only the noiseless foot-passenger is something of itself. No impudent hackmen or obstinate donkeys, as in other Italian cities, disturb the serenity of one's contemplations. In but few of the chief arteries is there ever any human press. The pavements are scrupulously clean. Beggars are obsolete under Austrian rule. No dust clouds the vision. Hoofs there are none to clatter over the smooth stones. Opposite houses almost meet at their eaves. There is an endless variety of turns—sharp corners, suggestive of passages ending in blank, impenetrable walls; occasional bits of earth, scanty verdure, or a few meagre flowers, exiles from the main land, water-sustained and imprisoned in cold stone borders; shops no larger than American entries, with their contents most temptingly thrust into the narrow streets; every few steps, arched bridges, from the parapets of which you watch the silent, melancholy gondola as it shoots underneath, its black blinds and funereal curtains shutting out all view of its occupants. In short, Venice is a creation by itself. Shut up amid its walls and canals, one momentarily forgets the glad earth, reveling in new emotions until their wearisome repletion recalls the familiar associations of nature's open skies and verdant fields.

A gondola and Venice are almost synonymous terms. Each pictures the other. Neither admits of other associations. If ever divided, both will lose their individuality, which, like happy matrimony, is complete only by union. The first object the stranger calls for is a gondola to conjure up his dream of Venice. Fortunately, they are innumerable and cheap—less than seventy-five cents per day for the best. For this sum, one of these magic vehicles will attend you as closely as a shadow from sunrise to midnight. Delicious is it to lounge on their luxurious cushions, shrouding one's self wholly from the world, and, gliding over still waters with all the repose of a pleasing dream, revel in sensuous ease. If your companion be one of the dark-eyed, warm-hearted beauties of the sea-girt city or Italy's burning soil, then the terrestrial enchantment is complete. Draw the curtains and throw open the blinds. It is toward sunset in June. The Grand Canal swarms with gondolas filled with fair women, gallant men, and joyous children. They pass and repass with the silence and rapidity of swallows, the gondoliers, now straining every muscle in effort to outspeed their rivals, then quietly and gracefully bending their flexible forms to the propelling oar, sending their gondolas as slowly and easily over the water's surface as clouds float through a serene sky. Friendly nods, waving handkerchiefs, and meaning glances are exchanged, but there is no levity even now in Venice. Seldom do its real sons and daughters appear in public. They are a sad and impoverished remnant of a race that won the rule of the waves. When seen, they still maintain the serious yet benign dignity which characterized their ancestors, sighing over the Past, and effortless to know the Present.

The graceful form of the gondola is rarely given by the artist. It floats swan-like on the water; in appearance, though not in reality, is as easily moved as if it had instincts and powers of its own. Fair weather is its true element, for it has no storm qualities. A worse sea-boat was never contrived. Flat, long, low, and rising sharply from the water at either end in serpent-like crests; luxuriously carpeted, cushioned, and richly carved; at once affording the most complete privacy, or, with its top off, entire freedom of vision, it combines in still water more advantages than any other mode of conveyance. Unlike the row-boat, there is no jerking motion of oars. Whether quick or slow, it invites repose and suggests dreamy fancies, for which Venice affords ample food. Consequently, for the invalid or idler its effect is paradisiacal. The gondolier being at the back, he is not seen. We glide, however, with trout-like quiet and ease over the water, without even the suggestion of labor to mar the soothing effect.

Formerly the gondolas were ornamented with various colors, rich gilding, and every decoration which could add to their brilliancy and sumptuousness. Then the canals must have glistened with opalescent tints, and the general effect been exceedingly rich, especially as the national costumes, and even the architecture, all showed the same fondness for deep and rich coloring. Now the gondolas are all clothed in sombre black. Were it not for their graceful forms and light motions, they would be taken for water-hearses. As it is, their mournful livery suggests mysterious fancies connected with the fate of the republic, but the true reason, I believe, for their uniform color arises from an old sumptuary decree of the state, which, to check the extravagant expense lavished upon gondolas, ordained the present equality in hue. General poverty and depression continue to enforce the obsolete law, so that we shall probably never see a change in this respect, because, although Venetians must continue to go, for ages to come as for a thousand years back, to church and theatre, to their baptisms and their burials, to their marriages and their lawsuits, to Opera and office—in short, every where business, pleasure, or necessity call them, in gondolas, yet the soul of Venice has left its body. There is nothing Venetian at heart. The real Venice is dead — dead and buried in the irrevocable Past. That which we now see is only the cast-off garment, here and there betraying its original fashion, but disfigured with many a sad rent and uncongenial repair. Modernism has set its practical seal upon all that constituted its pride and glory. Picturesque costumes have vanished before the Christian hat and trowsers. Old Jewdom, in its modern phase of homely, unpicturesque apparel, reigns triumphant over the quays of Venice. A few Greeks and Turks, men from Africa or the Ionian Isles, as yet refuse to bow down before modern unity in dress. Some fishermen retain, with their manly forms and finely-bronzed complexions, their red caps and colored sails, with quaint devices. But in general, the universal black hat and coat of Christendom are fast triumphing over color and variety even here, in their firm-set seat and richest expression, while the wheels of steam froth its waters and send panic to the frail gondolas.

All is not lost, however. The architecture retains a portion of its adamantine hues, which time and the restorer still respect. Jasper, porphyry, serpentine, those precious stones which Venetians, in their love for their city and feeling for the beautiful, so lavishly wrought into their palaces and churches in harmonious combinations and deep meaning, still faintly throw their shadows over the waters, which lovingly give back their hues. Changed though the outer form may be, and weakened the force of man's works, yet the same warm sun, as it sinks behind the far-off hills, bathes dome and tower in trembling purple mist, lighting up with golden brightness sea and sky, while soft, vapory, variegated clouds, warm and tender, brilliant with nature's loveliest hues, arch the heavens in almost imperceptible gradation from their sinking source of beauty in the west. Toward this the eye wanders in an aerial perspective, deeper and deeper into space, and finding no end save as night slowly shrouds the glories that follow the sun in its course to gladden other hearts. Nearer by, and lower down, the long reaches of the great canals let the eye into shorter perspectives ; shadowed water and palace reflecting ; soft streams of hazy, twinkling brightness; deep, luminous shadows, a mingled horizon of sea and city blending into each other, and wrapped in one tender robe of twilight, harmonizing with the hues of heaven's painting. Toward the Adriatic, the long, low line of the Lido lies like a thread upon the water. Beyond, the setting sun glances upon white sails, that, ghost-like, seem to have no bodies, for the hulls of the vessels are covered by the intervening land. Between the Lido and Venice rise numerous sunlit islands, their white walls sparkling in golden light, heightened by an occasional bit of deep green, from the few trees that grow thereupon. But what words can reflect that beautiful sheet of water between the Guideca and the Ducal Palace, on which is mirrored all this loveliness? The summer's eve brings with it a goodly company of worshipers, who repose in sensuous delight on its surface, spell-bound by the enchantment. From many gondolas, music steals lovingly over the waters, caressing and caressed by the zephyr that bears it harmoniously on its wings. The general silence best proclaims the soothing romance of the scene. Occasionally a chorus of youthful voices breaks forcibly upon the ear in some well-known Venetian strain, now rising loudly on the still air, then dying away amid the intricacies of distant canals. The lights from the Piazza San Marco, as night shuts in the scene, come out brightly and joyfully in the distance. Towering far above all other objects, dark, stern, and majestic, is the tower of St. Mark's, the noblest beacon-pile reared by modern man. Below it rise the clustered domes and forest of shafts of the Cathedral; a Christian thought in Oriental form and color; pregnant with the spoils of paganism, written all over with the story of the new revelation—the world's creation and man's redemption; eternal and legible as enduring precious material can make them; the faith of Venice pictured for all time, and gathered into one fantastic and yet glorious edifice, emblematic in the richness and variety of its decorations of all the races of men, their artistic triumphs and their garnered knowledge, who are yet to come up to the new Jerusalem, and sit in peace within its sanctuary. Who can tread the wave-like mosaic floor of this venerable church, as it rises and falls like the swell of the sea, and not feel that its foundations are indeed laid upon the sands of the deep?

"Jacomo, land me at the Piazzetta." "Yes, excellent sir." I had been dreaming away an hour or more, indolently reclining upon the cushions of my gondola, amid the above scene, after my return from my usual plunge into the sea on the farther side of the Guideca. The prow of the gondola soon touched the quay, and in another second I found myself wandering among the throng. An Austrian band was playing in the square. Thousands were promenading on its smooth and clean pavements. It was brilliantly lighted. The cafés and shops added greatly to the illumination. Groups of children, ladies and their cavaliers, sat in front of each favorite café, eating ices, chatting, and listening to strolling musicians. It was a musical soiree in the open air to which all Venice was free to come, yet none but well-bred and well-clad people had gathered to the festival. Here they sat and walked, in quiet enjoyment of the clear sky above and the enlivening scene beneath, until late into the night. There is but one St. Mark's Place in the world, and but one spectacle of complete out-door domesticity, refined and sensuous, like this.

Venice existed as a state nearly fourteen hundred years. The common associations with her name are those derived through the poet and novelist. They are, unfortunately, connected chiefly with her vices and her crimes. We think of Venice and the Bridge of Sighs—more of her damp dungeons than her lovely palaces—her tortures than her festivals—her crimes than her piety; while, as we glide over her waters, our eyes shudderingly turn from the bosom of that canal into which no fisherman was allowed to cast his net from fear that dead men might rise and tell tales. Venice to the popular mind was a vast political inquisition, remorseless as the grave in her state craft, and in her private life full of selfish luxury, treachery, and prostitution. This was *not* the Venice of mediæval ages. Had it been, the spoiler would have laid his hand upon her long before. Her polity was not a perfect one. It generated weaknesses. Wealth and pride, as they ever do, cankered her heart. But for a thousand years her bones were sound, while for centuries her strength was the bulwark of Christendom. She had character; a noble and vicious compound, it is true, but the mingled devotion and enterprise that kept her for so long a period in the van of civilization leavened her whole system with faith and energy.

Catholic herself, she resisted the Popes as successfully as she did the Turks. Devout, but not fanatic, the state, and not the Church, ruled within her borders. She was as successful in repelling the interdicts of the Roman pontiffs as in checking the spread of Mohammedanism. Unlike Spain, the Inquisition took not root in her soil. The free spirit of commerce could ill brook such a nightmare upon its energies. Liberal and just in her policy, Jew, Greek, and Gentile lived, trafficked, and worshiped in security beneath the shadow of her lion-wings. While all Italy was convulsed with civil wars and the dissensions of rival families, Venice always presented a firm and united front to her enemies. Without and within, she was ever a unity. Nobles and people have loved Venice as no other country has been loved. The individual was merged into the nation. From the time that the first settlers, flying before Alaric to the mother island of Tercello, saw in the distance the sky reddened with the flames of their late homes on the mainland, until Bonaparte deposed their last doge, the

Venetians have ever been animated with a fanatic love of country. Patriotism in them was a passion, narrowed to a selfish policy, which sacrificed citizen or stranger alike to its own end, governed at times wisely, but often misdirected, until, in contact with stronger selfishness, it fell shivered to the ground like a thing of glass.

There must have been much that was true and lofty in the soul of Venice to have preserved its independence during a period which extends far beyond the existence of any modern state. In the sixteenth century, we find her the residence of the greatest artists. Emperors and kings, at a time when Francis I. of France and Charles I. of Spain rivaled each other in their patronage of art, and the Medici corrupted Italy in lavish expenditure and bastard taste to the enrichment of artists, sought to win from Venice her noblest names. Like Sansovino, they replied, that, having the happiness to live under a republic, it would be folly to change for a monarchy. Her patricians, unlike the ignorant nobility of the rest of Europe, cultivated literature. Their doges, at once generals and admirals away from Venice, on their return exchanged the sword for the pen. Some, like Andrea Dandolo and Marco Foscarini, became historians; others, of the noble families of the Carnaro, Justiniani, Morosini, Contarini, and Mocenigo, were professors or simply librarians. All labored to instruct and exalt Venice. It was owing to the profound respect shown to art and literature by her noblest citizens, extending as it did to all classes, that so many distinguished artists, few of whom were born within her limits, were led to make their homes on her congenial soil.

The cultivation of her intellect was therefore one source of her long and refined existence. Among others, in her policy, must not be overlooked her jealous resistance to the spiritual and temporal encroachment of Rome. Her clergy were subordinate to the state. Churchmen were not only excluded from the Grand Council, but were declared ineligible to civil employments. In 1434, even the *relatives* of priests were prohibited from the post of embassador at Rome. When ecclesiastical matters were discussed in the national councils, all those members whose votes were liable to be influenced by the ties of blood were expelled. Unlike other countries at that epoch—the fifteenth century—a priest guilty of infraction of the civil law was amenable to the police, without reference to the tribunals of the Church. In 1484, a clergyman assaulted a clothier with a drawn weapon. He was taken immediately and *hanged*. This fact shows the severity and impartiality of their law.

To avoid all pretense of Rome to intervene in their political affairs, the Venetians respected scrupulously her religious dogmas. They took no part in the heresies, councils, or religious wars of the times. They were no less inflexible in preserving their system of toleration. By commerce they lived and prospered. No illiberal doctrines were allowed to check the prosperity of trade. All sects were permitted their houses of worship. Even burial in churches was not refused to heretics. With all this latitude, so unusual at that age, Venice preserved her reputation for the purity of her faith. "We are *first* Venetians, then Christians." This was her maxim, indicative of her unalterable resolution that no partial or foreign policy should interfere with the sovereignty of the state.

The Jesuits, in particular, were objects of suspicion. No one of that order could remain in Venice more than three years. The slightest disobedience to the authority of the government was punished by imprisonment. Noble families were not allowed to have their children educated at their colleges. No Venetian could enter their order unless by the sanction of the government. It was forbidden to will them property. Such were some of the jealous safeguards with which the state fortified itself against a foe as insidious, implacable, cold, secret, and selfish as its own policy, but more deadly, because joined to a hydra-headed versatility of principle, which made its professed friendship more to be dreaded than its open enmity.

The governing spring of Venetian policy was her commercial interest. With her it was a restricted, purely selfish interest, looking only to her own aggrandizement, at whatever expense of blood and prosperity to other nations. She did not comprehend the wider maxims of modern civilization, which see in general peace and prosperity the firmest foundations for individual success. On the contrary, she sought to rise on the ruin rather than the competition and consequent enlargement of the fields of commerce foreign to her own channels of traffic. She brooked no rival. Insults to her honor might be overlooked, but peril to her trade, never. Her aspiration was to be the commercial heart of the world. The policy which gave her tolerance in religion, a firm protective government, encouragement to art and science, attracting within herself talent, capital, and enterprise, was wise and successful. But, inasmuch as she resorted to fraud and violence without, sacrificing great truths to special interests, estimating conquests only by the spirit of the ledger, their justice graduated only by their facility, Venice in time corrupted herself. From being the prey of her own avarice and wantonness, she passed into the sordid embraces of the Northern stranger, who coveted even the remains of a beauty he could never hope to rival. This was a legitimate end for a nation that trafficked its piety, exacting from united Europe the highest price for its aid against the infidel, and finally broke faith and betrayed religion for selfish gain.

The taint that pervaded the commercial veins of Venice

was a necessary consequence of her unscrupulous devotion to Mammon. But throughout her history, especially in the first thousand years, and particularly when moral worth and tried talent were the choice of the people to their highest offices, we find repeated and continued evidences of individual and national nobility of feeling. There was a sound current in her blood, that repeatedly brought her back to healthful action. If it could not save Venice in the final turmoil of nations, it constantly exalted her career, giving her power and might, glorifying her existence even amid much error and abasement. Her saving grace arose from her piety. Founded in disaster, nursed in warfare, passing rapidly from the greatest reverses to the loftiest triumphs, the national feeling has ever been devotional. Even when the rest of Italy was far gone in infidelity, Venice maintained an external religious decorum, which preserved her nationality intact, and sustained her reputation to the very verge of her final fall. National policy subjected private piety to worldly ends, but the latter gave strength and vigor to the former from its own fount of sincerity and enthusiasm. Virtue may often be misapplied, but its own strength of lofty motive ever remains the same. Hence selfishness is never more powerful and dangerous than when it blinds religion to aid its designs. Occasionally we find, from its inherent strength and purity, that it subjects its tyrant and becomes the guide, trampling upon temporary expediency and short-sighted state-craft. At such times the whole body politic becomes inoculated with new life. The habit of confessing God in all the transactions of life, begun in sincerity, and continued in serious and simple familiarity, *feeling* that there is a "Father in heaven" whose name is ever to be hallowed in thought and action, has an important influence upon human character. To this may be traced much of the dignity and heroism of the Venetian mind, coupled with serenity and energy of will, even when unworthily employed. Its fullness was commensurate with the greatness of Venice, and its decline with her gradual and complete degradation, the more conspicuous from her previous nobility, as the grossest corruption proceeds from the richest soils. The same sun of righteousness flowed in upon her mind, but it was no longer humble or sincere; instead, there were festering selfishness and cankering avarice; the heart that would have warmed humility and sincerity into divine life and wisdom turned selfishness and avarice into putrefaction. Religion in Venice became mere formalism more slowly than elsewhere, owing to the innate vigor and warmth of the national mind. At present, her piety, as her beauty, is but the shade of her former self. The shallow lagoons, with their dull gray surface and grassy bottoms, the habitations of slimy eels, truly reflect the fallen image of that city, whose throne in ivory, gold, and precious stones shone for ten centuries over the waters of the Mediterranean, and whose flag so often triumphantly upheld the Cross before the Crescent. Even the Turks were not insensible to the nobility of Venetian character in their most indefatigable foe. Upon learning the death of Luigi Mocenigo, they spontaneously put on mourning, draped their galleys in black, and caused them to pass with respectful homage before the place of his burial.

At Windsor Castle we see the portraits of England's distinguished men appareled in gaudy cloth, covered with gilt and precious stones, the trappings of power, pride of state, and haughty self-consciousness of rank legible in every touch of the brush; brave men, no doubt, strong in their own intellect, but, like Nebuchadnezzar's image of gold, set up to be worshiped by the soulless throng. What have we in Venice? We see her great men, doges and generals, pictured in all the vitality of existence by the pencils of Bellini, Titian, and Tintoretto, not in the paraphernalia of external power, but in their dignified costumes, serious and devout in mien, humbly kneeling before the images of their faith, the divine Mother and Son, to whom they offer their crowns of success, indicative of their trust in and homage to that Being who alone creates and casts down, exalts and abases. This feeling is consistent with the devotion of that doge who was carried in his dying hour to the foot of the altar of St. Mark's, saying with his departing breath, "Into thy hands, O Lord, I commend my spirit and the republic." So also Lorenzo Priuli, elected doge at a moment when his country was suffering from the threefold plague of war, pestilence, and famine, commenced his inaugural address with the devout ejaculation, "Even though I walk in the valley of the shadow of death, I shall fear no evil, because thou art with me."

A prolific source of greatness to Venice lay in wise incorporation of other natural elements of industry and strength into her own system. She continually reinvigorated her own blood by fresh streams from without. This was owing to the liberal tone of commerce, which ever seeks for itself the best, irrespective of origin. Consequently, we find in Venice, especially in architecture, a variety that tells of Oriental, Byzantine, Lombard, and Gothic origin, yet fused by Venetian taste into one consistent whole, each style adding value to the other. Over all the earlier architecture there is thrown the spiritual mantle of religious feeling. Borrowing largely as they did from their Arab enemies their delicate and graceful architecture, with its rich coloring and prolific ornamentation, the Venetians, in transforming it to the service of their own loftier faith, caused it to glow with hues that savored of celestial glories, while its walls spoke to them in adamantine energy of its mystic truths. Every where amid the public and private architecture of old Venice we find evidence of the devotion of its citizens. They were not ashamed to confess their God equally in their bed-chambers and their council-halls. Their continual going down to the sea in ships and incessant conflicts with infidel foes, and having their homes, as they did, upon the restless ocean, kept alive within them a constant and sincere recognition of Him who holds the elements in the hollow of his hand, and controls the destinies of nations by the breath of His will. Hence their devout and serious character. They gloried not so much in their own strength as in divine protection. Nature had warmed their skies with the most glorious of her hues. Commerce had made them familiar with the brilliant tints of the Orient. Pearls and precious stones, and all the rich stuffs of Arabian manufacture, were gathered into her bosom for profit and adornment. From the West and the North there poured into her canals a continuous throng of commercial pilgrims or crusading heroes. Her conquests were marked by a rapacity inoculated by the spirit of trade. Wealth and monopoly were her axioms; enterprise, cunning, and force, her agents; at times, high principles and pure aspirations directed her councils; at others, selfish maxims and short-sighted policy; but her progress for ten centuries, in harvesting to herself the riches of the earth, gathering within her narrow limits the tastes, civilization, and knowledge of all nations, making a highway of the ocean, centring all roads into her own lagoons, was steadily onward. Palace-built Venice, with her jeweled shrines, wave-washed walls of porphyry and jasper, her mystic sculpture and allegorical mosaics, imbued with thought, and burning with the colors of revelation, her lone, lofty watch-tower, and her myriad of heaven-directed spires, her marble-checkered pavements, and her half Western and half Oriental homes, combining the energy of the one quarter with the sensuous and jealous life of the other, all beautiful and bright, like a sea-born pearl—such was the Venice that grew up amid the mud and shallows of the Adriatic. So long as she held to her devotional energy, expanding her thought with her fields of enterprise, she shone forth on the waters their queen, splendid and prosperous. But when, in a fatal hour, she adopted the renaissant paganism of Italy, the vitality of her faith and the life of her action departed. Enervated by luxury, corrupted by vice, commerce sought new channels. Gleams of former virtue occasionally illumined her dark horizon, but her brightness and her beauty no longer shone with a pure flame, and she became a glittering corpse.

The renaissance had much to do with this—not so much as the active agent, as the exposition of a changed heart. Architecture is among all nations the exponent of its inner thought. We can read the ruling ideas in its form and ornament. Every curve and color can be made to tell the feeling of a people, whether cold or passionate, pure or base, serene or false, religious or sensual, with all their gradations from nobility to meanness. The youth of Venice was passed in prayer and tribulation. Her earlier architecture was simple, sincere, and symbolical. Inherited from Christian Rome, it partook of its severely graceful and classical forms; the noble arch and rich capital; in which Lombard energy, with its rude and vigorous imagination, wrote its homely and mystic thoughts, symbolical of northern life and freedom. From this element sprang hardihood and enterprise; vigor in war, sincerity in worship, and commercial activity in peace. It embodied religious dogmas into material forms, tending in the common mind to substitute the worship of the thing created for the Creator. To counteract the idolatrous tendency of imaginative worship founded upon the creature was the mission of the Arab, who, rolling like a lava-stream from the hot South upon the decaying fragments of Roman civilization, proclaimed with ferocious energy the unity and spirituality of a new creed. That which he could not warm into a new life, he consumed. No other cry to heaven was allowed where his sword flashed but that which from his minarets told "There is no god but God." This element, to the extent of its civilization, but not of its faith, found a home at Venice, and mingled its grace and beauty with Gothic fancies and energy. Thus we have the dome and minaret, arabesque and grotesque, the profuse imagery of Europe and the brilliant colorings of Asia, all united into a mixed and not pleasing architecture at Venice, the central point around which revolved the two great conflicting principles of religion.

The decadence of Venice became rapid from the period when she abandoned those styles of architecture which sprang from faith and were the offspring of devotional feeling dedicating its riches to the service of the sanctuary, for self-glorification and enervating ease. The Renaissance was the offspring of modern infidelity. In proportion as Venice had been pure in her faith, in that degree she became corrupt in her idolatry. True, she did not go back to pagan mythology for objects of worship. She did worse. Her idols became wholly of sense, the external glorification of her own weakened power, and the sensual expression of her own vitiated tastes. Better by far had she worshiped the intellectual creatures of classical ages, exalting humanity by elevating its types. But no. She preferred the orgies of worldly pleasure to the excitements of mental pursuits. The pride of power and luxury of life, amalgamated into a sensualized existence, betraying themselves in cold mansions, stately and selfish, emblazoned with insignia of state-rank or individual pride, and ornamented with incongruous classicalism, now drove humility and belief in spiritualities into exile from their once cherished homes. The lecherous and beastly decorations derived from corrupted pagan imaginations became the rule for Christian architecture. All that was pure and good in spirit in classical architecture was carefully sifted and set aside. All that was impure and bad was extracted, and still farther tainted by the foul fancies of the sensualized imaginations of modern art. Hence, although some grace of design, convenience, and adaptation to physical comfort may be allowed to the bastard architecture of modern Venice, yet its spirit is wholly of the earth, earthy. It rooted itself in her decline, and is symbolical of the vices that hastened her fall.

In viewing Venice, therefore, the traveler should carefully distinguish between the several styles of her architecture as illustrative of her ruling principles in the different epochs of her existence. As plainly as character is typified in human features, as legibly are the virtues and vices of nations to be read in their architecture. Back amid sea-weed, choked canals, silent and deserted, the time-stained shutters half dropping from time, rust-eaten hinges, with basements water-stained and foundations cracked and broken, the sea each tide oozing lazily in and out their stones, do we find many mansions before which it will do us more good to pause than before the stately piles of Palladio and less worthy architects, who have usurped the sites of so many of the older and purer palaces on the principal canals. In their obscurity, deserted and poverty-struck, they are perishing piecemeal; but on their venerable fronts are still to be seen the records of the *feeling* in which they were built. Symbols of Christian faith, the noble abstraction of its pure tenets, each in its day "a word in season" to the indweller and passer-by.

For ornament we see pure and simple forms of nature, elaborately wrought or rudely carved, amid masses of richly-colored stones, each suggestive of life and beauty, and leading the thought to the nobler forms and hues of God's own works. Pause well before such buildings. There is a moral written on their fronts that modernism, in its dainty devices and puerile fancies, its science-worship and ease-coveting, is in danger of forgetting. We whiten our sepulchres, and forget the dead men's bones within. So long as we keep our soul undefiled, the intellect active and sincere, loving beauty as the gift of its author, and not debasing it to administer to selfish and sensual desires, just so long need we take no heed to outer expression. That will reflect the harmony and truth that reigns within. But if we seek to disguise our own falsities by external show, we shall as plainly expose the concupiscence that burns within, as did Venice, when in her pride and infidelity she practically denied the living principles that had raised her to power and dominion.

THE END.

www.ingramcontent.com/pod-product-compliance
Lightning Source LLC
LaVergne TN
LVHW020123110826
845151LV00001B/253
* 9 7 8 1 4 2 5 5 4 1 1 8 7 *